Visit us at

www.syngress.com

Syngress is committed to publishing high-quality books for IT Professionals and delivering those books in media and formats that fit the demands of our customers. We are also committed to extending the utility of the book you purchase via additional materials available from our Web site.

SOLUTIONS WEB SITE

To register your book, visit www.syngress.com/solutions. Once registered, you can access our solutions@syngress.com Web pages. There you may find an assortment of valueadded features such as free e-books related to the topic of this book, URLs of related Web sites, FAQs from the book, corrections, and any updates from the author(s).

ULTIMATE CDs

Our Ultimate CD product line offers our readers budget-conscious compilations of some of our best-selling backlist titles in Adobe PDF form. These CDs are the perfect way to extend your reference library on key topics pertaining to your area of expertise, including Cisco Engineering, Microsoft Windows System Administration, CyberCrime Investigation, Open Source Security, and Firewall Configuration, to name a few.

DOWNLOADABLE E-BOOKS

For readers who can't wait for hard copy, we offer most of our titles in downloadable Adobe PDF form. These e-books are often available weeks before hard copies, and are priced affordably.

SYNGRESS OUTLET

Our outlet store at syngress.com features overstocked, out-of-print, or slightly hurt books at significant savings.

SITE LICENSING

Syngress has a well-established program for site licensing our e-books onto servers in corporations, educational institutions, and large organizations. Contact us at sales@syngress.com for more information.

CUSTOM PUBLISHING

Many organizations welcome the ability to combine parts of multiple Syngress books, as well as their own content, into a single volume for their own internal use. Contact us at sales@syngress.com for more information.

SYNGRESS®

Nagios 3 Enterprise Network Monitoring Including Plug-Ins and Hardware Devices

Max Schubert
Derrick Bennett
Jonathan Gines
Andrew Hay
John Strand

KEY	SERIAL NUMBER
001	HJIRTCV764
002	PO9873D5FG
003	829KM8NJH2
004	BAL923457U
005	CVPLQ6WQ23
006	VBP965T5T5
007	HJJJ863WD3E
008	2987GVTWMK
009	629MP5SDJT
010	IMWQ295T6T

PUBLISHED BY
Syngress Publishing, Inc.
Elsevier, Inc.
30 Corporate Drive
Burlington, MA 01803

Nagios 3 Enterprise Network Monitoring Including Plug-Ins and Hardware Devices

Printed in the United States of America
1 2 3 4 5 6 7 8 9 0

ISBN 13: 978-1-59749-267-6

Publisher: Andrew Williams
Copy Editor: Beth Roberts
Page Layout and Art: SPi Publishing Services

For information on rights, translations, and bulk sales, contact Matt Pedersen, Commercial Sales Director and Rights, at Syngress Publishing; email m.pedersen@elsevier.com.

Authors

Max Schubert is an open source advocate, integrator, developer, and IT professional. He enjoys learning programming languages, designing and developing software, and working on any project that involves networks or networking. Max lives in Charlottesville, VA, with his wife and a small herd of rescue dogs. He would like to thank his wife, Marguerite, for her love, support and tolerance of his wild hours and habits throughout this project, his parents for stressing the importance of education, writing, and for instilling a love of learning in him. In addition, Max would like to express his gratitude to the following people who provided him guidance and assistance on his portion of this project: Sam Wenck, for his help in creating the early outline for the security chapter and for his friendship, Ton Voon and Gavin Carr for Nagios::Plugin and for allowing me to use the Nagios::Plugin::SNMP namespace for my own Perl extension to Nagios::Plugin, Joerg Linge and Hendrik Bäcker for the Nagios PNP perfdata / RRD graphing plugin, which I used extensively in this book, my friends Luke Nabavi and Marty Kiefer for their extensive encouragement during the writing of the book, many other friends who encouraged me when I was feeling overwhelmed, and a big thank you to all of the Nagios core developers, plugin authors, and enhancement contributors who's works we have discussed in this publication; it is you who make Nagios the wonderful framework it is today. I would like to also personally thank Andrew Williams, our fearless Publisher, for his encouragement, humor, and ability to make solid and rational decisions to keep us all on track. Finally, my heartfelt thanks to everyone on this writing team; we have produced what I feel is a very solid book in a very short period of time. Thank you all for making this an exciting and satisfying experience.

Derrick Bennett has been working professionally in the IT Field for over 15 years in a full spectrum of Network and Software environments. Being born a bit too late and missing the Assembly bandwagon I started with computers and programming with the Commodore Vic-20 and Basic language programs. From there my time has been spent between both the software and hardware. In the 90's as BBS Sysop, to the mid 90's as an MCSE supporting a large Windows network for a major corporation, to today working with customers of all types to deliver real world solutions for their environments. During that work I was first exposed to Network monitoring on a global scale, and the pitfalls of trying to monitor enterprise networks over frame-relay and dial up links. While working in the corporate world and supporting large scale environments I also worked with smaller startups and new companies. This was during the initial years of the commercialization of the Internet and many small companies were working hard to provide commercial class service on low end budgets. It was through this work on both enterprise networks and small 5 servers shops that the true advantage of open source projects found their home for me. Since then I have continued working for various large networks where monitoring has always been key. It was through this work that I contributed source code changes to the NRPE project for Nagios adding in SSL encryption along with other updates for the Nagios Core. I have deployed Nagios in over 20 unique environments from 20 servers to a complete NOC covering hundreds of systems spread across every country. A majority of my work has been in integrating Nagios and other tools into existing applications, environments, and processes and making the job of running a system easier for those that maintain it. Even today I find my attraction to the systems and their software to be the same as when I programmed my first basic goto to today when I install a new server and its applications. In a never ending desire to reduce repetitive maintenance and to reduce downtime I hope that everyone reading this will find something that helps make their systems run even better than before. Like most the co-authors on this project I can be found on the Nagios-Dev mailing list nagios-devel@lists.sourceforge.net or at dbennett@anei.com.

I am thankful to those who have done all the great programming before me and to my parents Pat and Fred who not only inspired my involvement with computers but supported my obsessive love for them once I plugged the first one in. I also want to thank Charles and all the other people out there willing to financially support people, employees, or family, who are working on open source projects and supporting the future of great applications. Last I want to say thank you to Ethan, he has been truly devoted to the Nagios project and has contributed more than anyone else ever could. His true support of Nagios and the community is what makes all of these Nagios related resources so worthwhile and has made a good idea into a great application.

Jonathan Gines is a systems integrator, software engineer, and has worked for major corporations providing telecommunications and Internet services, healthcare management, accounting software development, and of course, federal government contracting. His experience includes serving as an adjunct professor for Virginia Tech, teaching database design and development (yes, including relational algebra, relational calculus, and the ever dreadful normalization forms), developing modeling and simulation models in C++, and good ol' software development using open source programming technologies such as Perl, Java/J2EE, and some frustrating trial and error with Ruby. Jonathan has a graduate degree from Virginia Tech, and holds several certifications including the CISSP and the ITIL Foundation credential.

While not performing UNIX systems administration or troubleshooting enterprise software applications, Jonathan has just completed his doctorate coursework in Bio-defense at George Mason University, and stays busy preparing for the PhD candidacy exam. Jonathan would like to thank his friends and immediate family for their loving support, but offers special acknowledgment to his brother, Anthony S. Gines. Anthony, thanks for always willing to lend a helping hand, and serving as an inspiration to try your best.

Andrew Hay is a security expert, trainer, and author of The OSSEC Host-Based Intrusion Detection Guide. As the Integration Services Program Manager at Q1 Labs Inc. his primary responsibility involves the research and integration of log and vulnerability technologies into QRadar, their flagship network security management solution. Prior to joining Q1 Labs, Andrew was CEO and co-founder of Koteas Corporation, a leading provider of end-to-end security and privacy solutions for government and enterprise. His resume also includes various roles and responsibilities at Nokia Enterprise Solutions, Nortel Networks, and Magma Communications, a division of Primus.

Andrew is a strong advocate of security training, certification programs, and public awareness initiatives. He also holds several industry certifications including the CCNA, CCSA, CCSE, CCSE NGX, CCSE Plus, Security+, GSEC, GCIA, GCIH, SSP-MPA, SSP-CNSA, NSA, RHCT, and RHCE.

Andrew would first like to thank his wife Keli for her support, guidance, and unlimited understanding when it comes to his interests. He would also like to thank Chris Fanjoy, Daniella Degrace, Shawn McPartlin, the Trusted Catalyst Community, and of course his parents, Michel and Ellen Hay, and in-laws Rick and Marilyn Litle for their continued support.

John Strand currently teaches the SANS GCIH and CISSP classes. He is currently certified GIAC Gold in the GCIH and GCFW and is a Certified SANS Instructor. He is also a holder of the CISSP certification. He started working computer security with Accenture Consulting in the areas of intrusion detection, incident response, and vulnerability assessment/penetration testing. He then moved on to Northrop Grumman specializing in DCID 6/3 PL3-PL5 (multi-level security solutions), security architectures, and program certification and accreditation. He currently does consulting with his company Black Hills Information Security. He has a Masters degree from Denver University, and is currently also a professor at Denver University. In his spare time he writes loud rock music and makes various futile attempts at fly-fishing.

Contents

Foreword

The primary benefit, for anyone picking this book up and reading this Foreword, is to understand that the primary goal here was to explain the advanced features of Nagios 3 in plain English. The authors understand that not everyone who uses Nagios is a programmer. You also need to understand that you do not need to be a programmer to leverage the advanced features of Nagios to make it work for you. Gaining a better understanding of these advanced features is key to unlocking the power of Nagios 3.

The authors start by taking you through the new features of Nagios 3. Scaling Nagios 3, by understanding and implementing the advanced features of Nagios, is also discussed in detail. Understanding these features will help you to take 10 monitored hosts and scale to 100,000 monitored hosts similar to Yahoo! Inc. or Tulip It Services in India. These organizations didn't simply install the default Nagios configuration and start monitoring 100,000 hosts. As you can imagine, a rigorous tuning exercise was performed that included custom security and performance modifications to assist in the monitoring of hosts on their network.

The Plug-ins chapter alone is worth the price of this book. Never has such detail been put into the explanation of plug-in creation and use. As I said before, you don't need to be a programmer to understand the value of this chapter. The authors take the time to ensure that the scripts are explained in plain English so that anyone, from the new Nagios user to the seasoned professional, knows how to use the plug-ins to their advantage.

A real-world case study rounds out the book by explaining how fictional Fortune 500 Company ACME Enterprises implements Nagios 3 to monitor its offices in North America, Europe, and Asia. Most readers will benefit from the description of the ACME implementation and parallel it with the configuration of their own network.

Having just finished writing the *OSSEC Host-Based Intrusion Detection Guide,* I still had the writing bug. When my publisher asked me to contribute to a new book on Nagios 3, I jumped at the opportunity. Since I had previously used Nagios in both an enterprise environment and at home, I thought I could offer insight into my challenges and experiences with the product. I was introduced to my coauthors and was amazed to hear about their level of expertise with Nagios and past contributions to the project. It was obvious that Max Schubert, Derrick Bennett, and Jonathan Gines would be the teachers in this book, and I would be learning as much as I could from them.

In talking with my new coauthors, we realized we needed some additional help with the *Intrusion Detection and Security Analysis with Nagios* chapter. I had experience with intrusion detection and security analysis, but not with respect to Nagios. I reached out to my friend and colleague John Strand to see if he'd be interested in joining the authoring team. He had previously mentioned that he had used Nagios extensively during his incident handling engagements. John was thrilled to join the authoring team and we started immediately.

My coauthors and I hope you use this book as a resource to further your knowledge of Nagios 3 and make the application work for you. If Nagios 3 doesn't do what you need it to out of the box, this book will show you how to create your own custom scripts, integrate Nagios with other applications, and make your infrastructure easier to monitor.

—Andrew Hay, Coauthor
Nagios 3 Enterprise Network Monitoring

Introduction

A Brief History of Nagios

Nagios Timeline

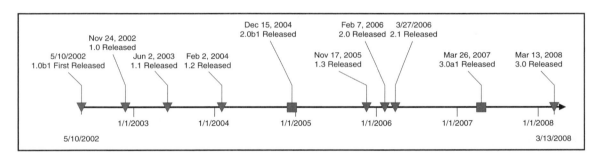

In the Beginning, There Was Netsaint

Shortly after the first week of May 2002, Nagios, formerly known as Netsaint, started as a small project meant to tackle the then niche area of network monitoring. Nagios filled a huge need; commercial monitoring products at the time were very expensive, and small office and startup datacenters needed solid system and network monitoring software that could be implemented without "breaking the bank." At the time, many of us were used to compiling our own Linux kernels, and open source applications were not yet popular. Looking back it has been quite a change from Nagios 1.x to Nagios 3.x. In 2002, Nagios competed with products like *What's up Gold*, *Big Brother*, and other enhanced ping tools. During the 1.x days, release 1.2 became very stable and saw a vast increase in the Nagios user base. Ethan had a stable database backend that came with Nagios that let administrators persist Nagios data to MySQL or PostgreSQL. Many users loved having this database capability as a part of the core of Nagios, Nagios 2.x and NEB, Two Steps Forward, One Step Back (to Some).

Well into the 2.0 beta releases, many people stayed with release 1.2 as it met all the needs of its major user base at that time. The 2.x line brought in new features that started to win over users in larger, "enterprise" organizations; at this time, Nagios also started to gain traction the area of application-level monitoring. Ethan and several core developers added the Nagios Event Broker (NEB), an event-driven plug-in framework that allows developers to write C modules that register with the event broker to receive notification of a wide variety of Nagios events and then act based on those events. At the same time, the relational database persistence layer was removed from Nagios to make the distinction clear between core Nagios and add-ons/plug-ins and to keep Nagios as flexible as possible. NDO Utils, a NEB-based module for Nagios, filled the gap the core database persistence functionality once held. During the 2.x release cycle, NDO Utils matured and was adopted by the very popular NagVis visualization add-on to Nagios.

Enter Nagios 3

With the 3.x release, we see the best of 1.x and 2.x and significant gains in configuration efficiencies and features that make using Nagios in larger environments much easier. The template system now supports multiple inheritance and custom, user-defined variables, a huge win for making maintainable and readable configurations. A number of configuration settings have been added specifically to make Nagios perform more efficiently when used with large numbers of services and hosts. Nagios will now parse and ingest multiline output from scripts, making it much easier to output stack traces, HTML errors, and other longer status messages. The GUI now makes a clear separation between "handled" (acknowledged) service and host problems, making Nagios even easier to use to focus on service and host problems that require attention.

Nagios in the Enterprise—a Flexible Giant Awakens

Move forward six years from the days of Netsaint, and Nagios is now a product that has proven to be a best-in-class open source monitoring solution. It competes well against most commercial applications, and in our opinion, it will in most cases have a lower cost to deploy and a higher level of effectiveness than many commercial applications in the same market. It has become an application that is both flexible and relatively easy to maintain. For every issue we have seen, there has been a way to monitor it through Nagios using plug-ins from the Nagios community or to create a way to monitor so that 100% meets the needs of the environment Nagios is in. In the progression of Nagios, we have seen the majority of attention paid to core features and functionality. No marketing team has dictated what new color needs to be in the logo, no companies have bought each other to re-brand a good product and leave new development on the floor. We see continued development that only improves on a tool no system or network administrator should be without. The 3.0 Alpha release saw 25 major changes from 2.0 documented in the change log. With almost every subsequent 3.x release, there has been a list of more than 10 new features per version.

As a measure of any good project, one needs to look at the community using it. Since 2.0, the Nagios-Plugins and Nagios Exchange Web sites have grown dramatically— nagiosexchange.org demonstrates the large community involvement in Nagios with custom plug-ins, add-ons, and modifications that have been freely contributed to improve and extend this application. Need to visualize service and host data? NagVis, PNP, nagiosgrapher, and other add-ons will let you do that. Want to give users who are not familiar with Nagios a GUI to edit and create an initial configuration? Use a Web-based GUI add-on—Fruity, Lilac, and NagiosQL are just a few of the administration GUIs available. Want to receive alerts via your blog? Or IM? Or Jabber? Scripts exist to let you do just that. Do not want to create your own integration of Nagios with other network and system monitoring products? A number of choices exist for that as well.

The future looks bright for Nagios in the enterprise; all of the authors on this project firmly believe this, and we believe our book can help you to make best use of Nagios by showing you the wide variety of features of Nagios 3, describing a number of useful add-ons and enhancements for Nagios, and then providing you a cookbook-style chapter full of useful plug-ins that monitor a variety of devices, from HTTP-based applications to CPU utilization to LDAP servers and more. We hope you enjoy this book and get as much out of it by reading and applying the principles and lessons shown in it as we did during the process of writing it.

—The Authors

## Chapter 1

Nagios 3

Solutions in this chapter:

- **What's New in Nagios 3?**
- **Backing up Your Nagios 2 Files**
- **Migrating from Nagios 2**

What's New in Nagios 3?

Nagios 3 has many exciting performance, object configuration, and CGI front-end enhancements. Object configuration inheritance has been improved and extended. Nagios now supports service and host dependencies along with service and host escalations. You can add arbitrary custom variables to services and hosts and access those variables in notifications and service and host checks. The CGI front end now has special subtabs for unhandled service, host, and network problems. The performance data output subsystem is very flexible and can even write to named pipes. The Nagios Event Broker (NEB) subsystem has been improved and enhanced. Finally, a number of new performance tuning features and tweaks can be used to help optimize the performance of your Nagios installation.

Storage of Data

There have been several enhancements to how Nagios 3 stores application-specific data.

Scheduled Downtime

In Nagios 2, scheduled downtime entries were stored in their own file as defined by the *downtime_file* directive in the main configuration file. Nagios 3 scheduled downtime entries are now stored in the status file, as defined by the *status_file* directive in the main configuration file. Similarly, retained scheduled downtime entries are now stored in the retention file, as defined by the *state_retention_file* directive in the main configuration file.

Comments

Previously stored in their own files in Nagios 2, host and service comments are now stored in the status file, as defined by the *status_file* directive. Similarly, retained comment entries are now stored in the retention file, as defined by the *state_retention_file* directive in the main configuration file.

Also new in Nagios 3, acknowledgment comments marked as non-persistent are only deleted when the acknowledgment is removed. In Nagios 2, these acknowledgment comments were automatically deleted when Nagios was restarted.

State Retention

With Nagios 3, status information for individual contacts, comments IDs, and downtime IDs is retained across program restarts. Variables have also been added to control what host, service, process, and contact attributes are retained across program restarts.

The *retained_host_attribute_mask* and *retained_service_attribute_mask* variables are used to control what host/service attributes are retained globally across program restarts. The *retained_process_host_attribute_mask* and *retained_process_service_attribute_mask* variables are used to control what process attributes are retained across program restarts. Finally, the *retained_contact_host_attribute_mask* and *retained_contact_service_attribute_mask* variables are used to control what contact attributes are retained globally across program restarts.

Status Data

Contact status information is saved in the status and retention files. Please note that contact status data is not processed by the CGIs. Examples of contact status information include last notification times, notifications enabled, and notifications disabled contact variables.

Checks

Several new service, host, and freshness check features have been added to Nagios 3 with a focus on enhancing system performance.

Service Checks

By default Nagios 3 checks for orphaned service checks. There is a new *enable_predictive_service_dependency_checks* option that control whether Nagios will initiate predictive dependency checks for services. Nagios allows you to enable predictive dependency checks for hosts and services to ensure the dependency logic will have the most up-to-date status information when it comes to making decisions about whether to send out notifications or allow active checks of a host or service.

Additionally, regularly scheduled service checks no longer impact performance with the implementation of new cache logic in Nagios 3. The new cached service check feature can significantly improve performance, as Nagios can use a cached service check result instead of executing a plug-in to check the status of a service.

Host Checks

Scheduled host checks running in serial can severly impact performance. In Nagios 3, host checks run in parallel. As with service checks, the new cached check feature also applies to host checks. This feature can significantly improve performance.

Two new options have been added to increase host check performance. The new *check_for_orphaned_hosts* option enables checks for orphaned hosts in parallel. Similar to the *enable_predictive_serivce_dependency_checks* option for service checks, the *enable_predictive_host_dependency_checks* option controls whether Nagios will initiate predictive dependency checks for hosts.

In Nagios 3, passive host checks that have a DOWN or UNREACHABLE result can now be automatically translated to their proper state as the Nagios instance receives them. Using the *passive_host_checks_are_soft* option, you can also control how Nagios sets the state for passive host checks instead of leaving the default HARD state.

Freshness Checks

A new *freshness_threshold_latency* option has been added to allow you to change the host or service freshness threshold that is automatically calculated by Nagios. To make use of this option, specify the number of seconds that should be added to any host or service freshness threshold.

Objects

Objects are the defined monitoring and notification logical units within a Nagios configuration. The objects that make up a Nagios configuration include services, service groups, hosts, host groups, contacts, contact groups, commands, time periods, notification escalations, notification dependencies, and execution dependencies.

In Nagios 3, changes have been made to object definitions and object inheritances that can result in a Nagios configuration that is easier to maintain and grow than configurations with Nagios 2 were.

Object Definitions

In the past, you may have wanted to create service dependencies for multiple services that are dependent on services on the same host. In Nagios 3, you can leverage these host dependencies definitions for different services on one or more hosts. The *host-group*, *servicegroup*, and *contactgroups* configuration types have also been enhanced with the addition of several key attributes. The *hostgroup_members*, *notes*, *notes_url*, and *action_url* attributes have been moved from the hostextinfo type to the *hostgroup* type. The *servicegroup_members*, *notes*, *notes_url*, and *action_url* attributes have been moved from the extserviceinfo type to the *servicegroup* type. Finally, the *contactgroup_members* attribute has been added to the *contactgroups* type. This flexibility allows you to include hosts, services, or contacts from subgroups in your group definitions.

The contact type now has new *host_notifications_enabled* and *service_notifications_ enabled*, and *can_submit_commands* directives that better control notifications to the contact and determine whether the contact can submit commands through the Nagios Web interface.

Extended host and service definitions (*hostextinfo* and *serviceextinfo*, respectively) have been deprecated in Nagios 3. All values that form extended definitions have also been merged with host or service definitions. Nagios 3 will continue to read and process older extended information definitions, but will log a warning. The Nagios development team notes that future versions of Nagios will not support separate extended info definitions. Also deprecated in Nagios 3 is the *parallelize* directive in service definitions. By default, all service checks now run in parallel.

To limit the times during which dependencies are valid, host and service dependencies now support an optional *dependency_period* directive. If you do not use the *dependency_period* directive in a dependency definition, the dependency can be triggered at any time. If you specify a *timeperiod* in the *dependency_period* directive, Nagios will only use the dependency definition during times that are valid in the *timeperiod* definition.

You can also use extended regular expressions in your Nagios configuration files if you enable the *use_regexp_matching* configuration option. A new *initial_state* directive has been added to host and service definitions. This directive allows you to tell Nagios that a host or service should default to a specific state when Nagios starts, rather than UP for hosts or OK for services.

Finally, there are no longer any inherent limitations on the length of host names or service descriptions.

Object Inheritance

Specifying more than one template name in the *use* directive of object definitions allows you to inherit object variables/values from multiple templates. When you use multiple inheritance sources, Nagios will use the variable/value from the first source that is specified in the *use* directive so the order you list templates in is very important. Services now inherit *contact groups*, *notification interval*, and *notification period* from their associated host unless otherwise specified. Similarly, hosts and service escalations now inherit *contact groups*, *notification interval*, and *escalation timeperiod* from their associated host or service unless otherwise specified. Table 1.1 lists the object variables that will be implicitly inherited from related objects if their values are not explicitly specified in your object definition or inherited them from a template.

Table 1.1 Object Variables

Object Type	Object Variable	Implied Source
Services	*notification_period*	*notification_period* in the associated host definition.
Host Escalations	*escalation_period*	*notification_period* in the associated host definition.
Service Escalations	*escalation_period*	*notification_period* in the associated service definition.

Specifying a value of *null* for the string variables in host, service, and contact definitions will prevent an object definition from inheriting the value set in parent object definitions. In addition, most string variables in local object definitions can now be appended to the string values that are inherited. This "additive inheritance" can be accomplished by prepending the local variable value with a plus sign (+). The following example shows how to use the additive inheritance:

```
define host{
        host_name            andrewserver
        hostgroups           +internal-servers,dmz-servers
        use                  generichosthosttemplate
        }
```

Operation

Numerous operational improvements have been added to Nagios 3, including several performance improvements, changes to the IPC mechanism, an overhaul of the *timeperiod* directives, enhanced debugging information, and more.

Performance Improvements

The pre-caching of object configuration files and exclusion of circular path detection checks from the verification process has greatly improved Nagios 3 performance. A number of improvements have been made in the way Nagios deals with internal data structures and object relationships. This results in substantial performance improvements in larger deployments of Nagios.

Two additional options have been added to increase performance specifically in large deployments. The *use_large_installation_tweaks* option allows the Nagios daemon to take certain shortcuts that result in lower system load and better performance. The *external_command_buffer_slots* option determines how many buffer slots Nagios will reserve for caching external commands that have been read from the external command file by a worker thread, but have not yet been processed by the main thread of the Nagios daemon.

Inter-Process Communication (IPC)

There have been significant changes to the IPC mechanism Nagios users to transfer host/service check results back to the Nagios daemon from child processes. The IPC mechanism has been changed to reduce load and latency issues related to processing large numbers of passive checks in distributed monitoring environments.

Check results are now transferred by writing check results to files in a directory specified by the *check_result_path* option. Additionally, files older than the *max_check_result_file_age* option will be deleted without further processing.

Time Periods

Everyone involved with the Nagios project agreed that the manner in which *timeperiods* functioned required a major overhaul. Time periods have been extended in Nagios 3 to allow for date exceptions including weekdays by name of day, days of the month, and calendar dates.

NOTE

The *timeperiods* directives are processed in the following order: calendar date (e.g., 2008-01-01), specific month date (e.g., January 1st), generic month date (e.g., Day 15), offset weekday of specific month (e.g., 2nd Tuesday in December), offset weekday (e.g., 3rd Monday), normal weekday (e.g., Tuesday).

Nagios Event Broker

When events within Nagios the Nagios Event Broker's (NEB) callback routines are executed to allow custom user-provided code to interact with Nagios. Using the NEB, you can output the events generated within your deployment to almost any application or tool imaginable.

Modules are libraries of shared code the NEB calls when an event occurs. The events are checked by the NEB to see if there is a registered callback associated with that particular type of event. If the event matches what the callback expects, the event is forwarded to your module. Once received, the module will execute any custom code associated with the event.

The event broker in Nagios 3 contains a modified callback for adaptive program status data, an updated NEB API version, additional callbacks for adaptive content status data, and a pre-check callback for hosts and services. The hosts and services pre-check callback allows modules to cancel or override internal host or service checks.

Debugging Information

In Nagios 3 debugging information can be written to a separate debug file. This file is automatically rotated when it reaches a user-defined size. The benefit of this enhancement is that you no longer have to recompile Nagios to debug an issue.

Flap Detection

The host and service definitions now have a *flap_detection_options* directive that allows you to specify what host or service states should be considered by the flap detection logic. When flap detection is enabled, hosts and services are immediately checked, and any hosts or services that are flapping are noted on the Nagios GUI. Percent state change and state history are also retained for both hosts and services even when flap detection is disabled.

Notifications

Notifications in Nagios 3 are sent for flapping hosts/services or when flap detection is disabled on a host or service. When this occurs, the *$NOTIFICATIONTYPE$* macro will be set to "FLAPPINGDISABLED". Notifications can also be sent out when scheduled downtime starts, ends, and is cancelled for hosts and services. The *$NOTIFICATIONTYPE$* macro is set to "DOWNTIMESTART" when the scheduled downtime is scheduled to start, "DOWNTIMEEND" when the scheduled downtime completes, and "DOWNTIMECANCELLED" when the scheduled downtime is cancelled.

The *first_notification_delay* option has been added to host and service definitions to introduce a delay between when a host/service problem first occurs and when the first problem notification goes out.

Usability

Several usability enhancements have been included in Nagios 3. The Web interface layout has been updated, Perl scripts can now tell Nagios to use the embedded Perl interpreter, *timeperiods* can be changed on demand, and plug-in output is now multiline and extended to 4096 bytes of output.

Web Interface

Similar to the TAC CGI, important and unimportant problems are broken down within the *hostgroup* and *servicegroup* summaries. Some minor layout changes around the host and service detail views have also been implemented. Additional check statistics have been added to the *Performance Info* screen.

Splunk integration options have been added to various CGIs within Nagios 3. This integration is controlled by the *enable_splunk_integration* and *splunk_url* options in the CGI configuration file. The *enable_splunk_integration* option determines whether integration functionality with Splunk is enabled in the Web interface. If enabled, you will be presented with *Splunk It* links in various places throughout the Nagios web interface. The *splunk_url* option is used to define the base URL to your Splunk interface. This URL is used by the CGIs when creating links if the *enable_splunk_integration* option is enabled.

External Commands

In Nagios 2, the *check_external_commands* option was disabled by default. In Nagios 3, however, this option is enabled by default so the command file will be checked for commands that should be executed automatically. Custom commands may now also be submitted to Nagios. Custom command names are prefixed with an underscore and are processed internally by the Nagios daemon.

Embedded Perl

Perl-based plug-ins can now explicitly tell Nagios whether they should be run under the embedded Perl interpreter. Two new variables now control the use of the embedded Perl interpreter. The *enable_embedded_perl* variable determines whether the embedded Perl interpreter is enabled on a program-wide basis. The *use_embedded_ perl_implicitly* variable determines whether the embedded Perl interpreter should be used for Perl plug-ins/scripts that do not explicitly enable/disable it. Please note that Nagios must be compiled with support for embedded Perl for both variables to function.

Adaptive Monitoring

Using the adaptive monitoring capabilities in Nagios 3, the *timeperiod* for hosts and services can now be modified on demand with the appropriate external command. The *CHANGE_HOST_CHECK_TIMEPERIOD* command changes the valid check period for the specified host. The *CHANGE_SVC_CHECK_TIMEPERIOD* command changes the check *timeperiod* for a particular service to what is specified by the *check_timeperiod* option.

Plug-in Output

One of the biggest enhancements in Nagios 3 is that multi-line plug-in output is now supported for host and service checks. The maximum length of plug-in output has also been increased from the 350-byte limit in Nagios 2 to 4096 bytes. The 4096-byte limit exists to prevent a plug-in from overwhelming Nagios with too much output. Additional lines of output (beyond the first line) are now stored in the *$LONGHOSTOUTPUT$* and *$LONGSERVICEOUTPUT$* macros.

TIP

To modify the maximum plug-in output length, simply edit the *MAX_PLUGIN_ OUTPUT_LENGTH* definition in the *include/nagios.h.in* file of the source code distribution and recompile Nagios. As of this writing, you will also have to manually modify the p1.pl script to have it output more than 256 bytes of output from scripts run under ePN, the embedded Nagios Perl interpreter.

Custom Variables

The ability to create user-defined, custom variables is seen as a huge advantage in Nagios 3. Custom variables allow users to define additional properties in their host, service, and contact and then use the values of these custom variables in notifications, event handlers, and host and service checks. When you define a custom variable, you must ensure that the name begins with an underscore (_) character.

Custom variables are case insensitive so you cannot create multiple custom variables with the same name, even if they differ by using a mix of uppercase and lowercase letters. Like normal variables, custom variables are inherited from object templates. Finally, scripts can reference custom variable values with macros and environment variables.

The following example shows how you could use custom variables for a host object that indicate when one of your Oracle servers (oraclepci334) was installed and when it was secured:

```
define host{
host_name oraclepci334
_installed_on_date February 24, 2008 ;
_secured_on_date February 26, 2008 ;
…
}
```

Macros

Nagios 3 includes 40 new macros to help you simplify your commands. These macros allow you to reference information from hosts, services, and other sources in your commands without having to explicitly declare the same values every time. Table 1.2 describes the new macros.

Table 1.2 New Macros in Nagios 3

Macro	Description
$TEMPPATH$	The *temp_path* directory variable Nagios uses to store temporary files during the monitoring process. This directory is specified in the *nagios.cfg* for your Nagios installation using the *temp_path=<dir_name>* format (e.g., temp_path=/tmp).
$LONGHOSTOUTPUT$	The full text output from the last host check.
$LONGSERVICEOUTPUT$	The full text output from the last service check.
$HOSTNOTIFICATIONID$	The unique number that identifies the host notification. This notification ID is incremented by one each time a new host notification is sent out.
$SERVICENOTIFICATIONID$	The unique number that identifies the service notification. This notification ID is incremented by one each time a new service notification is sent out.
$HOSTEVENTID$	The unique number that identifies the current state of the host. The event ID is incremented by one for each state change the host undergoes. If the host has not experienced a state change, the value returned will be zero.
$SERVICEEVENTID$	The unique number that identifies the current state of the service. The service ID is incremented by one for each state change the service undergoes. If the service has not experienced a state change, the value returned will be zero.
$SERVICEISVOLATILE$	Indicates that the service is being marked as volatile (1) or not volatile (0).
$LASTHOSTEVENTID$	The last unique event ID given to the host.
$LASTSERVICEEVENTID$	The last unique event ID given to the service.
$HOSTDISPLAYNAME$	The alternate display name as defined by the *display_name* directive in the host definition configuration.

Continued

Table 1.2 Continued. New Macros in Nagios 3

Macro	Description
$SERVICEDISPLAYNAME$	The alternate display name for the host as defined by the *display_name* directive in the host definition configuration.
$MAXHOSTATTEMPTS$	The alternate display name for the service as defined by the display_name directive in the service definition configuration.
$MAXSERVICEATTEMPTS$	The maximum number of check attempts defined for the current service.
$TOTALHOSTSERVICES$	The total number of services associated with the host.
$TOTALHOSTSERVICESOK$	The total number of services associated with the host that are in an OK state.
$TOTALHOSTSERVICES WARNING$	The total number of services associated with the host that are in a WARNING state.
$TOTALHOSTSERVICES UNKNOWN$	The total number of services associated with the host that are in an UNKNOWN state.
$TOTALHOSTSERVICE SCRITICAL$	The total number of services associated with the host that are in a CRITICAL state.
$CONTACTGROUPNAME$	The short name of the contact group this contact is a member of as defined by the *contactgroup_ name* directive in the contactgroup definition configuration.
$CONTACTGROUPNAMES$	The comma-separated list of contact groups this contact is a member of.
$CONTACTGROUPALIAS$	The long name of either the contact group name passed as an on-demand macro argument or the primary contact group associated with the current contact. This value is taken from the alias directive in the contactgroup definition.
$CONTACTGROUPMEMBERS$	The comma-separated list of all contacts passed as an on-demand macro argument or the primary contact group associated with the current contact.
$NOTIFICATIONRECIPIENTS$	The comma-separated list of all contacts that are being notified about the host or service.

Continued

Table 1.2 Continued. New Macros in Nagios 3

Macro	Description
$NOTIFICATIONISESCALATED$	Indicates that the notification was escalated (1) or sent to the normal contacts for the host or service (0).
$NOTIFICATIONAUTHOR$	The name of the user who authored the notification.
$NOTIFICATION AUTHORNAME$	The short name (if applicable) for the contact specified in the *$NOTIFICATIONAUTHOR$* macro.
$NOTIFICATION AUTHORALIAS$	The alias (if applicable) for the contact specified in the $NOTIFICATIONAUTHOR$ macro.
$NOTIFICATIONCOMMENT$	The comment that was entered by the notification author.
$EVENTSTARTTIME$	Indicates the point in time after *$PROCESSSTARTTIME$* when Nagios began to interact with the outside world.
$HOSTPROBLEMID$	The unique number associated with the host's current problem state. The number is incremented by one when a host or service transitions from an UP or OK state to a problem state.
$LASTHOSTPROBLEMID$	The previous unique problem number that was assigned to the host.
$SERVICEPROBLEMID$	The unique number associated with the service's current problem state. The number is incremented by one when a host or service transitions from an UP or OK state to a problem state.
$LASTSERVICEPROBLEMID$	The previous unique problem number that was assigned to the service.
$LASTHOSTATE$	The last state of the host. The possible states are UP, DOWN, and UNREACHABLE.
$LASTHOSTSTATEID$	The numerical representation of the last state of the host (e.g., 0 = UP, 1 = DOWN, 2 = UNREACHABLE).

Continued

Table 1.2 Continued. New Macros in Nagios 3

Macro	Description
$LASTSERVICESTATE$	The last state of the service. The possible states are UP, DOWN, and UNREACHABLE.
$LASTSERVICESTATEID$	The numerical representation of the last state of the service (e.g., 0 = UP, 1 = DOWN, 2 = UNREACHABLE).
$ISVALIDTIME:$	The on-demand macro that indicates if a particular time period is valid (1) or invalid (0); e.g.,
	$ISVALIDTIME:24×7$ will be set to **1** if the current time is valid within the **24×7** time period. If not, it will be set to **0**.
	$ISVALIDTIME:24×7:timestamp$ will be set to **1** if the time specified by the **timestamp** argument is valid within the **24×7** time period. If not, it will be set to **0**.
$NEXTVALIDTIME:$	The on-demand macro that returns the next valid time for a specified time period; e.g.,
	$NEXTVALIDTIME:24×7$ will return the next valid time from, and including, the current time in the **24×7** time period.
	$NEXTVALIDTIME:24×7:timestamp$ will return the next valid time from, and including, the time specified by the **timestamp** argument in the **24×7** time period.

TIP

You can determine the number of seconds it takes for Nagios to start up by subtracting *$PROCESSSTARTTIME$* from *$EVENTSTARTTIME$*.

Nagios macros can be used in one or more of 10 distinct command categories, and not all macros are valid for every type of command. Table 1. 3 describes the 10 categories of Nagios commands.

Table 1.3 Nagios Command Categories

Macro	Description
Service checks	Checks the availability of services in your Nagios deployment at regular intervals, as defined by your service definitions, or on-demand (as required).
	Certain *Host* and *Service* macros cannot be used, and none of the *Contact* or *Notification* macros can be used.
Service notifications	Used to define how notifications are handled for service state (i.e., OK, WARNING, UP, DOWN, etc.) changes.
	Certain *Host* macros cannot be used.
Host checks	Checks the availability of hosts in your Nagios deployment at regular intervals, as defined by your host definitions, or on-demand (as required).
	Certain *Host* macros cannot be used, and none of the *Service*, *Contact*, or *Notification* macros can be used.
Host notifications	Used to define how notifications are handled for host state (i.e., OK, WARNING, UP, DOWN, etc.) changes.
	None of the *Service* macros can be used.
Service event handlers and/or a global service event handler	Global service event handlers are run for every service state change that occurs, immediately prior to any service-specific event handler that may be run. Individual services can have their own event handler command that should be run to handle state changes.
	Certain *Host* and *Service* macros cannot be used, and none of the *Contact* or *Notification* macros can be used.
Host event handlers and/or a global host event handler	Global host event handlers are run for every host state change that occurs, immediately prior to any host-specific event handler that may be run. Individual hosts can have their own event handler command that should be run to handle state changes.
	Certain *Host* macros cannot be used, and none of the *Service*, *Contact*, or *Notification* macros can be used.

Continued

Table 1.3 Continued. Nagios Command Categories

Macro	Description
OCSP command	Obsessive Compulsive Service Processor (OCSP) commands allow you to run a command after every service check.
	Certain *Host* and *Service* macros cannot be used, and none of the *Contact* or *Notification* macros can be used.
OCHP command	Obsessive Compulsive Host Processor (OCHP) commands allow you to run a command after every host check.
	Certain *Host* macros cannot be used, and none of the *Service*, *Contact*, or *Notification* macros can be used.
Service performance data commands	Internal performance data that relates to the actual execution of a service check.
	Certain *Host* and *Service* macros cannot be used, and none of the *Contact* or *Notification* macros can be used.
Host performance data commands	Internal performance data that relates to the actual execution of a host check.
	Certain *Host* macros cannot be used, and none of the *Service*, *Contact*, or *Notification* macros can be used.

The Nagios developers have been kind enough to provide a full list of all available standard macros for Nagios 3 at http://nagios.sourceforge.net/docs/3_0/macrolist.html. The Nagios on-demand macros and macros for custom variables are detailed at http://nagios.sourceforge.net/docs/3_0/macros.html. These sites should be considered the most up to date resources available as both pages are actively updated as new features are introduced into the Nagios 3 product stream.

Backing up Your Nagios 2 Files

With any application, it is recommended to back up your current configuration files prior to upgrading to a newer version of that same application. Aside from being a good part of any disaster recovery plan, backing up your files prior to an upgrade allows you to revert to your running configuration with minimal downtime.

Before starting your Nagios 3 upgrade, ensure that you back up the files listed in Table 1.4.

Table 1.4 Nagios Files to Back Up

Nagios File	Description
nagios.cfg	The main Nagios configuration file, typically located at /usr/local/nagios/etc/nagios.cfg.
resource.cfg	The resource configuration file, typically located at /usr/local/nagios/etc/resource.cfg.
cgi.cfg	The CGI configuration file, typically located at /usr/local/nagios/etc/cgi.cfg.
retention.dat	The retention data file, typically located at /usr/local/nagios/var/retention.dat.
nagios.log	The current Nagios log file, typically located at /usr/local/nagios/var/nagios.log.

You should also back up all of your Nagios object definition files. These are the *.cfg* files that typically reside in the /usr/local/nagios/etc/objects/ directory. You may also want to back up any archived Nagios log files for forensic, or purely sentimental, reasons. These archived *.log* files typically reside in the /usr/local/nagios/var/archives/ directory.

Migrating from Nagios 2 to 3

If you have a current installation of Nagios 2 you can install Nagios 3 and leverage your existing configuration without having to retune your deployment for your network. Although possible, this is not recommended as you will miss out on many of the enhancements in Nagios 3.

There are several important points to consider prior to upgrading your Nagios 2 installation to Nagios 3. The *service_reaper_frequency* variable in the main configuration file has been renamed to *check_result_reaper_frequency*. This option allows you to control the frequency in seconds of check result *reaper* events. *Reaper* events process the results from host and service checks that have finished executing. These events constitute the core of the monitoring logic in Nagios.

The *$NOTIFICATIONNUMBER$* macro has been deprecated in favor of the new *$HOSTNOTIFICATIONNUMBER$* and *$SERVICENOTIFICATIONNUMBER$* macros. The *$HOSTNOTIFICATIONNUMBER$* macro is the current notification number for the host. The notification number increases by one each time a new notification is sent out for the host, with the exception of acknowledgments, which do not cause the notification number to increase. The *$SERVICENOTIFICATION NUMBER$* macro is the current notification number for the service. The notification number increases by one each time a new notification is sent out for the service, with the exception of acknowledgments, which do not cause the notification number to increase.

Several directives, options, variables, and definitions have also been removed or depreciated and should no longer be used in Nagios 3. The *parallelize* directive in service definitions is now deprecated and no longer used, as all service checks are run in parallel. The *aggregate_status_updates* option has been removed. All status file updates are now aggregated at a minimum interval of one second. Extended host and extended service definitions have been deprecated. They are still read and processed by Nagios 3, but it is recommended that you move the directives found in these definitions to your host and service definitions, respectively.

The *downtime_file* file variable in the main configuration file is no longer supported, as scheduled downtime entries are now saved in the retention file. The *comment_file* file variable in the main configuration file is no longer supported, as comments are now saved in the retention file.

TIP

To preserve existing downtime entries and existing comments, stop Nagios 2 and append the contents of your old downtime and comment files to the retention file.

Upgrading Using Nagios 3 Source Code

One way to upgrade your Nagios 2 deployment to Nagios 3 is to download the latest source code from the Nagios project's SourceForge.net page. The downloaded archive can be obtained using any Internet connected system and transferred to your Nagios server or it can be downloaded directly to your Nagios server using the *wget* command:

```
# wget http://osdn.dl.sourceforge.net/sourceforge/nagios/nagios-3.tar.gz
```

Depending on the current Nagios release, or the Nagios release you wish to download, you will have to adjust the filename accordingly. Once downloaded, you need to extract the files from the archive and install the Nagios software. If your server does not have the necessary development and dependant packages installed, the installation may not complete or operate as expected. At the time of this writing, regardless of your operating system type, the following dependencies must be installed prior to installing Nagios 3: the Apache HTTP server, the GCC compiler and development libraries specific to your distribution, and the GD graphics library.

> **NOTE**
>
> SourceForge.net is a source code repository and acts as a centralized location for software developers to control and manage open source software development. The Nagios project page on SourceForge is located at http://sourceforge.net/projects/nagios/.

The Apache HTTP server is required to provide a Web interface to manage your Nagios deployment. Some operating system distributions recommend certain versions of the Apache HTTP server over another. For example, when installing Nagios on an Ubuntu Linux or openSUSE distributions, Apache2 is recommended. Some older Linux distributions may not have the capability to run the Apache2 release and you may be forced to install on Apache 1.3.

The GNU Compiler Collection (GCC) is a set of compilers used to compile the raw Nagios code into a working application. Without the development libraries GCC relies on to build the application, the Nagios compile, and subsequent installation, will fail.

TIP

If your Unix, Linux, or BSD operating system has a package management utility installed, you usually need only specify that the GCC and development "tools" packages be installed. The package management utility is usually smart enough to automatically resolve any dependency issues for you.

The GD graphics library is an open source code library for the dynamic creation of images by programmers. Nagios uses the GD graphics library to generate the graphical representations of your collected data so it is easy to work with.

With the dependencies satisfied, and the Nagios archive downloaded, all that remains is to extract the archive and install it using the following commands:

```
# tar xzf nagios-3.tar.gz
# cd nagios-3
# ./configure --with-command-group=nagcmd
# make all
# make install
# /usr/local/nagios/bin/nagios -v /usr/local/nagios/etc/nagios.cfg
# /sbin/service nagios restart
```

If there are no errors generated during the compilation or installation, your Nagios installation has succeeded. If, for some reason you do receive errors, please review the exceptions for hints on how to resolve the issue and try the installation again.

If you alpha- or beta-tested the Nagios pre-released code, you need not worry about starting your Nagios deployment from scratch. Using the same source code installation process you can upgrade your pre-released Nagios deployment to the generally available final release, or any subsequent release, without losing your configuration information.

Generally speaking, this means that when a development release of Nagios is released you will have the ability to update from your final release, to several development releases, and eventually, to the final release of the new Nagios code.

If this is a production server, however, it is probably a good idea not to install pre-released Nagios code as there may be instabilities and vulnerabilities in the development version of Nagios.

Upgrading from an RPM Installation

The team behind Nagios releases the latest and greatest code in the form of compressed source code archives. Package-based releases for various operating systems—such as RPM for Red Hat distributions or DEB files for Debian distributions—are developed by members of the Nagios community and are usually driven by community demand.

To upgrade from your package-based Nagios 2 release to the source-based Nagios 3, you need to:

1. Back up your Nagios 2 configuration, retention, and log files. See the *Backing up Your Nagios 2 Configuration Files* section earlier in this chapter.

2. Uninstall the Nagios 2 package using the package management tools specific to your operating system distribution. For example, if using a Red Hat based Linux distribution, you could use the *rpm -e* command to uninstall the Nagios 2 package.

3. Install Nagios 3 from source. See the *Upgrading Using Nagios 3 Source Code* section earlier in this chapter.

4. Restore your Nagios 2 configuration, retention, and log files.

5. Verify your Nagios 3 configuration. Since we have copied an archived version of your Nagios 2 files, we should verify that there are no conflicting configuration issues by using the command:

```
# /usrs/local/nagios/bin/nagios -v /usr/local/nagios/etc/nagios.cfg
```

TIP

If there is an error in your configuration file, the error generated by the *nagios -v* command will point you to the line in the configuration file that appears to be causing the problem. If a warning is encountered the check will pass, as they are typically recommendations and not issues.

6. Start your Nagios 3 server. Now that you have verified that your configuration file will work with your new Nagios 3 installation, run the following command to start the server:

```
# /sbin/service nagios restart
```

Converting Nagios Legacy Perl Plug-ins

The Nagios software employs plug-ins to perform checks on managed hosts and services. In addition, these plug-ins may either be compiled executables, or human-readable scripts written in Perl or any of the Unix shells. For perl-based plugins Nagios provides the option of having the plug-ins interpreted via embedded Perl for Nagios (ePN).

If your Nagios installation is not using ePN there is nothing to use the plugins with Nagios 3. If, however, you have perl plugins that you wrote for Nagios 2 running under ePN, you will need to modify your plugins to specify that they wish to use ePN or set the variable use_embedded_perl_implicitly to 1 in the nagios.cfg configuration file. Add one of the following lines to your Perl plug-in within the first 10 lines of the plugin to instruct ePN to either execute the plugin by calling an external perl intrepreter or to execute the plug-in with ePN:

```
# Use embedded Perl for Nagios (ePN)
# nagios: +epn
```

   or

```
# Do NOT use ePN; use the Perl interpreter outside of Nagios
# nagios: -epn
```

## Chapter 2

Designing Configurations for Large Organizations

Solutions in this chapter:

■ **Fault Management Configuration Best Practices**

■ **Planning Your Configuration**

■ **Nagios Configuration Object Relationship Diagrams**

■ **Notification Rules and Output Formats**

Introduction

In this chapter, chapter we discuss how to create Nagios configurations that are easy to navigate, easy to maintain, and meet the needs of a larger customer. First we cover a few simple rules to follow as you design and implement your configuration. We then cover planning, a critical part of configuration that is often overlooked when implementing a fault management system. We then visually depict and discuss some important Nagios configuration object relationships that can help make your Nagios configuration easier to maintain and manage. We then discuss notification and escalation best practices. Finally we show you how to make the best use of the flexible and powerful object-oriented configuration language that is at the core of Nagios 3.

Fault Management Configuration Best Practices

We now discuss some basic principles that can make your life as a Nagios administrator and integrator easier. Given the variety of groups in an organization that monitoring systems touch, defining a change and growth process for your Nagios implementation is important. Readers who are familiar with software development might recognize some of these rules.

Solicit Input from Your Users First

Users should drive your implementation. Whether they are technicians fixing problems, customers expecting service-level agreements to be met, or managers wanting to know the status of applications that support projects they manage, users determine whether your monitoring implementation lives or dies. Pay close attention to what they want and your implementation will be successful. Before you write one line of configuration code, talk to each of these groups and find out how Nagios can best make their workdays (and nights) easier.

Use a "Less Is More" Approach

What is the fastest way to overwhelm the human brain? Send it too much information at once. What is the fastest way to make enemies out of your users? Bombard them and yourself with notifications for every little event that happens. We recommend you always prioritize your configuration and focus on what is most important.

- Only notify people who can do something about a problem unless someone outside the scope of responsibility for an area explicitly asks to be notified.

- Only monitor services on your systems that are indicators of failure. While it might be fun to see how many users are present on your systems, unless having too many users on a system at once has caused problems in the past, do not monitor that metric.

- Only monitor hosts and devices that matter. Can you monitor the health of the black-and-white printer down the hall? Sure. If it is only used a few times a week, should you monitor it? Probably not.

Take an Iterative Approach to Growing Your Configuration

Show the value of your system early on by adding a few important users in your organization to Nagios as contacts and by implementing checks of a few critical devices or services to Nagios. Grow your configuration as you learn more about your users' needs and what is important to them. Over time you will end up with a system your users pay attention to and one that helps track device and service problems. As with software development, implementing checks and notifications incrementally will help you create a system that matters.

Only Alert on the Most Important Problems

It can be very intimidating to be brought into a large organization to implement monitoring; determining what is important can become confusing, especially when politics are involved. Here are some rules to help you determine what services and devices are important to monitor:

- **Financial impact** If a service or device problem means a financial loss to your organization, monitor it.

- **Organizational impact** If a service or device outage means missing an important deadline or hurting a customer relationship, monitor that service or device.

- **Personal impact** If an outage means loss of job, income, or respect in a group for you or anyone on your team, help by implementing monitoring for that device or service.

Let Your Customers and Users Tell You What Is Important

Allow your user base to drive your configuration with regard to what is important and your system will be a success with your users. Talk to domain experts of the applications you will be monitoring and let them educate you about how their applications are designed to run and what indicates failure within each application. There is one exception to the "what is important" rule: Unless one or more of your users or managers are Nagios experts they should not tell you how to best implement their requirements.

Planning Your Configuration

Now that we have covered some basic configuration development principles, we will look at the process of planning your configuration. Users are key to this process and should be as much a part of the requirements process as they can be given restraints of time and resources. In this section we guide you through a top-to-bottom planning process you can use to implement a Nagios configuration for your organization.

Soliciting Requirements from Your Customers and Users

We cannot stress enough the importance of bringing the customer into the requirements process. Ask any network or systems administrator who has been in charge of implementing monitoring for an organization and you will hear story after story of implementations that failed because 1) the customer was not involved in developing requirements for the monitoring software; 2) the customer was not involved with prioritizing the system and application checks done on devices and applications in the organization; or 3) the customer was not involved in determining who should get notified how often and during which time periods.

Start by finding out what is important to monitor. Speak with the customer, project managers, and team leads. Initially it can be very useful to have meetings with both the customer and managers present to determine what is important. Keep the meetings short and to the point. Have a written agenda. It is very easy when discussing monitoring for the meetings to get sidetracked by political, budgetary, or organizational issues that have little to do with the basic questions:

- What is important to monitor?
- Who knows what the important devices and applications in your organization are?
- Who needs to know about outages?

Start High-Level and Work Down the Application Stack

Nagios makes it very easy to monitor devices. Once you are comfortable with developing service and host checks, you may be tempted to monitor every possible aspect of every device you can find. If you find yourself heading down this path, pause and take a deep breath. Ask yourself how monitoring the aspect of the device or application you are focusing on helps you meet the requirements you gathered from your customer and users. Most users do not care if the paging rate of a Unix system goes about 400 pages a second. Most system administrators will not care about this either unless it is a system that hangs and crashes when I/O paging rates hit that limit.

Most consumers of your data care more about whether their applications perform within acceptable boundaries than whether each system is performing as efficiently as it possibly can. Does monitoring CPU utilization help determine whether an application is performing properly? It can. Does performing an HTTP-based robotic test do a better job of telling you that same information? Absolutely. Why? It much more closely mirrors what users of the application might do and therefore has a much better chance of alerting on an application problem at a level your users care about. After an application test fails does the CPU test then mean more? Yes, it does; the CPU test now helps you determine or eliminate potential causes for the application problem, and helps you focus on lower level system and network issues that might be causing the failure or performance problem.

Start with checks that test functionality at a level that is closest to how your users judge whether your application is responding properly, and then work down toward metrics like CPU utilization, paging rates, network errors, and so forth. Your users will thank you by caring about what you have implemented for them, and your operational staff will thank you for eliminating some of the angry "it is 2 A.M. and Joe in Hawaii just called me, the CEO, to tell me he cannot log in!" calls.

Find Out What Applications Are the Most Important to Your Users

Sounds obvious, and it is. Sometimes, the application that continually has the most problems in an organization is not the most important application to that organization. Talk with your managers, customers (if you are allowed to), and users, and ask them what the most important applications are. Make a prioritized list based on the feedback you get from each group, keeping in mind that the customers' wants take highest priority. Your users will often be able to share important information with you about what applications are the most important to the customer as well.

Find Out What the Most Important Indicators of Application Failure/Stress Are

The key is to ask questions and talk with your peers, managers, and customers. Guessing only leads to useless or ignored alerts. Spend time (as much as you are able to) reading architectural, workflow, and other diagrams and documents created for the applications you are to monitor. You need to understand how the applications you are monitoring work before you can provide meaningful alerts.

Start By Only Monitoring the Most Critical Indicators of Health/Failure

Once you have a framework set up that easily lets you monitor various elements of a device or aspects of an application, it can be very tempting to monitor everything on that device or application. Resist this temptation. Start by monitoring the most obvious aspects of a device or application, and then add monitors for less obvious indicators as your understanding of the device or application matures. Keep your focus on what is important and you will help your user community and yourself; monitor everything and you will create chaos and confusion. Always remember that monitoring frameworks are first and foremost tools to facilitate communication and provide meaningful information on the state of a network and the applications on it.

Device Monitoring

Every organization will have a different focus. Use the flexibility of Nagios to your advantage. If a shop has separate groups that manage systems based on the operating system type, create host groups in Nagios based on the type of operating system. If your organization organizes machines based on environments (integration, development, production), group hosts based on those identifiers. If your customer only has staff who deal with problems on an application level, group devices by the application they support.

Application Monitoring

If your place of work focuses primarily on monitoring important applications, an approach you can take to get up and running quickly is to add each device the application lives on to Nagios, add one service check to each device, and then quickly move on to application-level tests. Keep in mind that application-level tests involve more than just testing if a network service port is listening. Work with your development staff or development managers, find use cases that typify what users do with the application you are monitoring, and then write tests that model those interactions. Your tests will serve two purposes: they will show when the application path you have simulated fails, and will provide useful baseline performance indicators. Even if your test does not fully simulate a user interaction (for example, by automating a browser GUI as opposed to just scripting HTTP directly), the performance numbers from each test run will show average response over time and also point out deviations in response time that can prove very useful.

Think like a tester. When an application fails and that failure is corrected, find out what happened and, if you can, write a test that simulates that path or modify your existing tests to catch that error and output a message that embodies the trouble-shooting steps you learned from the people who corrected the problem (or yourself if you were the troubleshooter). The more troubleshooting knowledge you can embed in your monitoring application, the less precious brainpower you and others have to spend remembering obscure troubleshooting paths.

Nagios Configuration Object Relationship Diagrams

Nagios has excellent documentation. One addition we have always wanted is diagrams showing how the various Nagios configuration objects relate to each other. Here are some diagrams representing relationships between the various configuration objects available in Nagios 3. We initially created a diagram with all relationships shown on one graph, but that turned out to be completely unreadable. We have broken down these relationships into smaller pieces, which makes for graphs that are more readable. We provide notes on each diagram to help point out some of the more useful relationships between Nagios configuration objects.

Hosts and Services

Note that services and hosts can both be members of hostgroups; this pair of relationships can make your Nagios configurations much easier to grow over time. For example, you could define a cisco-snmp group, write a slew of useful SNMP-based checks for your routers and switches, and then quickly add those checks to every Cisco device on your network by just adding the devices to the cisco-snmp group (Figure 2.1).

Figure 2.1 Service Configuration Object Relationships

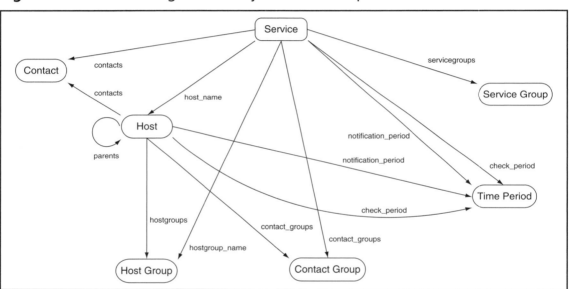

Contacts, Contact Groups, and Time Periods

Contact groups can help keep your configuration simple as they allow you to associate access control by groups. You can associate a user with one or more contact groups using the **contactgroups** attribute of the contact object, or you can associate contacts from the contact group itself by enumerating them in the **members** attribute.

Note also the flexibility Nagios gives users re time periods. User objects have the **service_notification_period** and **host_notification_period** to limit when they receive notifications, and time periods can use other time periods as exclusions to limit the range of the time period. Hosts and services have time periods associated with them that limit when host checks are performed (**check_period**) and when notifications are sent (**notification_period**) (Figure 2.2).

Figure 2.2 Contact and Time Period Configuration Object Relationships

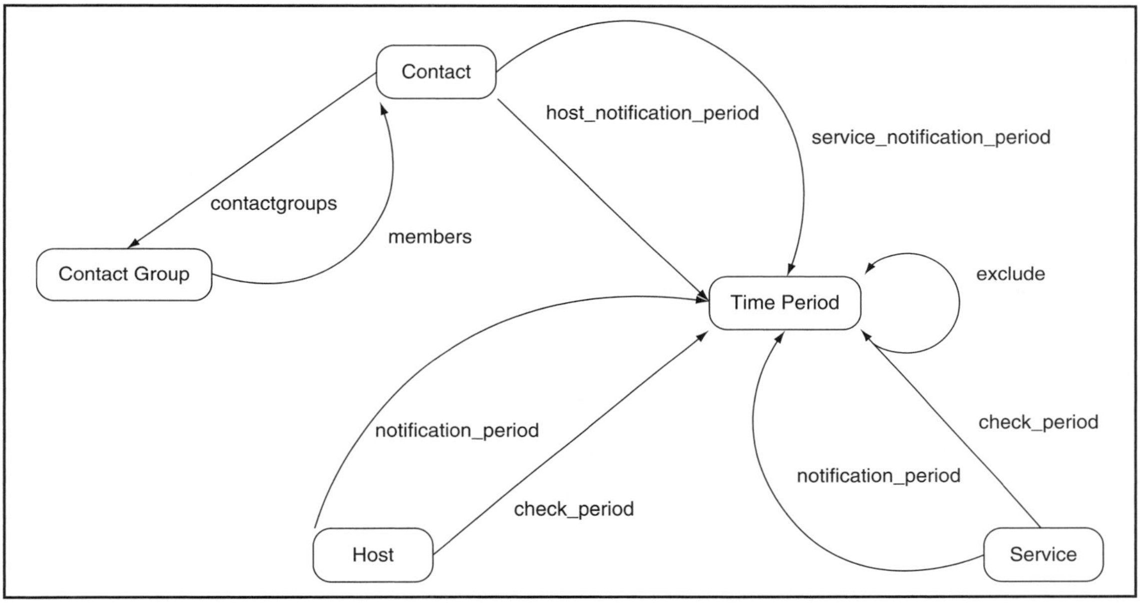

Hosts and Host Groups

Host groups are great for reporting and for associating groups of related devices with groups of related service checks. For example, an ISP might create a unique host group for each customer. The ISP can then run or create scripts to regularly run availability and trend reports for each customer. Also note that host groups can have host groups as members; this lets an administrator associate a device with a host group that has other host groups as members where each child host group has multiple services associated with it. For example, we might have a host group for Solaris servers and a host group for Apache servers with a parent group call unix_web_servers (Figure 2.3).

Figure 2.3 Host and Host Group Object Relationships

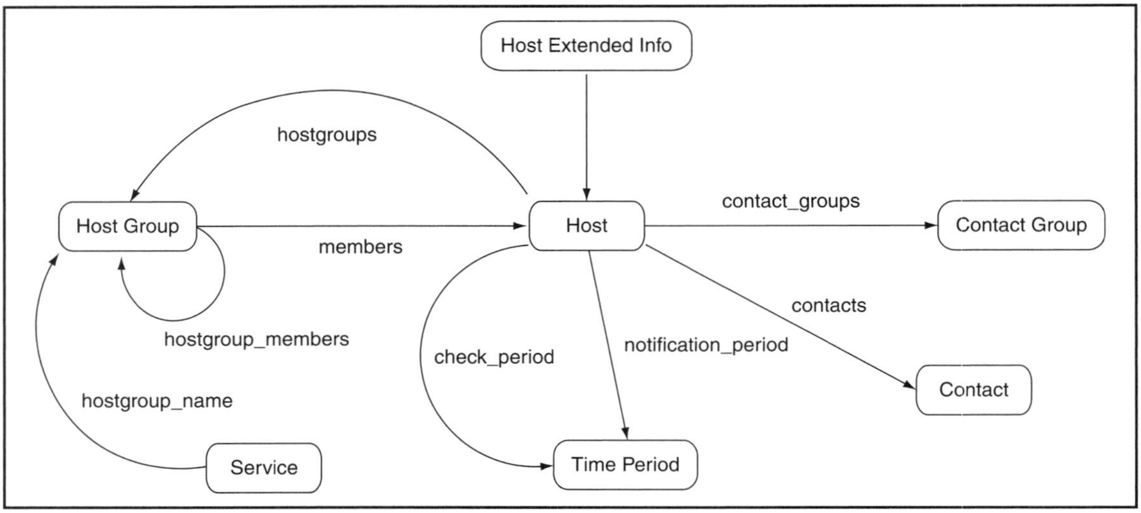

Services and Service Groups

A nice division of responsibility that Nagios uses is the separation of check periods and notification periods. For example, we can have a service that is checked 24×7 and only triggers notifications during working hours, meaning availability and trend reports will show all service changes and the people responsible for the health of the services only are notified during hours they are at work. Note also that with Nagios 3, service groups can have other service groups as members; this allows Nagios users and administrators to run SLA reports for management that aggregate trends and availability of groups of services across your organization (Figure 2.4).

Figure 2.4 Service and Service Group Object Relationships

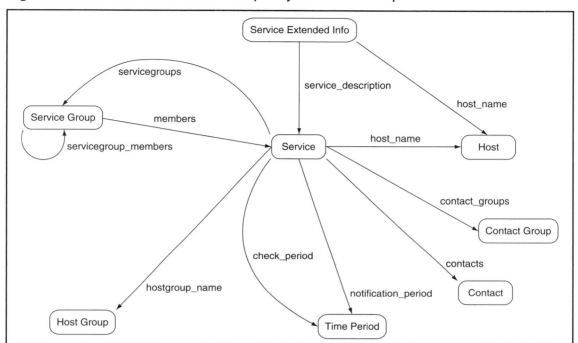

Hosts and Host Dependencies

Nagios allows administrators to set up dependencies between hosts. This relationship can be useful in modeling real-life host dependencies. For example, the application tier of an application might be completely useless if the database server it relies on is unreachable or down; in this case we may wish to suppress notifications for the application tier when the database server is down as the application server is totally dependent on the database server. Note that host dependencies have time periods associated with them so you can limit when the dependency is in effect. The Nagios documentation recommends that host dependencies should *only* be used when the hosts that depend on each are related to each other by functional relationships; for hosts that depend on each other for network connectivity, the basic child to parent relationship attribute *parents* should be used (Figure 2.5).

Figure 2.5 Hosts and Host Dependencies Object Relationships

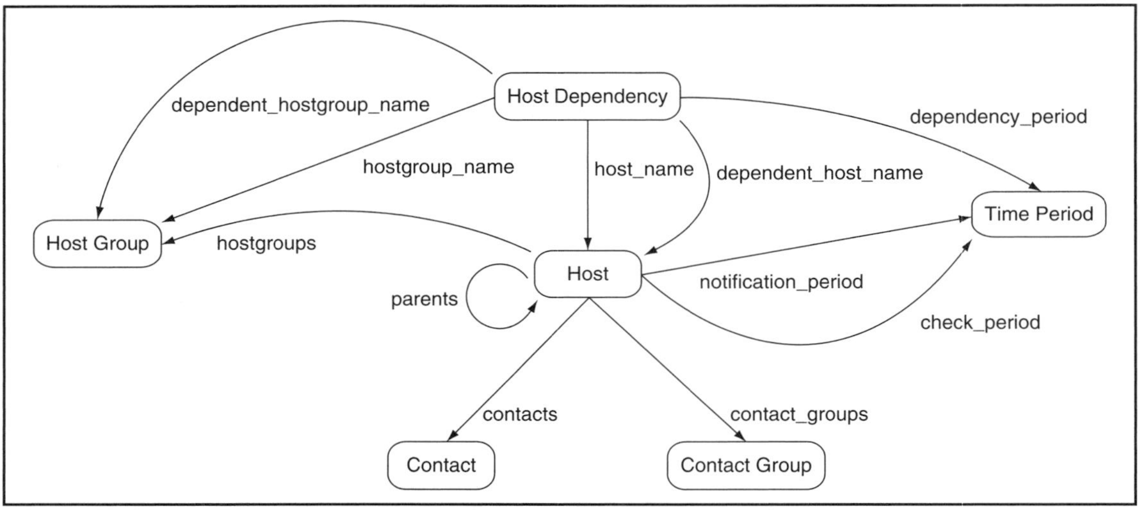

Services and Service Dependencies

Some services in an organization may only function if other services are working properly; Nagios lets us model this situation using service dependencies. When master services fail, checks will be suppressed for services that depend on them. For example, if an organization is using a service-oriented architecture (SOA), it might have one Web service that provides information on employees within the organization: name, contact numbers, where the employee sits, and so forth. Another service might use this service to retrieve employee data and display it on a centralized Web site; if the employee data provider stops functioning properly, there is no point in verifying with a check that the Web site used to display that data is working properly, as it completely depends on the data provider. Note that as with host dependencies, service dependencies use time periods (dependency_period) to allow for limiting when the dependency is in effect (Figure 2.6).

Figure 2.6 Services and Service Dependencies Object Relationships

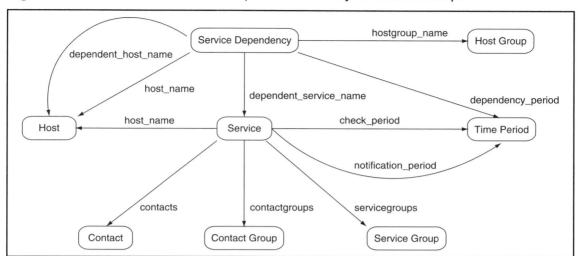

Hosts and Host Escalations

Host escalations let Nagios easily integrate with tiered support systems. They allow the Nagios administrator to set up notification rules that instruct Nagios to alter or add to the groups notified when a host is in a particular state based on the numbers of notifications that have been sent for a state. For example, an organization might have a dedicated tier 1–2 Unix system administration group. When a Web server becomes unreachable, this group would be the first to work to get the host back online. If the tier 1–2 group is unable to bring the host back to an operational state after two notifications, then a tier 3 group at central corporate would be notified and begin to investigate the issue to resolve it within established service-level agreement times set up between the customer and the service provider. Note that as with dependencies, host escalation time periods can be limited if desired; host escalations can also be associated with host groups, making it easy to maintain escalation procedures across large groups of hosts (Figure 2.7).

Figure 2.7 Hosts and Host Escalations Object Relationships

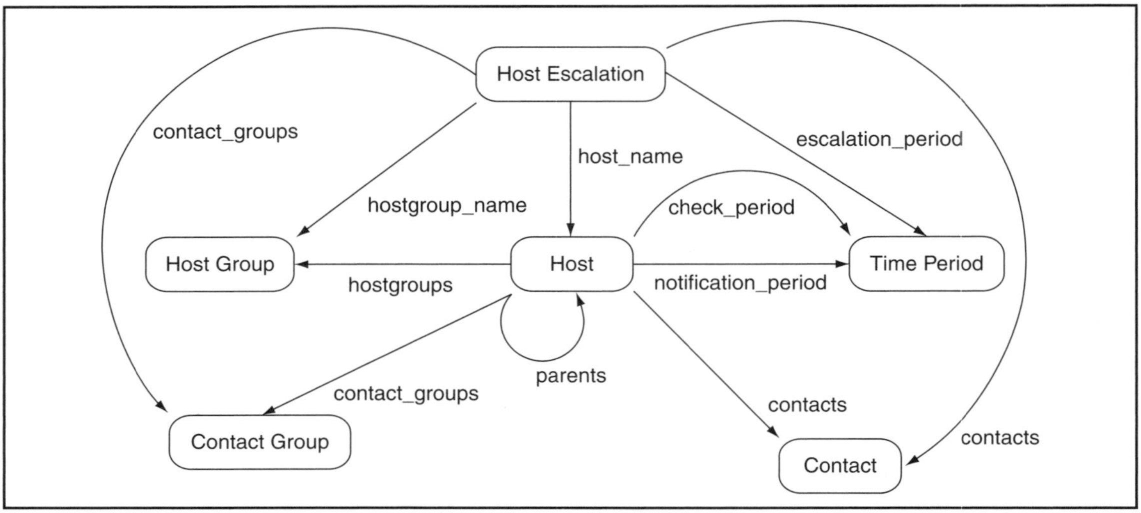

Services and Service Escalations

As with host escalations, service problems can be escalated to different groups in an organization based on the length of time a problem occurs. Notice that service escalations can be associated with both hosts and host groups but not service groups. If services that need to be escalated are associated with host groups rather than hosts or services, it is then easy to create service escalation policies that apply across an organization. For example, an organization might have a host group named *web servers* that holds all Web servers in an organization along with all service checks needed for them. Under this scenario, any new host added to the *web servers* group immediately inherits the service escalation policies created for the host group (Figure 2.8).

Figure 2.8 Services and Service Escalations Object Relationships

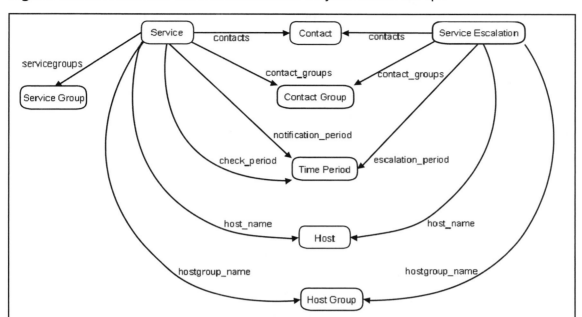

Version Control

Nagios' configuration language is like a stripped-down programming language with object-oriented features; treat your Nagios configuration as you would any other application source code. The larger and more heterogeneous the environment is, the more complex configurations can become, even when designed carefully to take advantage of the inheritance model the Nagios configuration language supports. In an environment where there is enough trust to give coworkers the ability to manage their own configurations, the risk of losing important configuration code increases. Finally, there is the risk of losing a configuration should an intruder break in to the host Nagios runs on.

Version control can help resolve all of these situations. It mitigates the risks associated with having multiple authors working on the same code at the same time. It provides an easy way to have live backups of Nagios configurations and lets administrators see who changed what, and when. In this section, we show how version control can help make your configuration easier to use, change, and share.

The larger the configuration, the trickier it becomes to remember the changes made to the configuration. Place the configuration under version control and it becomes easy to see what changes have been made to the configuration. Additionally, the comments provided give context and rationale for why changes were made. Version control also allows for tagging specific releases of a configuration. If an organization has implemented a redundant cold backup system, a version control system can easily compare two configuration releases and quickly synchronize a live system and a cold backup system. Finally, most version control systems also provide a Web interface that allows users to browse the source, compare arbitrary revisions, and create and associate actions with code (trouble tickets, bug reports, etc). This can make it easy for an administrator to keep track of what has changed and remember why changes were made in the first place.

As mentioned before in this book, Nagios can facilitate communications between groups in an organization and help them communicate the status of managed devices and services within an organization to operational staff. Once an organization starts seeing the value Nagios can provide in these areas, domain experts within an organization might start to develop their own ideas of what they want to monitor and how they want to monitor the services and hosts that are important to them. Eventually trust might develop between the administrators and these users and you may decide to allow users to make their own configuration changes. Even with this trust in place administrators probably do not want users to make configuration changes to service and host monitoring policies that other groups in an organization have established. Version control systems can be used to control access to areas of a configuration tree by setting up group-specific subdirectories that are stored in projects made specifically for each group. For example, if there is a Unix group, a Windows group, and a router group, the configuration directives in nagios.cfg might look like this:

```
cfg_dir=/usr/local/nagios/etc/groups/windows
cfg_dir=/usr/local/nagios/etc/groups/unix

cfg_dir=/usr/local/nagios/etc/groups/router
```

Each subdirectory could then be set up as a version-controlled repository. This allows each group to check out its own configuration project, make changes to it, and check changes back in. They never need interactive login access to the physical monitoring host. After changes are made, a code review can be done (very important), the configuration can be tested, and the new code can then be applied to the system. Version control will not keep people from writing malicious code or creating files with incorrect syntax, so make sure a human reviews each group's changes before they are applied to the Nagios host.

This way of thinking about configuration can also be very useful for a consulting business. For example, a business might have a client with whom there is a fair amount of trust, yet that client requires service or hosting checking functionality specific to their application or network. Administrators might not be comfortable giving clients SSH access to the Nagios host as it contains configurations from other customers. In this case, the Nagios configuration tree might look something like Figure 2.9.

Figure 2.9 Example Nagios Configuration Tree for a Consulting Business

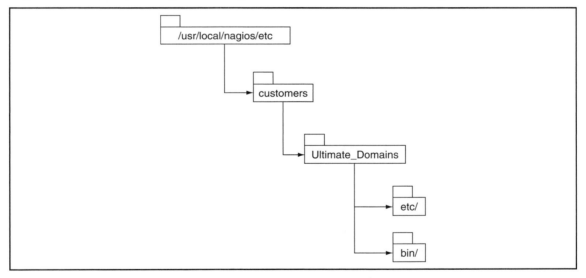

The Nagios cfg_dir section might look like this:

```
cfg_dir=/usr/local/nagios/etc/customers/Ultimate_Domains/bin
cfg_dir=/usr/local/nagios/etc/customers/Ultimate_Domains/etc
cfg_dir=/usr/local/nagios/etc/customers/CVK9_Services/bin
cfg_dir=/usr/local/nagios/etc/customers/CVK9_Services/etc
```

For each customer custom scripts would be stored in the bin/ subdirectory, and custom configurations in the etc/ subdirectory. We also recommend making use of the custom attributes feature of Nagios 3 to create base host or service configuration for each customer that contains company-specific information. This meta-data can later be used in notifications to provide contact information or other company-specific information to the people receiving the alerts. A base service configuration with custom attributes is shown in this example:

```
define service {

use generic-service # Inherit from the generic-service definition that comes with
Nagios

name                    ud-base

hostgroups              ultimatedomains

notification_interval   120

notification_period     24×7

contact_groups          ultimatedomains

__ud_base               /usr/local/nagios/etc/clients/Ultimate_Domains # Custom
                        commands can refer to this

__customer_notes        Ask for Jarred if you need to speak to someone who knows
                        all the applications well

__customer_address      111 Example Avenue, Sometown, Florida. 00000

__customer_phone        555-1212

register                0
}
```

We recommend using a double-underscore "__" as a prefix to custom attributes; when the variables are used in services or hosts the _HOST or _SERVICE prefix is separated from the variable name by a single underscore. For example, in a command definition, __customer_phone becomes:

```
$_SERVICE_CUSTOMER_PHONES$
```

An example check command that uses the __ud_base and other custom variables:

```
define command {
    command_name check_ud_keyword_search
    command_line $_SERVICE_UD_BASE$/bin/check_keyword_search.pl -s
    $_SERVICE_UD_KEYWORD_SEARCH_TERM$ -e $_SERVICE_UD_KEYWORD_SEARCH_ENV$ -w
    $_SERVICE_UD_KEYWORD_SEARCH_WARN$ -c $_SERVICE_UD_KEYWORD_SEARCH_CRIT$
    }
```

Losing a configuration, whether it is due to mistyping, a system break-in by an attacker, or system failure is painful. Set up a revision control repository for the Nagios monitoring host on a host that is separate from Nagios on the network so that even if the monitoring host is compromised or fails, there is a recent backup to roll back to quickly. Version control should never be used as *the* backup system for a host, yet it certainly makes an excellent addition to backup systems and is a very fast way to restore a configuration should something bad happen.

Version control of configuration code is often not considered at all when implementing a monitoring system with Nagios. Nagios' configuration language is rich and can help model services and hosts in complex environments—making the loss of a well-designed configuration a painful event. Make wise use of version control and there will be peace of mind for administrators, flexibility for users, and customers can have control over their custom service checks and the ability to easily see what changes are made to their monitoring configuration.

Notification Rules and Output Formats

Designing notification rules is one of the most important activities done in the management of a Nagios configuration. Design rules that provide the right information to the right people at the right times and coworkers will notice. Do a poor job of designing notification rules, send out too much information or too little to the wrong people, and coworkers will notice in a negative way and there will be much unhappiness (trust us on this) in the office and users will ignore the alerts Nagios sends out.

Notification via Email

Less is more when it comes to email notifications. Most professionals in IT receive hundreds or more emails a day. While many email clients make it easy to prioritize, flag, and tag messages, it is still a normal human tendency to be annoyed at too much information and to ignore email when we receive too much of it from a single source. Customizing your notifications to fit in with the email system the client uses can really help you sell your monitoring services to your customer/clients.

Minimize the Fluff

We repeat this often because it is so important. Send out email notifications only when a problem requires human intervention immediately. If CPU utilization on a system hits 100% during one five-minute poll, you certainly want to capture that event by having your service check return a CRITICAL state to Nagios, but you most likely should not send out an email to a system administrator. If CPU utilization stays pegged at 100% utilization for several hours, it might then be time for a person to investigate. Use host and service dependencies to escalate alerts when needed and to suppress alerts for hosts and services that should not be checked because dependent services and hosts are not available.

Make Notification Emails Easy to Filter

Always use a standard subject prefix to your emails so users can filter your emails into custom folders if they want to. A fixed subject prefix also makes it easy to see which emails are sent from Nagios.

Enhancing Email Notifications To Fit Your User Base

Customers use a variety of email systems; some support open standards for displaying priority, importance, or status. Some support HTML, others do not. Take the time to learn your customer's email system so that you can make your emails as precise and easy to digest as possible. There are a variety of enhancements and customizations you can make to your email notification scripts that will allow you to target your customers' specific needs. These include graphics, custom information about the servers you are sending alerts for, standard operating procedures, and links to other information systems that can provide troubleshooting insight to the recipients of the emails.

Brains get overloaded with too much text. While some hard core IT employees might tell you that graphics are only for pointy-haired managers, the truth is that meaningful graphics convey a lot of information quickly when done properly. For example, some email systems support HTML and allow you to associate custom icons with email that indicate urgency (IMPORTANT, URGENT, etc). Associate these custom icons with WARNING and CRITICAL states in your email notifications and your technicians immediately know how urgent an alert is without even opening it.

For some environments, including a trending graph from Nagios in alert emails is also useful. A host trend graph in a host down email can tell a technician if the host that is now down has been experiencing multiple outages recently or if this is a unique event. This additional information lets the technician know the level of troubleshooting they need to engage in; if a host is just down once in the time on the trending graph in the email (A 3 day trend for example) then the technician can maybe just reboot the host, do some relatively basic troubleshooting / investigating and close the ticket. If, on the other hand, the host has been up and down repeatedly over the last three days, then the technician knows that he or she should do much more in-depth troubleshooting to attempt to find and resolve the issue that is causing the host to have such instability.

Custom information about a device that is having an issue can add significant value to alert emails. Nagios 3 lets us specify custom attributes in host and service definitions; staff at an organization can use these attributes to convey additional important information about devices with problems. Rack location, key personnel names / numbers, manager names, type of server, support contract number, all of this information can help the technician troubleshooting a problem with a server or network device more quickly resolve whatever issues are causing the device to crash or be unreachable. When working under pressure this can be a real time-saver and keep anxiety levels low.

As the monitoring teams and personnel at an organization gain experience troubleshooting applications within the organization, they should also take the time to develop standard operating procedures to make fixing problems that re-occur easier. These procedures can include common troubleshooting steps and who to contact if the problem cannot be resolved. If these procedures are stored on a web server and given names that map to Nagios service descriptions, then the script that creates the Nagios alert email can include links to standard troubleshooting procedures or even include troubleshooting steps in the email alert sent to end users.

Most organizations maintain a number of internal tools that provide configuration management or other important information on devices and services hosted within the organization. It is very common for larger organizations to use commercial or open source configuration management tools to track hardware object manufacturers, peripherals, CPU type / speed, RAM, etc. In organizations in which technicians work on a large variety of hosts and network devices, this additional configuration information could prove to be very useful to the technician, providing them insight on the power and stability of the hardware they are investigating before they even touch it.

Finally, providing links to other types of network-accessible knowledge base systems within an organization in notifications can be very useful to technical staff. Wikis are becoming more and more common in organizations of all sizes; information in Wikis ranges from troubleshooting tips to software development requirements to contact information for key personnel. You might find that providing links to this information in your notifications helps speed up the troubleshooting process by eliminating a lot of the initial knowledge gathering that sometimes happens between technical staff when a problem arises. An on-call technician might receive an email at 2 AM about a web service that he or she is not familiar with. If the email includes links to an accessible Wiki that has information on the web service, that technician may be able to spend a few minutes reading and then remotely login to the server to troubleshoot the problem rather than spending two hours trying to reach someone by email or phone who can get the technician up to speed on how this little-used web service works.

Figure 2.10 Use Nagios notifications to communicate more than just simple status

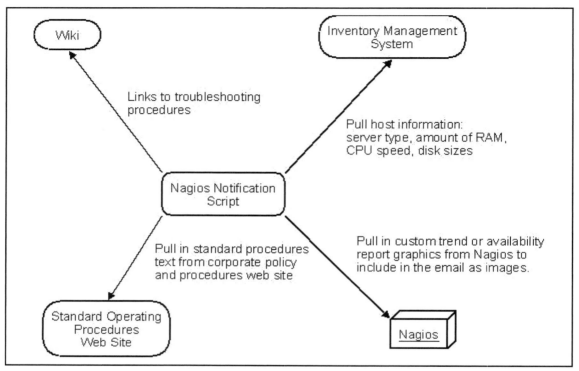

Email is the most-used notification method with Nagios or any other fault management system. Make use of the flexibility Nagios provides to give your users every bit of information they request, be that trending graphs, device information, knowledge base links, or standard operating procedures. Help your 2 AM web service troubleshooting expert to resolve his or her issue quickly; there is nothing technicians like more than being able to go to sleep at a reasonable hour.

Notification Via Pager/SMS

Minimize Included Information

Notifications need to convey information quickly and concisely. Even though many of us have phones and pagers capable of receiving and displaying large documents, the last thing we want to do as system and network managers is clog up mail networks with too much information. Ask your customers and users what they want to see in their notifications. Include only the most important facts: host name, IP address, service description, maybe a customer-specific piece of meta-data like a contact phone number. Avoid graphics and long service output strings in notifications to pagers/SMS devices.

Only Notify in the Most Important Situations

The larger the set of hosts and services you monitor, the more important this rule is; it also takes time to tune service and host checks so they are not triggered when situations do not warrant it. In general it is better to start with no notifications and then add notification rules as necessary rather than send too many notifications out for service and host outages and have them ignored. One of us was in a situation where a coworker called Nagios "the spaminator" because this co-author had not implemented notifications properly and users were getting notified of service state changes too frequently. A five-minute discussion with another member of the team led to a quick and happy resolution thanks to the rich configuration language Nagios includes.

Respect Working Hours and Employee Schedules

Make sure you find out from managers and your customers when they want to be notified. Nothing is more annoying to a technician or manager than receiving an alert during a time when he or she is supposed to be off the clock. Make it easy for people to contact you to request changes to schedules, and implement those changes promptly when users request them.

Alternative Notification Methods

For most situations, email is the preferred method of notification. However, there are plenty of situations in which administrators might prefer to send or receive alerts using methods other than email. In this chapter, we cover sending alerts that use Instant Messenger and polling Nagios for alerts and then translating them into speech using text-to-speech.

Instant Messenger

For some organizations, certain systems or services are so critical that users want to be notified as close to the time of the event as possible. Other groups, like software teams, might leave a chat room open for team discussion and interaction; these developers might also want alerts about system or host problems for development systems to be sent to their chat room. The Instant Messenger protocol can be used to satisfy this kind of requirement.

We will now show an example notification script that uses AOL instant messenger, a very stable and well-documented Instant Messenger protocol with a wide variety of clients available. To send an Instant Message, we will need to first establish a user account with AOL and then save our username and configuration in our Nagios configuration. Since this information is sensitive, we recommend you put it in the resource.cfg file and tighten down the permissions on resource.cfg so only root can read/write it. Here we will set our username in user variable 50 and our password in user variable 51 in the Nagios configuration file resource.cfg:

```
$USER50$=myusername
$USER51$=mypassword
```

Since the resource.cfg file is readable only by root, we will need to restart Nagios after changing it, as Nagios reads the resource.cfg file as root *before* it drops privileges to the nonroot user ID Nagios runs as (you are running Nagios as a nonprivileged user we hope).

Here is an example script that will send an instant message using AOL IM, written in ruby; for this example, we are calling it notify-by-aol-im.rb:

```ruby
#!/usr/local/bin/ruby

require 'rubygems'
require 'net/toc'

USAGE = <<EOF
#{$0} from-screen-name from-password to-screen-name message
EOF

screen_name = ARGV[0] || my_die("Missing from screen name")
password = ARGV[1] || my_die("Missing password")
to = ARGV[2] || my_die("Missing to screen name")
msg = ARGV[3] || my_die("Missing message to send")

client = Net::TOC.new(screen_name, password)

client.connect
client.buddy_list.buddy_named(to).send_im(msg)
client.wait(5)
client.disconnect

exit 0
```

Now we need to create a command definition in Nagios so we can access the new command from our Nagios configuration:

```
define command {
   command_name service-notify-by-im
   command_line $USER1$/notify-by-aol-im.rb '$USER50$' '$USER51$' '$ADDRESS1$'
   'Host: $HOSTNAME$\nHost state: $HOSTSTATE$\nTime: $LONGDATETIME$\nService:
   $SERVICEDESC$\nService state: $SERVICESTATE$\nService output: $SERVICEOUTPUT$\n' }
```

To send a message, we will need to know the end user's IM username. Since this information is not sensitive, we can embed it in the contact definition for the user as an *addressN* variable. Here is an example that sets the instant messenger username into the *address1* variable in a contact:

```
define contact {
   ...
   address1       myexampleIMname
   ...
}
```

Next we associate our notification command with the user who wants to be notified by IM:

```
define contact{
   ...
   service_notification_commands service-notify-by-im
   ...
}
```

Voilà! The user will start to receive service notifications via IM. If the user wants IM notifications only during special times or days in addition to the normal notifications he receives, we can create a second contact definition for the user that just holds the IM specifications:

```
define contact{
   contact_name                 joe-im
   alias                        Joe - Instant Messenger
   service_notification_period  9x5
   host_notification_period     never
   host_notification_options    n              # n == none
   host_notification_commands   dummy_command  # have to define a command for host
                                notifications
   service_notification_options u,w,c,r
   service_notification_commands service-notify-by-im
   address1                     myexampleIMname
}
```

A possible definition for dummy_command in the commands file, as we do not care about host notifications for this contact:

```
define command{
command_name dummy_command
command_line check_dummy 0
}
```

Keep in mind that services like AOL IM will disallow login access if an IM client connects and then disconnects too many times within a minute. For this reason, use IM only for the most critical alerts.

Text-to-Speech

We have encountered many situations where initially managers thought that having alerts spoken would be a great way to make their lives easier. Sometimes giving a manager the ability to hear alerts can help sell Nagios to an organization. The result is often that after a month or two, the manager and other employees get tired of hearing these alerts. This does not mean there is no value in text-to-speech. Some busy system administrators might appreciate not having to constantly switch their focus to Nagios to check for new problems, and certainly if there are staff at an organization who have problems with sight, text-to-speech can be very useful.

For text-to-speech, we prefer to have a script that actively polls Nagios for alerts rather than having Nagios call a script to perform the text-to-speech. Having the text-to-speech script poll Nagios means it can live anywhere on the network and even be deployed to multiple places within an organization if so desired; each instance can filter the alerts from the "Service Problems" and "Host Problems" screens to cater to the target audience for the script.

The script presented here uses Perl and the Microsoft Voice API to translate alerts into speech; we have found that most organizations use Windows workstations for end users. Porting the script to Linux or Unix is a simple matter, as the GPL Festival project (http://www.cstr.ed.ac.uk/projects/festival/) provides a very flexible and fairly easy to set up set of tools to translate text to speech for Unix and Linux.

If you wish to use a voice other than the default voice that comes with Windows, download the Microsoft SAPI5 speech SDK from http://download.microsoft. com/download/speechSDK/SDK/5.1/WXP/EN-US/speechsdk51.exe. Run the .msi installer from the package, and two additional voices—Sam (voice index 1) and Mary (voice index 2)—will be installed.

If you wish to use SSL URLs with this script on Windows, note that the SSL packages are no longer provided in the Activestate perl package repository due to Canadian cryptographic export restrictions. Instead, you will have to add the

University of Winnipeg repository to PPM and then install them. Example session using Activestate Perl 5.10 (please be aware that the repositories have different paths for versions 5.8 and 5.6 of Activestate Perl):

```
C:\>ppm-shell
ppm> add rep winnipeg http://cpan.uwinnipeg.ca/PPMPackages/10xx/
ppm> install Net::SSLeay
```

You will be asked a series of questions about retrieving `ssleay32.dll` and `libeay32.dll`. Answer yes to the questions, accept the defaults for any other questions related to the install of the SSL module, and the module will install without problems.

This script will also run under Cygwin (tested under version 1.5.25-7 with Perl 5.10). We tested the script with the default Perl 5.8.8; unfortunately with perl 5.8.8 Net::SSLeay dumps core when LWP attempts to retrieve SSL URLs using Net::SSLeay. Upgrading to Perl 5.10 and recompiling Net::SSLeay using the cpan front-end resolved the issue.

Here is the code for the daemon:

```
#!/usr/bin/perl

=pod

=head1 NAME

nagios-ttsd.pl

=head1 SYNOPSIS

Poll a Nagios host for alerts and translate them from text to speech bounded by
filters established within the configuration file.

=head1 CONFIGURATION

The configuration file has 3 sections: main, filters, and translations.

The main section contains information on where Nagios is on the network, how often
to poll it, and the username and password to use to log into Nagios to retrieve
service and host status. The account used for retrieving status should only be
able to view statuses; do not give it permission to execute commands, leave
comments, etc. Finally, there is a debug variable in the main section that will
cause the script to output verbose debugging information to a file if you set the
value of debug to a file name.

The filters section allows you to filter what alerts are retrieved from Nagios based
on service name, host name, and service or host state.

The translations section contains a list of words and replacements for them.

Often you will find that text to speech libraries do not handle English spellings
properly, so being able to replace proper spellings with phonetic spellings can
```

make alerts sound much more natural when spoken. Place new words or phrases between EOF markers and put %% between the word or phrase to catch and the translation of the phrase. Additionally the translations section contains host_ phrase_template and service_phrase_template variables; you can alter the template for host and service problem phrases to your liking.

See the included sample configuration file for more information on configuring this program.

```perl
=cut
use strict;
use LWP;
use Win32::OLE;
use Config::IniFiles;
use CGI;
use FindBin;

my $CF_FILE = shift || "$FindBin::Bin/nagios-ttsd.ini";

my %HOST_STATES  = qw(
    PENDING      1
    UP           2
    DOWN         4
    UNREACHABLE  8
);

my %SVC_STATES   = qw(
    PENDING      1
    OK           2
    WARNING      4
    UNKNOWN      8
    CRITICAL     16
);

my $CAN_SSL = 0;
eval{
    require Net::SSLeay;
    import Net::SSLeay;
};
$CAN_SSL = 1 unless $@;

my $CFG = read_config($CF_FILE);

my $DEBUG = $CFG->{'main'}->{'debug'} || '';
my $VERBOSE = $CFG->{'main'}->{'verbose'} || 0;
```

```perl
validate_config($CFG, $CAN_SSL, \%HOST_STATES, \%SVC_STATES);

debug("Starting");

my $TTS = Win32::OLE->new("Sapi.SpVoice")
             || die "Sapi.SpVoice failed";
$TTS->{'Voice'} = $TTS->GetVoices->Item($CFG->{'main'}->{'voice'});

my $SLEEP = $CFG->{'main'}->{'polling_interval'};

my @TRANSLATIONS = @{$CFG->{'translations'}->{'phrase_list'}};
my $HOST_PHRASE = $CFG->{'translations'}->{'host_phrase_template'};
my $SERVICE_PHRASE = $CFG->{'translations'}->{'service_phrase_template'};

while (1){
   speak("Checking for host alerts") if $VERBOSE;
   my @h = check_for_host_alerts($CFG, \%HOST_STATES);
   speak_alerts($HOST_PHRASE, \@TRANSLATIONS, @h);

   speak("Checking for service alerts") if $VERBOSE;
   my @s = check_for_service_alerts($CFG, \%SVC_STATES);
   speak_alerts($SERVICE_PHRASE, \@TRANSLATIONS, @s);

   speak("Sleep for $SLEEP seconds") if $VERBOSE;
   sleep $SLEEP;
}

exit 0;

sub read_config{

   my $cfg_file = shift;

   my %ini;
   tie %ini, 'Config::IniFiles', (-file => $cfg_file);

   return \%ini;

}

sub validate_config{
   my $cfg = shift;
   my $has_ssl = shift;
   my $host_states = shift;
   my $svc_states = shift;

   my @errors;

   my @main_req = qw(
     nagios_url nagios_user nagios_pass polling_interval
```

```perl
      voice
    );

    for my $param (@main_req){
      if ($cfg->{'main'}->{$param} eq ''){
        push(@errors, "Missing $param in main");
      }
    }

my $nagios_url = $cfg->{'main'}->{'nagios_url'};

if ($nagios_url ne ''){
    if ($nagios_url !~ m/^http/i){
        push(@errors,
        "Invalid nagios_url, must start with http or https");
    }
    if (($nagios_url =~ m/^https/i) && ($has_ssl == 0)){
     push(@errors,
        "nagios_url uses SSL but Net::SSLeay is not present");
    }
    $cfg->{'main'}->{'nagios_url'} =~ s/\/$//;
}

my $interval = $cfg->{'main'}->{'polling_interval'};
push(@errors, "polling_interval in main must be a number")
    unless $interval =~ m/^\d+$/;

my @ss = split(/\s+/, $cfg->{'filters'}->{'service_statuses'});

if (scalar(@ss) == 0) {
    $cfg->{'filters'}->{'service_statuses'} = '';
} else{
    my $ss_regexp = join('|', keys %{$svc_states});
    for my $s (@ss){
     if ($s !~ m/${ss_regexp}/i){
        push(@errors, "Invalid service state $s specified");
     }
    }
}

if ($cfg->{'filters'}->{'service_regexp'} eq ''){
    $cfg->{'filters'}->{'service_regexp'} = '.';
}
```

```perl
  my @hs = split(/\s+/, $cfg->{'filters'}->{'host_statuses'});

  if (scalar(@hs) == 0){
      $cfg->{'filters'}->{'host_statuses'} = '';
  } else{

   my $hs_regexp = join('|', keys %{$host_states});

   for my $s (@hs){
     if ($s !~ m/${hs_regexp}/i){
       push(@errors, "Invalid host state $s specified");
     }
    }
  }

  if ($cfg->{'filters'}->{'host_regexp'} eq ''){
   $cfg->{'filters'}->{'host_regexp'} = '.';
  }

  if (scalar(@errors) > 0){
   warn "Configuration file validation failed\n";
   die join("\n", @errors);
  }
  debug("Configuration file validated");
}

sub debug{

  return if $DEBUG eq '';

  if (! defined($main::DEBUG_FD)){
   open($main::DEBUG_FD, ">> $DEBUG")
     ||die "Can't append to debug file $DEBUG: $!";
  }

  my $msg = shift;

  print {$main::DEBUG_FD} scalar(localtime(time)) . ": $msg\n";
}

sub speak{
  my $msg = shift;
  debug("Speaking '$msg'");
  $TTS->Speak($msg, 0);
  $TTS->WaitUntilDone(-1);
}
```

```perl
sub speak_alerts{

   my $phrase_template = shift;
   my $translations_ref = shift;
   my @alerts = @_;

   for my $item (@alerts){

     my $phrase = substitute_phrase($item, $phrase_template);

     for my $t (@$translations_ref){

       my ($match, $replace) = split(/\s*%%/, $t);
       debug("Translation: s/$match/$replace/g");
       $phrase =~ s/$match/$replace/gie;
       # Substitute in $N variables from user-supplied replacements
       eval "\$phrase = qq{$phrase}";

     }

     speak($phrase);

   }

}

sub check_for_host_alerts{

   my $cfg = shift;
   my $host_states = shift;

   my $base = $cfg->{'main'}->{'nagios_url'};

   my $statuses_val = get_value_of_desired_states(
   $cfg->{'filters'}->{'host_statuses'}, $host_states);

   # http://www.example.com/nagios/cgi-bin/status.cgi?hostgroup=all
   # &style=hostdetail&hoststatustypes=12
   my $url = "${base}/cgi-bin/status.cgi?hostgroup=all&noheader=yes&" .
   "style=hostdetail&hoststatustypes=${statuses_val}";

   my $content = get_content($cfg, $url);
   debug("HOST content:\n==========\n$content\n==========");
   my @alerts = parse_host_content($content, $cfg);

   return @alerts;

}
```

```perl
sub check_for_service_alerts{

   my $cfg = shift;
   my $service_states = shift;

   my $base = $cfg->{'main'}->{'nagios_url'};

   my $statuses_val = get_value_of_desired_states(
     $cfg->{'filters'}->{'service_statuses'},
     $service_states);

   # http://www.example.com/nagios/cgi-bin/status.cgi?host=all&
    # servicestatustypes=28

   my $url = "${base}/cgi-bin/status.cgi?host=all&noheader=yes&" .
             "servicestatustypes=${statuses_val}";

   my $content = get_content($cfg, $url);
   debug("STATUS content:\n==========\n$content\n==========");

   my @alerts = parse_service_content($content);

   return filter_alerts(\@alerts, $cfg);

}

sub get_value_of_desired_states{
   my $states_string = shift;
   my $states_hash_ref = shift;

   my @wanted_states;

   if ($states_hash_ref ne ''){
     for my $state (split(/\s+/, $states_string)){
       debug("Adding state $state to wanted states array");
       push(@wanted_states, uc($state));
     }

   } else{
     @wanted_states = keys %{$states_hash_ref};
   }

   my $statuses_value = 0;

   for my $key (@wanted_states){
     $statuses_value += $states_hash_ref->{$key};
   }

   return $statuses_value;

}
```

```
sub get_content{

    my $cfg = shift;
    my $url = shift;

    my $user = $cfg->{'main'}->{'nagios_user'};
    my $pass = $cfg->{'main'}->{'nagios_pass'};

    my $ua = NagiosClient->new($user, $pass);

    debug("Retrieving URL $url");

    my $response = $ua->get($url);

    if (! $response->is_success){
        die("Could not retrieve $url: " . $response->status_line . "\n");
    }

    return $response->content;

}

sub parse_host_content{

    my $content = shift;
    my $cfg = shift;

    my @alerts;

    while ($content =~ m%
            <TD\s+align=left\s+valign=center\s+CLASS='statusHOST[A-Z]+'>
            .+?
            # Host name
            >([^<]+)</A>
            .+?
            # Status
            <TD\s+CLASS='statusHOST[A-Z]+'>([^<]+)</TD>
            .+?
            # Time
            nowrap>([^<]+)</TD>
            .+?
            # Duration
            nowrap>([^<]+)</TD>
            .+?
            # Status Information
            >([^<]+)</TD>
            .+?
        %xsmgi) {
```

```perl
        my $alert ={
            'type' => 'host',
            'host' => decode_html($1),
            'status' => decode_html($2),
            'time' => decode_html($3),
            'duration' => decode_html($4),
            'information' => decode_html($5)
        };

        if ($DEBUG ne ''){

            my $msg = "Host: ";

            for my $field (keys %$alert) {
                $msg .= "$field:$alert->{$field} ";
            }

            debug($msg);

        }

        push(@alerts, $alert);

    }

    return @alerts;
}

sub parse_service_content {

    my $content = shift;

    my @alerts;

    my $host;

    # HTML::Parser won't parse Nagios HTML, neither will HTML::ExtractTable
    (tried),
    # have to do it manually. Blech. Oh how nice it would be to have
    status.cgi
    # generate XML!

    while ($content =~ m%
(?:<TD\s+align=left\s+valign=center\s+CLASS='status(?:Even|Odd|HOST[A-Z]+)'>
            <A\s+HREF='extinfo.cgi
            .+?
            # Host name - will be empty TD pair if this is a continuation
            # of a host with multiple alerts
```

```
            '>([^<]+)</A>|<TD></TD>)
            .+?
            # ` Service description
            >([^<]+)</A>
            .+?
            # Status
            CLASS='status[A-Z]+'>([A-Z]+)</TD>
            .+?
            # ` Time
            nowrap>([^<]+)</TD>
            .+?
            # Duration
            nowrap>([^<]+)</TD>
            .+?
            # Attempts
            >([^<]+)</TD>
            .+?
            # Status Information
            >([^<]+)</TD>
            .+?
     %xsmgi) {

   # Host might be empty if this is a host with multiple alerts
   $host = ($1 ne '') ? $1 : $host;

   my $alert ={
        'type' => 'service',
        'host' => decode_html($host),
        'service' => decode_html($2),
        'status' => decode_html($3),
        'time' => decode_html($4),
        'duration' => decode_html($5),
        'attempts' => decode_html($6),
        'information' => decode_html($7)
   };

   if ($DEBUG == 1){

        print "Service: ";
        for my $field (keys %$alert){
             print "$field:$alert->{$field} ";
```

```
            }
            print "\n";

        }

        push(@alerts, $alert);

    }

    return @alerts;
}

sub decode_html{

    my $string = shift;
    $string = CGI::unescapeHTML($string);
    $string =~ s/nbsp//g;

    return $string;

}

sub filter_alerts{

    my $alerts_ref = shift;
    my $cfg = shift;

    my $host_regexp = $cfg->{'filters'}->{'host_regexp'};
    my $service_regexp = $cfg->{'filters'}->{'service_regexp'};

    my @filtered;

    for my $alert (@$alerts_ref){

        my $host = $alert->{'host'};
        my $service = $alert->{'service'};

        if ($host !~ /$host_regexp/) {
            debug("Host:'$host' Service:'$service' - host does not match,
            skipping");
            next;
        }

        if ($service !~ /$service_regexp/) {
            debug("Host:'$host' Service:'$service' - service does not match,
            skipping");
            next;
        }
```

```perl
        debug("Host:'$host' Service:'$service' - host and service match!");

        push(@filtered, $alert);

    }

    return @filtered;
}

sub substitute_phrase{

    my $vars_ref = shift;
    my $template = shift;

    my $phrase = $template;

    for my $var (keys %$vars_ref){
        $phrase =~ s/\%$var/$vars_ref->{$var}/gie;
    }

    return $phrase;
}

# Simple wrapper class to provide an overriden get_basic_credentials method
# to LWP::UserAgent so we can login as the user / password in the config
# file

package NagiosClient;

use strict;
use base qw(LWP::UserAgent);

our $USER = '';
our $PASS = '';

sub new{

    my $class = shift;
    $NagiosClient::USER = shift;
    $NagiosClient::PASS = shift;
    return $class->SUPER::new();

}

sub get_basic_credentials{
    main::debug("Returning credentials");
  return ($USER, $PASS);
}

1;
```

And here is a sample configuration file:

```
[main]
; Enter the name of a file to activate debugging, leave empty to disable
; debugging
debug = debug.log
; Put a one here to make the program a little verbose; program will tell
; you when it is about to poll and when it is about to sleep.
verbose = 1
; Base Nagios URL, https ok as long as you have Net::SSLeay installed
nagios_url = https://192.168.3.1/nagios
; User to authenticate as; must have read all permissions for all
; hosts and services
nagios_user = myuser
nagios_pass = mypass
; How often to check for events, in seconds
polling_interval = 900
; Which voice to use? 0: default, 1: Sam, 2: Mary
; Sam and Mary are only available if you install
; the Microsoft SAPI 5.x API.
voice = 2

[filters]
; Space-separated list of status to match; all others will be ignored.
; Use one or more of OK WARNING CRITICAL UNKNOWN
service_statuses = WARNING CRITICAL
; Regular expression to limit services we match. '.' matches all, all
; non-matching services (service description field) will be ignored.
service_regexp = .
; Space-separated list of host states to match; all others will be
; ignored.
; Use one or more of PENDING UP DOWN UNREACHABLE
host_statuses = DOWN UNREACHABLE
; Regular expression to limit hosts we match .. '.' matches all, all
; host names that do not match will be ignored.
host_regexp = .

[translations]
; Host and service phrase - templates to use for speaking host and
; service alerts. You can use the following variables, all are
; prefixed with %
```

```
;  *  %host - name of the host associated with the alert
;  *  %status - status of the alert
;  *  %type - type of alert, either 'host' or 'service'
;  *  %time - date/time of the alert in format 03-10-2008 10:54:34
;  *  %service - service description as defined in service definition
;  *  %duration - how long the alert has been in the current state,
;                    format '0d 0h 3m 40s'
;  *  %information - Status information, output from check plugin
;  *  %attempts - Attempt field from GUI
host_phrase_template = %host has been %status for %duration
service_phrase_template = %host … %service … %status … %information, for %duration
; Phonetic translation helpers. On the left side put the phrase you wish to
; match, on the right side of the %% put the phrase to replace it with.
Can make the
; text-to-speech output sound much more natural.
phrase_list = <<EOF
SSH%% ess ess Atche
-%% …
  0[dhms]%%
(\d+)d%% $1 days
(\d+)h%% $1 hours
(\d+)m%% $1 minutes
(\d+)s%% $1 seconds
\*\*ePN.+?"\.%% Check command failed to execute properly
EOF
```

To run the program, open a command Window or Cygwin bash shell, cd to the directory you have installed the script and configuration file in, and type:

```
nagios-ttsd.pl nagios-ttsd.ini
```

To stop it, just type **Ctrl-C** in the command window the daemon was started in.

On-Call Schedules
Rotating Schedules and Dynamic Notification

Later in this book we explore the role of the NOC (Network Operation Center) and the standard levels of support and escalation. When it comes to notifications there are several options. Excessive notifications to staff who are not directly responsible for resolving an issue will lead to complacency and reduce response to real issues. Nagios allows for numerous scheduling options for notifications and rotating schedules; full documentation can be found at (http://nagios.sourceforge.net/docs/3_0/oncallrotation.html). There are times, however, when you need customized notifications or notification schedules that match on-call staff rotations. The existing Nagios infrastructure does not lend itself well to a rotating notification schedule. Many organizations need to dynamically change who is on call or can use the more rigid fixed schedules built into Nagios. To adapt Nagios to work for this type of rotating schedule we need to set up some custom event handlers.

First, we establish a generic contact that contains an email alias we will use for the on-call staff member; for example we could name our alias *on-call*. We then use custom scripts to change our system's local mail alias file so that notifications sent to the custom mail alias are delivered to the on-call staff member. This allows us to use any scripting language to quickly change the on-call destination.

In the Web page shown in Figure 2.11, we have customized the Nagios default index.html. As you will see in the chapter in the book on scaling the Nagios GUI, we have changed the main section of the screen to only show services that are down. By modifying Nagios index.html page, we have added a message bar area at the top of the screen. This is a simple HTML frame. Inside that frame, we are able to add custom data pulled from a database or other text file using the scripting language of our choice. This dynamic data can include important contact information and use short refresh times to ensure that NOC staff can quickly see who is on-call to handle problems. For some sites, we have even implemented scrolling Java banners with constantly updated system information or performance data. The goal is to present the data that is needed in one simple location.

Figure 2.11 Nagios GUI Customized to Show On-Call Rotation Information

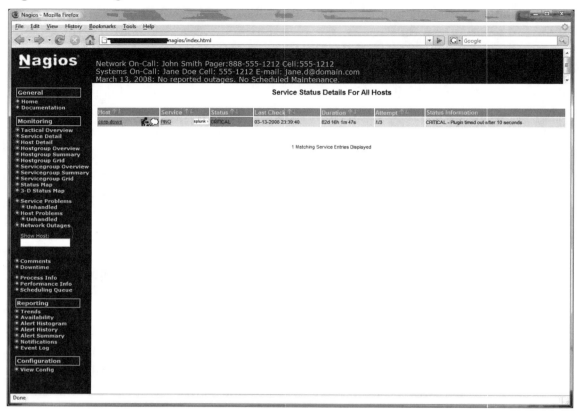

Dependencies and Escalations

You have a well laid-out configuration; services are associated with devices, contacts are associated with contact groups, and contacts and contact groups are associated with hosts and host groups. You are done, right? Wrong. Two days after implementing your configuration, you get a call from a system administrator in your lab. "Please do not alert me to host problems until the system integrators have been notified of them and have had a chance to fix them, as the SI team uses the lab to test new hardware and software configuration combinations." Host escalation rules will let you resolve this situation. A day later, you get a call from a developer. "Hey, just wanted to tell you that I am getting application test alerts over and over when Web services are turned off. If Apache and Tomcat are down, there is no need to perform application-level checks as the application will not run without those two services." Host and service dependencies will help you rework your Nagios configuration to handle that type of situation.

Host and Service Escalation Rules

In large organizations we are bound to encounter situations in which more than one group of people need to know about problems, especially problems that continue for longer periods of time: hours, days, or longer. Host and service escalation rules help make Nagios an excellent tool for communicating device and service status to the right people at the right time.

Escalate on a Host Level or a Service Level?

Whether to escalate on a host level or service level depends on the purpose of the monitoring. If an installation is designed to monitor devices and applications at both a central office and remote offices, it will be very useful to use host-based escalations. If the installation is designed to monitor clients for whom you provide consulting services, a service escalation might prove more useful.

If a Nagios installation is focused on the needs of a large organization with multiple offices, host escalations might prove very useful. Many organizations with remote offices will provide a small IT staff in each remote office. When host-based problems occur, they may wish to have Nagios *first* alert the local staff to the issues. If problems continue for some number of hours without resolution, they may then wish to have Nagios notify the IT staff at your central office. The following example Nagios code models this situation. For our example, office A has several hosts. When a host problem occurs, local IT staff are notified first. After five notification cycles, the central office will start to get notified if the problem has not been resolved and the central office will also continue to be re-notified every two hours until the problem is resolved (Figure 2.12).

Figure 2.12 Host Escalation Relationships

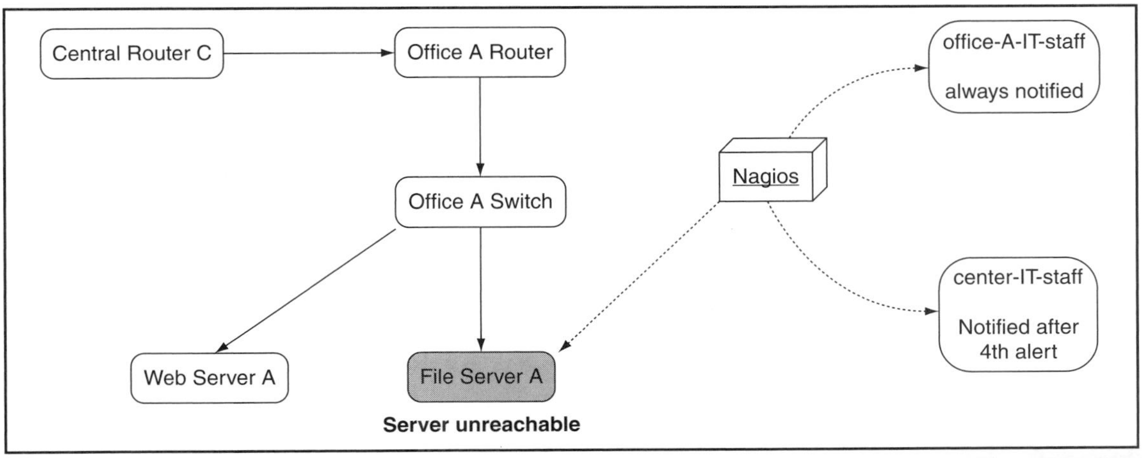

```
define host{
    name             office-A-base
    contact_groups   office-A-IT-staff
    hostgroup_name   office-A-hosts
    notification_period 24×7
    register 0
}

define host{
    use              office-A-base
    host_name        office_A_router
    parents          central_router_C
    …
}

define host{
    use              office-A-base
    host_name        office_A_switch
    parents          office_A_router
    …
}

define host{
    use              office-A-base
    host_name web_server_a
    parents          office_A_switch
}

define host{
    use              office-A-base
    host_name file_server_a
    parents          office_A_switch
}

define hostescalation{
    hostgroup_name     office-A-hosts
    contactgroups      central-IT-staff
    first_notification 5
    last_notification 0
    ; Only notify central staff every 2 hours
    notification_interval 120
    ; Rule is active at all times
```

```
    escalation_period 24×7
    ; Only trigger if hosts are down or unreachable
    escalation_options d,u
}
```

Service escalations are useful for managed applications, especially multi-tiered applications. For example, if there is an application with a database tier and a Web tier, administration staff might wish to first have general tier-1 and tier-2 staff notified of database problems. If the tier-1 and tier-2 staff are unable to resolve the problem after some time (or are not able to get to the problem quickly enough), administrators might then call on a production database team to investigate the issue. The production database team only provides direct support overnight and only wants to be notified if a service is in a critical state and the tier-1 and tier-2 staff have not been able to take care of the issue after three notification periods (Figure 2.13). The following code below models this situation.

Figure 2.13 Service Escalation Relationships

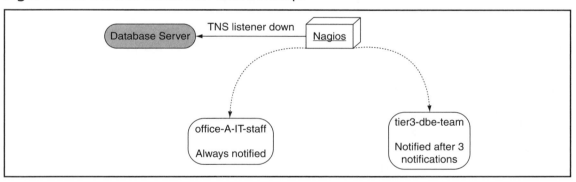

```
define service{
    name                office-A-svc-base
    contact_groups      office-A-IT-staff
    notification_period 24×7
    register 0
}
define service{
    use office-A-svc-base
    service_description TNS listener response
    hostgroup_name db-hosts
}
```

```
sevice_escalation{
    hostgroup_name  db-hosts
    service_description TNS listener response
    ; Our expert DB team
    contact_groups  tier3-dbe-team
    ; Notify after service alerts have gone to tier 1 and tier 2 staff 3 times
    first_notification 4
    last_notification 0
    ; Notify DB staff every hour until the issue is resolved or the time period
    expires
    notification_interval 60
    ; Only counts overnight
    escalation_period  2300-0600x7
    ; Only care about services in critical state
    escalation_options c
}
```

Host and Service Dependencies

An important feature of any good network and service monitoring framework is data reduction. Older network management platforms would alert repeatedly about a problem until it was resolved, leading to much frustration on the part of administrators (and sometimes even compounding an issue). Later network and service monitoring programs, like Nagios, notify once, and then suppress notifications until a problem is resolved or the interval you specify for re-notification is reached. Host and service dependencies take this data reduction concept one step further; if Web service N depends on hosts X, Y, and Z and services P, Q, and R, administrators can set up dependency rules so that Nagios will not even attempt to check the Web service if the hosts and services it depends on are down.

Figure 2.14 is an example of service dependency. Web service AcmeWeb has Apache on a Web host, Apache depends on MySQL on a database host and LDAP on an LDAP server to function properly.

Figure 2.14 Service Dependency Example

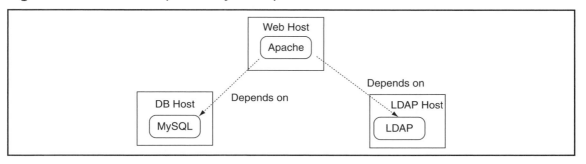

```
define service{
    host_name web_host
    service_description Apache
    check_command        check_http
    … more definition directives …
}

define service{
    host_name db_host
    service_description MySQL
    check_command        check_mysql
    … more definition directives …
}

define service{
    host_name ldap_host
    service_description LDAP
    check_command        check_ldap
    … more definition directives …
}

; Apache depends on MySQL, only want this in effect for critical states
defineservicedependency{
    dependent_host_name                web_host
    dependent_service_description      Apache
    host_name                          db_host
    service_description                MySQL
    inherits_parent                    0
    execution_failure_criteria         c
    notification_failure_criteria      c
    dependency_period                  24×7
}
```

```
; Apache depends on LDAP, only want this in effect for critical states
defineservicedependency{
    dependent_host_name                web_host
    dependent_service_description      Apache
    host_name                          ldap_host
    service_description                LDAP
    inherits_parent                    0
    execution_failure_criteria         c
    notification_failure_criteria      c
    dependency_period                  24×7
}
```

Figure 2.15 is an example of host dependency. File server B depends on NFS server B and SAN server C to function.

Figure 2.15 Host Dependency Example

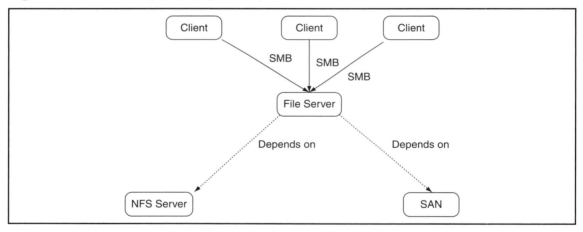

```
define host{
    host_name file_server
    … more host definition directives …
}
define host{
    host_name nfs_server
    … more host definition directives …
}
```

```
define host{
    host_name san_server
    … more host definition directives …
}

; File server depends on NFS server; we all know how touchy NFS
; can be ;).
define hostdependency{
    dependent_host_name              file_server
    host_name                        nfs_server
    inherits_parent                  0
    execution_failure_criteria       d,u
    notification_failure_criteria    d,u
    dependency_period                24×7
}

; File server depends on the SAN, file server loses too much disk space
; and functionality to bother checking if SAN goes away.
define hostdependency{
    dependent_host_name              file_server
    host_name                        san_server
    inherits_parent                  0
    execution_failure_criteria       d,u
    notification_failure_criteria    d,u
    dependency_period                24×7
}
```

Maximizing Templates

In this section we examine Nagios configuration templates. For templates and other configuration hacks, please remember one global rule: Never define a host or service that is not based on a template. If you are monitoring one system that has a number of well-defined services, you will usually find that you end up monitoring two or more servers with the same settings.

To maintain sanity define your templates in a separate file from your host or service configurations.

When someone first uses Nagios, they will often define all hosts in a single file. Once those are in your system and Nagios is actively monitoring them this person might think, "Wow this was easy, I can monitor anything." With Nagios, you can monitor host or device you can programmatically retrieve information from. We often encounter Nagios configurations that start with a few servers or networks and then quickly grow. This rapid growth leads to many host and service configurations that have much repeated data among them. Eventually you might end up with 200 Windows servers and realize that you need to change one setting on all services. This change has now become a task that may take you several days to complete. This is a listing of all of the attributes that can be used in a Nagios host template:

```
define host{
host_name                           host_name
alias                               alias
display_name                        display_name
address                             address
parents                             host_names
hostgroups                          hostgroup_names
check_command                       command_name
initial_state                       [o,d,u]
max_check_attempts                  #
check_interval                      #
retry_interval                      #
active_checks_enabled               [0/1]
passive_checks_enabled              [0/1]
check_period                        timeperiod_name
obsess_over_host                    [0/1]
check_freshness                     [0/1]
freshness_threshold                 #
event_handler                       command_name
event_handler_enabled               [0/1]
low_flap_threshold                  #
high_flap_threshold                 #
flap_detection_enabled              [0/1]
flap_detection_options              [o,d,u]
process_perf_data                   [0/1]
retain_status_information           [0/1]
retain_nonstatus_information        [0/1]
contacts                            contacts
contact_groups                      contact_groups
notification_interval               #
first_notification_delay            #
notification_period                 timeperiod_name
notification_options                [d,u,r,f,s]
notifications_enabled               [0/1]
stalking_options                    [o,d,u]
```

```
notes                                   note_string
notes_url                               url
action_url                              url
icon_image                              image_file
icon_image_alt                          alt_string
vrml_image                              image_file
statusmap_image                         image_file
2d_coords                               x_coord,y_coord
3d_coords                               x_coord,y_coord,z_coord
}
```

Quite a large number of attributes, and each host you manage will need to have many of them set for the host configuration to be valid. For most organizations many of the attributes in a host configuration will be the same between all hosts, yielding just three attributes that uniquely identify hosts to Nagios. This example shows what the host configuration looks like when we use a template to define all of the common attributes used for hosts within our configuration (in this case for all Unix hosts):

```
define host{
use unix-template-group1
      host_name unix1
      alias Unix Server 1
      address 192.168.0.2
}
```

With a little planning we have reduced our host configuration to just four lines; all common attributes are defined in the template used in the host configuration. We can additionally define the parents for this host in the host configuration, but again we can also define the parents in base templates for hosts that share the same parent network device. This has the additional benefit of making it easy to re-parent a set of devices by just changing the value of the *parents* attribute in the host template used by a group of hosts. When you combine the use of templates with careful organization of template files you can easily manage a large Nagios configuration. We start with where we store the Nagios configuration files.

Look in your nagios.cfg file:

```
cfg_dir=/usr/local/nagios/etc/servers
cfg_dir=/usr/local/nagios/etc/printers
cfg_dir=/usr/local/nagios/etc/switches
cfg_dir=/usr/local/nagios/etc/routers
```

With the preceding configuration, any files placed in the listed directories will be read in as object definition files. Inside the servers directory we can now create a file for "Main office."

By keeping configuration files in logically named files, you can easily manage your Nagios configuration as it grows.

How Do We Make a Template?

First, create a configuration file just for templates. Template configuration files look just like normal host configuration files with one additional attribute added to them to indicate the file is a template:

```
register 0 ; DONT REGISTER THIS DEFINITION - ITS NOT A REAL SERVICE,
JUST A TEMPLATE
```

register 0 tell Nagios that the definition is a template that will be used by real hosts or services in your Nagios configuration.

Here is an example service template:

```
define service{
name                          unix-service-host    ; The 'name' of this service
                                                     template
active_checks_enabled         1                    ; Active service checks are
                                                     enabled
passive_checks_enabled        1                    ; Passive service checks are
                                                     enabled/accepted
parallelize_check             1                    ; Active service checks should
                                                     be parallelized (disabling this
                                                     can le
obsess_over_service           1                    ; We should obsess over this
                                                     service (if necessary)
check_freshness               0                    ; Default is to NOT check
                                                     service 'freshness'
notifications_enabled         1                    ; Service notifications are
                                                     enabled
event_handler_enabled         1                    ; Service event handler is
                                                     enabled
flap_detection_enabled        1                    ; Flap detection is enabled
failure_prediction_enabled    1                    ; Failure prediction is enabled
process_perf_data             1                    ; Process performance data
retain_status_information     1                    ; Retain status information
                                                     across program restarts
retain_nonstatus_information  1                    ; Retain non-status information
                                                     across program restarts
is_volatile                   0                    ; The service is not volatile
```

```
    service_description        CP http
    check_command              check_http
    check_period               24×7        ; The service can be checked at
                                            any time of the day
    max_check_attempts         3           ; Re-check the service up to
                                            3 times in order to determine
                                            its final
    normal_check_interval      5           ; Check the service every
                                            10 minutes under normal
                                            conditions
    retry_check_interval       2           ; Re-check the service every
                                            two minutes until a hard state
                                            can be de
    contact_groups             admins      ; Notifications get sent out to
                                            everyone in the 'admins' group
    notification_options       w,u,c,r     ; Send notifications about
                                            warning, unknown, critical,
                                            and recovery e
    notification_interval      60          ; Re-notify about service
                                            problems every hour
    notification_period        24×7        ; Notifications can be sent out
                                            at any time
    register                   0           ; DONT REGISTER THIS DEFINITION
                                            - ITS NOT A REAL SERVICE, JUST
                                            A TEMPLATE
}
```

In this template we have defined all of our common attributes and have set the attribute *register* to 0 to tell Nagios we will be using the definition as a template for real services we are monitoring with Nagios. Using this template we can now define the following service:

```
define service{
    use       unix-service-host;
    host_name cp.localhost.net
    normal_check_interval 3
}
```

Notice how short the service definition has become. This example also shows that for specific implementations of templates we have written we can override settings as needed. For our check_http service we have decided to change the check_interval overriding the value set in the base template we use.

So now, we have discussed the principles and importance of templates to a Nagios configuration. Next, we will look at some lesser-known tricks that can be used in templates and config files. These are techniques you might not use often; when used they are real time savers. These can be applied to all Nagios definitions, and you can find the full list of Nagios object tricks and tips in the Nagios documentation online at http://nagios.sourceforge.net/docs/3_0/objecttricks.html.

Multiple Hosts

You can place multiple host names in the *host_name* definition of a service object to tell Nagios the service exists on all hosts:

```
define service{
    use      unix-service-host;
    host_name cp.localhost.net,server2.localhost.net,server3.localhost.net
    normal_check_interval 3
}
```

Multiple Host Groups

You have a host group that consists of Unix servers, and you want Nagios to ping each host in the group. This can be accomplished by changing the *host_name* attribute in the ping service to *hostgroup_name*:

```
define service{
    use      unix-service-host;
    hostgroup_name unix_servers,windows_servers
    normal_check_interval 3
}
```

In conclusion, when starting your Nagios configuration always think in terms of templates.

Regular Expression Tricks in Config Files

Most networks use naming conventions for hosts deployed within the organization. These conventions usually help identify a server's location, operating system, and function. Using this information and regular expressions, we can reduce the size and number of our configuration files. To start, you need to enable regular expression checking in the nagios.cfg configuration file by setting the configuration variable *use_regexp_matching* to 1 and then restarting Nagios.

Here we are using a naming standard based on operating system, function, and location. We have made the name DNS compatible as these names are part of our DNS database. For this example have a set of Windows 2000 servers that run a Web cluster in our Los Angeles office. For servers 1–9, the names would look like:

```
win2k-web01.la.localhost.net, win2k-web02.la.localhost.net --- win2k-web09.la.
localhost.net
```

These names tell us the operating system, major function, and office the systems are located in. Now we want to define our services for this host:

```
define service{
    use        win2k-service-host;
    host_name win2k-web.*.la.localhost.net
    service_description HTTP Service
    check_command check_http
}
```

By using the regex pattern of ".*" we tell Nagios, "Apply this service definition to any host that contains the sub-string 'win2k–web' followed by any number of additional characters followed by the sub-string '.la.hosthost.net'." This means that for each defined host this service will be checked. This will limit our check to just the Windows host in the LA office, but we can easily drop the LA portion and have it perform this service check for all the Windows Web servers. The option *use_regexp_matching* will only apply to host or service names that contain the characters *, ?, +, or \.. If you want regular expression matching to be used for all host and service names regardless of whether the names contain regular expression meta-characters, enable *use_regexp_matching* in your configuration file and then additionally set the option *use_true_regexp_matching* to 1.

## Chapter 3

Scaling Nagios

Solutions in this chapter:

- Scaling the GUI
- Detailed Information on Parameters Used by status.cgi
- Limiting the View to Read-Only
- Multiple GUI Users (Users/Groups)
- Clustering
- Failover or Redundancy
- The Future

Scaling the GUI

The Big Picture: Nagios is your monitoring tool. Whether used for a small office of 10 servers, or 400 servers and over 1000 services, the objective is still the same: you want to know how your systems are doing and you want to know quickly the health of your environment. The goal of any monitoring GUI is simple: tell end users and administrators in less than five seconds the overall status of managed systems and networks. Many professionals who manage systems and networks have had vendors tell us how we should view our network. Openview, Netview, and Tivoli have all kept to the same principle of having systems that show a top-down view that requires interaction to "drill-down" or zoom in to network problems while constantly displaying all the managed hosts and services at an organization that are not having problems. These interfaces provide excellent eye candy for overviews and presentations, but do little to provide a view that is useful to administrators and troubleshooting personnel. In general, two basic rules should be followed to allow you to keep an eye on real issues and a good idea on overall status. We now describe each of these rules and show how they will help make your Nagios implementation a success, regardless of the number of devices and services monitored or the size of the staff in charge of maintaining managed devices and services.

Rule 1: Only Show Outstanding Problems on Your Primary Display

Use color-coding to show how severe each alert is and to show which alerts have been acknowledged. Do not show scheduled outages, working services, flapping services, or other items that do not require immediate human intervention. Primary displays that show information that does not require action by support staff will be ignored. The display also needs to update itself automatically so that operators always see the latest set of alerts on it. Simplicity is the key to the success when it comes to implementing a useful 'heads up' display.

Rule 2: Keep Informational Displays Simple

The more data and more complicated the display, the more likely you have information displayed that will start to be ignored. Keep long-term trending data off of your primary display screen as it will only clutter up the display and overwhelm your support staff. Your primary status screen is your dispatcher; any new alerts that appear on it should require action by the staff in charge of the health of devices and applications within the organization.

Nagios allows us to meet both of these goals. Nagios 3 includes two new options in the GUI, "Unhandled Service Problems," and "Unhandled Host problems." These screens only show warning and critical host and service alerts that have not been acknowledged. We recommend you take this one step further and only show critical service and host alerts using customized status screens.

Let's examine the difference between what we normally see and what a custom configuration shows us (Figures 3.1 and 3.2).

Figure 3.1 Typical Nagios Status Display

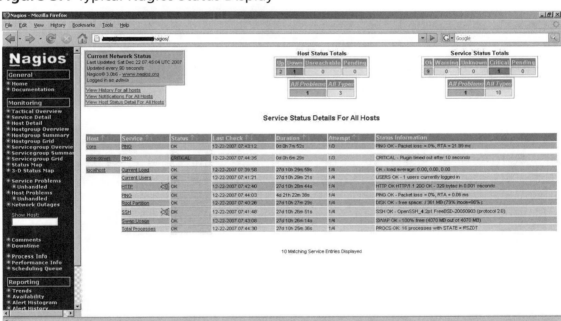

Figure 3.2 Status Screen Showing Only Critical Alerts

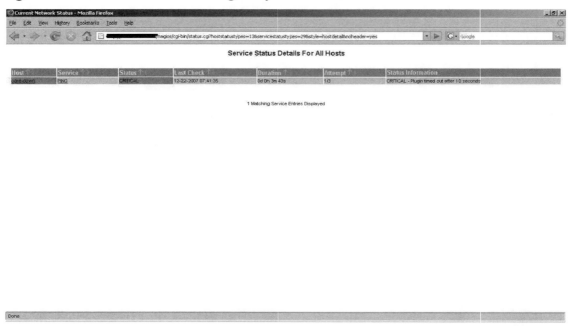

As you can see, the second screen shows us that one service is in a CRITICAL state. We have all the details about this service in one quick glance. We can create a custom view by changing the HTTP parameters that are passed to the Nagios status CGI, status.cgi.

Detailed Information on Parameters Used by status.cgi

The Nagios status.cgi program takes a number of HTTP parameters that allow us to alter the information it displays. In this section we show how to alter it to just display critical host or service alerts on the Nagios GUI. We recommend using HTML frames for your "heads up" critical host and service alert display; one frame displays critical host alerts, the other shows critical service alerts. An example of this is shown later.

Here is the Nagios status.cgi URL that the "Unhandled Host Problems" option in the Nagios 3 GUI links to by default

```
/cgi-bin/status.cgi?hoststatustypes=13&servicestatustypes=29&style=hostdetail&
noheader=yes
```

hoststatustypes

The *hoststatustypes* parameter stores an integer that indicates which host states status. cgi should display:

HOST_PENDING=1

HOST_UP=2

HOST_DOWN=4

HOST_UNREACHABLE=8

In our previous example, we used the number 13. Select the host states you want to view by adding together the values associated with the constants. A value of 13 tells us that status.cgi will show hosts that are in any state except HOST_UP (HOST_PENDING + HOST_DOWN + HOST_UNREACHABLE = 13).

servicestatustypes

The *servicestatustypes* parameter is also a variable that stores an integer that indicates which service states to display:

SERVICE_PENDING=1

SERVICE_OK=2

SERVICE_WARNING=4

SERVICE_UNKNOWN=8

SERVICE_CRITICAL=16

In our example, we see the value 29, which leaves out SERVICE_OK.

style

The *style* parameter allows us to change what data is displayed and how it is displayed. We use the value *detail* in our examples. Other values you can use are *overview*, *grid*, *summary*, and *hostdetail*.

noheader

The last HTTP parameter we use is *noheader*. This parameter does not require a value; if it is present in the query string, status.cgi will not display summary information before displaying alert detail. If summary information is wanted, we can display it in another frame or HTML page altogether by using ministatus.cgi, which can be found on the book web site. By trimming out header information from our alert display, we simplify the display and make it more useful to service desk staff.

Color is very important in any network or system monitoring system. From the time Nagios was called Netsaint until now, Nagios has used three distinct colors to show device and host status:

Green is OK

Yellow is WARNING

Red is CRITICAL

We start by removing green from status views. Why? Showing what is working properly uses up valuable screen space in the NOC. Our concerns rest in yellow and red status; for any hosts or services in the yellow (warning) state, we should start investigating the cause to resolve the issue, and for any hosts or services in the red (critical) state, we need to open a ticket for tracking our issue and work to resolve the issue and verify service restoration. In our previous example, we have a router showing a service failure. Initially, we should perform some basic checks to verify the service has failed. Once that is complete, we begin to "work" the issue. Since many NOCs utilize personnel located in multiple remote locations, we run the risk of multiple people working the same issue. To accommodate this reality of the NOC environment, Nagios added acknowledgement states for hosts and services; each type of acknowledgement can have a custom color associated with it. Alert acknowledgement allows staff members to see that a problem is being worked on and reduces the possibility of two or more people attempting to work the same problem independently. Nagios ships with status and acknowledgement colors set to the same color; By editing the <nagios-root>/share/stylesheets/status.css we find the items we need to update:

```
.statusHOSTDOWNACK { font-family: arial,serif; font-size: 8pt; background-color:
#F83838; }
.statusHOSTUNREACHABLEACK { font-family: arial,serif; font-size: 8pt;
background-color: #F83838; }
.statusBGUNKNOWNACK { font-family: arial,serif; font-size: 8pt; background-color:
#FFDA9F; }
.statusBGWARNINGACK { font-family: arial,serif; font-size: 8pt; background-color:
#FEFFC1; }
.statusBGCRITICALACK { font-family: arial,serif; font-size: 8pt; background-color:
#FFBBBB; }
```

```
.statusBGDOWNACK { font-family: arial,serif; font-size: 8pt; background-color:
#FFBBBB; }\
.statusBGUNREACHABLEACK { font-family: arial,serif; font-size: 8pt; background-color:
#FFBBBB; }
```

These are based on standard HTML colors. We recommend that you choose an acknowledgment color that is a deeper shade of the original status color so one can see the difference between a warning alert that has been acknowledged and a critical alert that has been acknowledged. Figure 3.3 shows the difference after changing the HOSTDOWNACK color to #FF9900 (orange).

Figure 3.3 Using Unique Colors to Make Acknowledged Alarms Stand Out

With the changes shown in Figure 3.3, we have now removed all nonessential data from our display for situations in which the primary task is to monitor and troubleshoot outstanding problems. As we progress through the Case Study, you will see how these items come together for a NOC of any size. Through the use of custom status screens, color-coded acknowledgments, and a quick view of the data that shows only hosts or services that are having problems, we simplify the display and help stop the apathy that can occur in a NOC when unimportant data is displayed or too much data is displayed on the "big screen"—only show what matters and what needs to be worked, and that work will much more likely be done. This is counter to what we have seen in many products in the past. Network and system monitoring products traditionally have been about showing how many hosts or services you are monitoring or how large or integrated your monitoring is. Nagios provides this data, and this should be used when looking at performance data, long-term trending, planning, and deeper issue isolation. However, it should never be the data your primary troubleshooters are required to watch all day. When looking at the screen in Figure 3.3 we can tell at a quick glance if any open issues need to be worked on and resolved. There is plenty of empty space available so that if new issues arise, they will be easily seen and addressed without any clicking or changing views.

Limiting the View to Read-Only

Nagios does a terrific job of conveying large amounts of information quickly, and in a manner most end users find intuitive. Anyone we have shown a Nagios status screen has instantly been able to identify that items in red need to be resolved. Many NOCs or service desks like to make status information available to other people in their company and even people outside their company, including outside customers and vendors. When implementing this "outsider view" they want to make sure they allow status data to be viewed, but also worry about these users making unauthorized changes to Nagios. The solution for this is a read-only user model. With this change to Nagios, we can allow specified accounts to access Nagios as read-only users. Through a combination of read-only users and custom URLs as described previously, we can provide custom status screens that are suitable for customer, vendor, or management view. This read-only functionality is currently not part of the core Nagios distribution. For read-only configuration to work, you need to install a patch to the CGI executables Derrick Bennet created; this patch is included on the Web site for this book for the current Nagios 3.x release. Once the patch is applied, we will modify our cgi.cfg file to add the following new option:

```
authorized_for_read_only=<user1>,<user2>
```

Add the same users to the *authorized_for_all_hosts* and *authorized_for_all_services* if you wish to allow them to see all hosts and services.

In figure 3.4 we show a snapshot of an unaltered detail screen; in figure 3.5 we show a snapshot for a detail screen with the read-only user patch applied to Nagios.

Figure 3.4 Typical Host Status Screen

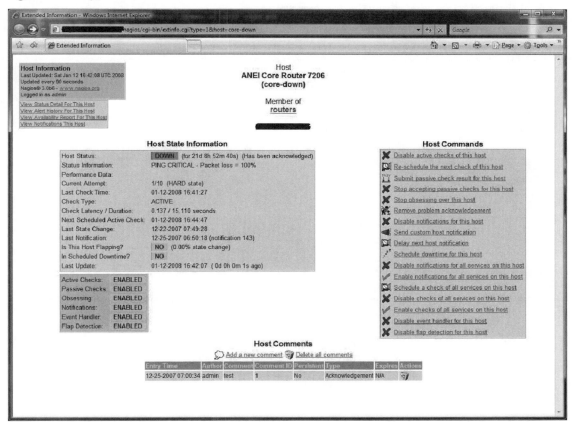

When logged in as a normal user, we can see both the Commands screen and any comments associated with this host or service.

Figure 3.5 Host Status Screen for a Read-Only User

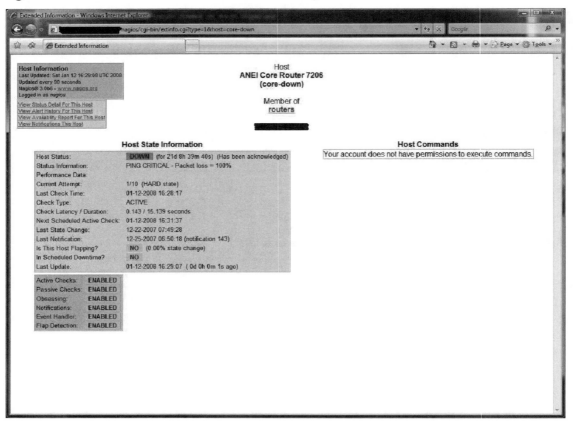

In Figure 3.5, we logged in with a shared account called "nagios" that is set as a read-only user. On the detail screen, we can see that the commands section informs the user that his account does not have access. In addition, the comments section has been removed completely. The read-only patch prevents the Nagios CGIs from sending comments and commands data to the browser for read-only user accounts. We now have a safe way to allow semi-trusted users to view systems and hosts within Nagios without worrying about them changing the state of Nagios or viewing private comments made by operational staff as they work to resolve outstanding problems.

Through a combination of custom status.cgi URLs and the read-only user patch to Nagios, we can create custom web pages outside of Nagios that include system and host status from Nagios without revealing private information or allowing untrusted users the ability to change the state of Nagios as it runs.

Multiple GUI Users (Users/Groups)

Often, multiple users in an organization want to have access to Nagios. Several approaches can be taken to meet this type of requirement. In this section, we briefly discuss each technique to help you decide which will work best for your organization.

One Administrator, One Shared Read-Only Account

This scenario is common for organizations that started small and are growing, or for environments like development shops, where fine-grained access control is not critical. In this mode, the Nagios administrator merely has to define one account in the CGI configuration file with administrative rights and a second account with read-only access. The read-only account may or may not have the capability to perform GUI-based actions like resubmitting service checks, acknowledging service or host problems, or disabling notifications. Whether an administrator chooses to allow those actions will depend on the local security policies and the level of trust an administrator has with his users.

One Administrator, Multiple Read-Only Accounts

In organizations in which Nagios is deployed in production environments, or the number of users actively checking Nagios is larger, or groups of users need access to specific groups of checks, this scenario works well. The read-only accounts might be shared accounts used by groups of people. The accounts might even map to email groups. For example, if an organization has a windows_admins email alias, the administrator might create a Nagios user named windows_admins. The windows_admins user would use the email address windows_admins and the account would have access limited to only the Windows servers on the organization's network by making use of the fine-grained access controls in the Nagios CGI configuration file.

Multiple Administrators, Multiple Semi-Privileged Accounts, One Read-Only Account

In the largest organizations, there may be multiple administrators, semi-privileged accounts, and a read-only account. In this scenario, a single sign-on framework using LDAP might be employed to centralize access. While Nagios does not directly support LDAP, a number of LDAP modules for Apache can be used to authenticate users, including mod_authnz_ldap. The problem with using LDAP directly this way is that for each LDAP user, entries have to be added to the CGI configuration file to give permissions to the user that extend beyond the roles granted to the default user. For this reason, we recommend an administrator set up a nightly script to query and write out the CGI configuration file for each user granted access. Desired roles can be kept in a database or other file store, and the script can then create all user configurations and the main CGI configuration file to give the fine-grained permissions needed for a large organization. A template for the CGI configuration can be employed that hard codes the read-only account in the configuration file template.

Clustering

One of the first bottlenecks organizations will run into is performance when monitoring a large number of hosts and services. This can occur even earlier if you are using performance handlers on your service or host checks. One way to resolve performance problems is to cluster Nagios; clustering is also very useful when there are a number of remote sites that need to be monitored by Nagios. We will first discuss a very common scenario in which there is a central Nagios installation used to monitor a single local site and several remote sites. Our example scenario has two separate offices with individual hosts and services that need to be monitored; between the two offices is a single network (WAN) connection. For performance reasons, we do not want to run all our monitoring checks over this single connection from our central office. We also want the remote office to be able to monitor their systems locally. Using the configuration shown in Figure 3.6 (below), we can distribute host and service monitoring across several Nagios servers. This reduces the load on each individual Nagios server (compared to having all monitoring done from a central server) and also has a nice side-effect of reducing site-to-site network traffic as remote site monitoring is performed by a Nagios instance local to the site.

We will set up the master Nagios server in our main office; this server will hold both the master and remote Nagios server configuration file trees. The master server will also run the NSCA daemon and will accept passive reporting from the remote instance. The master server will then present a whole view of the network and systems being monitored.

Figure 3.6 Clustered Nagios Data Flow

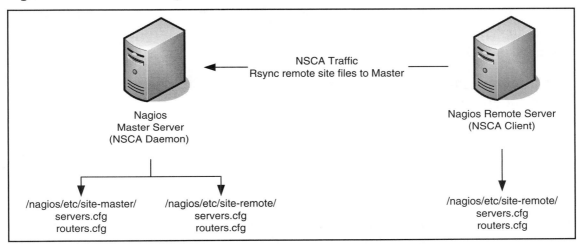

With this setup, we can disable notifications on the remote server if that is desirable. In many cases, it may be easier to define notifications, escalations, and other non-system-specific details in the master server, as this simplifies administration. In this case, make sure *enable_notifications* is set to 0 in the nagios.cfg file on the remote server. In addition, for any host or service defined at the remote site you must have the same configuration in place for your master server (Figure 3.7).

TIP

Since Nagios allows you to monitor directories for configuration files, it is recommended that you set up a /<nagios_prefix>/etc/site-remote/ directory and use a cron job to import file changes on a daily basis. This allows the master and remote servers to synchronize without user intervention (as we will show later in this section).

Figure 3.7 NSCA Data Flow between Clustered Servers

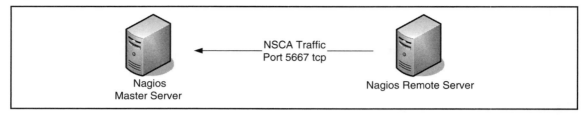

First we configure the remote site; install Nagios as normal on the server and then change the following parameters in nagios.cfg to allow it to function properly in our Nagios cluster:

> **enable_notifications = 0 #** We do not want this instance sending out notifications.

> **obsess_over_services=1 #** We want the remote server to obsess over services so all changes will be reported back to the master server.

> **oscp_command=nsca_send_result #** This is a custom script shown next.

With these configuration changes in place, the remote Nagios server will call the command *nsca_send_result* after every service check executed on the remote host. The *nsca_send_result* script will then forward the service check results to the master Nagios server. Place the following definition for *nsca_send_result* in your commands configuration file (commands.cfg by default):

```
define command{
  command_name nsca_send_result
  command_line /usr/local/nagios/libexec/nsca_send_result
$HOSTNAME$ '$SERVICEDESC$' $SERVICESTATE$ '$SERVICEOUTPUT$'
}
```

Now we create the *nsca_send_result* shell script on the remote server (this version is taken from the Nagios 3.0 manual):

```
#!/bin/sh
   # Arguments:
   # $1 = host_name (Short name of host that the service is
   #    associated with)
   # $2 = svc_description (Description of the service)
   # $3 = state_string (A string representing the status of
   #    the given service - "OK", "WARNING", "CRITICAL"
   #    or "UNKNOWN")
   # $4 = plugin_output (A text string that should be used
```

```
#       as the plugin output for the service checks)
#
# Convert the state string to the corresponding return code
return_code=-1
case "$3" in
  OK)
            return_code=0
        ;;
      WARNING)
          return_code=1
            ;;
      CRITICAL)
          return_code=2
            ;;
      UNKNOWN)
          return_code=-1
            ;;
esac
# pipe the service check info into the send_nsca program, which
# in turn transmits the data to the nsca daemon on the central
# monitoring server
/bin/printf "%s\t%s\t%s\t%s\n" "$1" "$2" "$return_code" "$4" | /usr/local/
nagios/bin/send_nsca central_server -c /usr/local/nagios/etc/send_nsca.cfg
```

Data flow from the remote server to the master server is:

1. Host and service checks are executed on the remote server.

2. The remote server takes the raw results of checks, and through the
   oscp_command function sends them to the master server.

We use NSCA to send the checks from the remote server to the master server in
this scenario. After we discuss how to configure NSCA to accomplish the remote-to-
master data flow, we will discuss using rsync and ssh to accomplish the same task.

NSCA and Nagios

NSCA is written and maintained by Ethan, the creator of Nagios. NSCA allows a
remote client to send an asynchronous event to a Nagios server using a TCP-based
protocol that includes data encryption and password-based authentication; the server
side of NSCA will even spool passive check results on the server side if Nagios is not
running at the time the check result is received. The default port for the NSCA
daemon is 5667; this can easily be changed as needed. NSCA is available as a separate

software package from the downloads section of http://www.nagios.org; like Nagios, it is well-documented and installation is relatively easily. Once you have configured and compiled NSCA you will have five files to install:

- The NSCA daemon startup script needs to be placed in /etc/ (/etc/init.d on Linux or Solaris) and properly linked to appropriate startup levels so NSCA starts up when the Nagios server enters multi-user mode with networking (run level 3 on most Unix and Unix-like operating systems).

- The NSCA configuration file needs to be set up and placed on the server; the default location is <nagios-prefix>/etc/nsca.cfg.

- The NSCA daemon needs to be copied to the Nagios installation; typically, it is installed as <nagios-prefix>/bin/nsca.

- The NSCA client binary, send_nsca, needs to be copied to the remote client that will be sending events to the NSCA server. The recommended installation location on the remote server for this binary is /<nagios-prefix>/libexec/send_nsca.

- The NSCA client needs a configuration file to work properly; you can either copy an existing NSCA client configuration file to the remote server or create one locally and then copy it to the remote server based on the example configuration included with the NSCA package. The recommended location for the NSCA client configuration file is <nagios-prefix>/etc/nsca.cfg on the NSCA client host.

NOTE

It is important that the password you set in the NSCA client and server configuration files match; if the passwords do not match the NSCA server will reject checks sent to it by the NSCA client.

Passive Service Checking

Once we have the NSCA daemon running on the master server and the send_nsca client configured on the remote server, we are now ready to continue our configuration. In our example scenario, the master server is performing checks for hosts and services located at the master site. It is important that we make sure that the master server **only** checks local services; if we are not careful with our master server configuration it might start to check remote services as well. We now describe how to configure the master server so that it accepts check results from the remote server but does not attempt to actively check remote services itself.

First we add a new service template that we will use as the base template for all service checks results sent to the master server from the remote server. In this template we disable active checks of the remote services by the master server by setting the parameter *active_checks_enabled* to 0. In some situations it may seem desirable to have the master server perform checks on hosts monitored by the remote server should the remote server fail. In this case we would set *check_ freshness* to 1. Please note that if this setting is enabled, **all** checks that the remote server runs to monitor remote hosts and services need to be present on the local master and need to be able to reach all hosts and services on remotely monitored hosts. This adds significant complexity and main- tenance cost to the Nagios cluster and we recommend that you do not allow the master server to actively check services monitored by the remote Nagios host. It is important to clearly define the logical path from the local master server to the remote Nagios server. We recommend that the local master monitor the remote Nagios server to ensure it is up and running. We also recommend that all remotely monitored hosts and services have the remote Nagios server set as their parent; this will ensure that all hosts and services monitored by the remote site will be marked as unreachable on the master Nagios GUI should the remote Nagios host become unavailable or unreachable. Here is an example service template that can be used on the master Nagios host as a base template for all services checked by the remote Nagios server in our cluster:

```
define service
C          name          remote-service    ; The 'name' of this service template
active_checks_enabled          0    ; Active service checks are enabled
passive_checks_enabled         1    ; Passive service checks are enabled/accepted
parallelize_check              1    ; Active service checks should be parallelized
                                      (disabling this can lead to major performance
                                      problems)
obsess_over_service            1    ; We should obsess over this service
                                      (if necessary)
check_freshness                1    ; Default is to NOT check service 'freshness'
notifications_enabled          1    ; Service notifications are enabled
event_handler_enabled          1    ; Service event handler is enabled
flap_detection_enabled         1    ; Flap detection is enabled
failure_prediction_enabled     1    ; Failure prediction is enabled
process_perf_data              1    ; Process performance data
retain_status_information      1    ; Retain status information across program
                                      restarts
```

```
retain_nonstatus_information    1        ; Retain non-status information across
                                           program restarts
is_volatile                     0        ; The service is not volatile
check_period                    24x7     ; The service can be checked at any time of
                                           the day
max_check_attempts              3        ; Re-check the service up to 3 times in
                                           order to determine its final (hard) state
normal_check_interval           10       ; Check the service every 10 minutes under
                                           normal conditions
retry_check_interval            2        ; Re-check the service every two minutes
                                           until a hard state can be determined
contact_groups                  admins   ; Notifications get sent out to everyone in
                                           the 'admins' group
notification_options            w,u,c,r  ; Send notifications about warning,
                                           unknown, critical, and recovery events
notification_interval           60       ; Re-notify about service problems every hour
notification_period             24x7     ; Notifications can be sent out at any time
register                        0        ; DONT REGISTER THIS DEFINITION - ITS NOT
                                           A REAL SERVICE, JUST A TEMPLATE!
}
```

Once we have our new template in place we need to copy the remote site's service configuration files to the remote service configuration directory on the master host. After the files are copied over we can do a global search and replace on all service checks in this directory so that they use our passive check template as their base template. To do this, we must replace any 'use <template-name>' lines in the configuration files with the line 'use remote-service.' If this is a new installation, we may chose to create the remote service configuration files on the master server and then push them to the remote server. After the push to the remote server, we can clean out the local server's remote site configuration directory, copy all services into the directory, and then perform the search and replace to replace the base template in all files. Throughout the creation of our configurations for this Nagios cluster we strive to create and use templates wherever possible to keep our overall configuration as simple and maintainable as possible.

Now is a good time to confirm that our configuration changes on the remote and local master make sense and are functioning as expected. Check the remote Nagios server to ensure that notifications are disabled, verify that *obsess_over_services* is enabled, and ensure that *oscp_command* is defined and that the command set in the variable exists and works as expected.

Notes from the Underground

translate_passive_host_checks and Distributed Monitoring

When working with distributed monitoring, host checks are usually completed from the master server. If your network configuration does not allow this, you may need to set up the local master Nagios server to accept passive host check results from the remote Nagios server as well. If you chose to do this, be very aware of how point of view can affect perception of whether a host is reachable or not. When the master server shows you that server A at the remote site is down, it is because the server was not reachable from the point of view of the remote server. However, it may be that the server is *only* unreachable from the remote server. To resolve this point of view conflict Nagios provides the *translate_passive_host_checks* option. With this option enabled, the master server will translate check results sent by the remote server and determine if server A should be shown as down on the master GUI. While the *translate_passive_checks* option might be useful for some clustered environments, in most distributed monitoring situations, you will want the master Nagios server to display remote check results from the point of view of the remote Nagios server and this option should be left disabled. (Figure 3.8).

Figure 3.8 Nagios Clustering and Outage Point of View

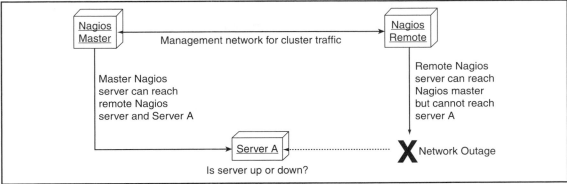

Passive Host Checking

Our master server and remote site are both now performing active checks on systems and services. We now need to determine if we wish to have all host checks for host monitored by the remote Nagios server done from the remote server. Host checks are only done by Nagios if all service checks have failed and the system needs to determine if the host is physically still reachable. If a network configuration or firewall prevents the master server from polling the remote server, we will need to have the remote Nagios server perform all host checks for remotely monitored servers and have the remote server submit check results to the local master server. To do this, make the following configuration changes on the Nagios servers in the cluster:

On the master server:

1. Enable the configuration parameter *passive_host_checks* by setting it to 1 in the nagios.cfg configuration file.

On the remote server:

2. Set the parameter *obsess_over_hosts* to 1 in the nagios.cfg configuration file (similar to what we did for services in the previous section).

3. As with our service configuration in the previous section, we need to configure the remote server to send passive host check results to the master server by setting the nagios.cfg parameter *obsess_command* to *nsca_send_result*.

Sending Data without NSCA

Earlier in this chapter we stated that we can send data from the remote server to the master server without using NSCA. Regardless of how we send passive checks from the remote server to the local master server, on the local master server passive service checks are submitted to Nagios by writing commands to the external command file in Nagios. This external command file allows Nagios plug-ins to submit passive check results to Nagios by writing the check timestamp, type, host, status, and output to the file. Nagios regularly reads this file and acts on the check results in it as if the results had been collected by Nagios executing a local plugin to check a service. Here is an example of what a passive service check output line looks like:

```
[1205044608] PROCESS_HOST_CHECK_RESULT;router1;0;0
```

This means that using ssh and a cron job on the master server, we can send data between our two servers and cat or pipe the data directly to the /<nagios_prefix>/var/rw/nagios.cmd file where it will then be processed.

Failover or Redundancy

In the previous section, we looked at clustering and how to share the load of our Nagios monitoring. Clustering helps lower network utilization for checks performed on remote sites and helps reduce the load on the primary Nagios server used to monitor both local and remote sites. If you have taken the time and effort to implement clustering, most likely monitoring is an important part of the operations and maintenance side of your organization and the last thing you want is to lose your monitoring server or the metrics collected by it. Failover and redundancy are two concepts that we can implement in the server and software infrastructure we use to host Nagios that can reduce the possibility of loss of data or loss of monitoring in our organization.

Depending on your specific situation and requirements, you will need to decide if your system needs failover or redundancy. In failover mode you create a second system that sits in standby mode, ready to take over the functions of the master server should it detect a failure or be manually brought up to master status. In a redundant configuration there are two Nagios systems that are online and running simultaneously; should the master server in the redundant pair fail the secondary server immediately takes over the tasks the master is unable to perform. In redundant mode, the secondary server performs the same checks as the master server and no service or host check result data is shared between servers. We give a brief description in this chapter of how redundancy might be implemented with Nagios; due to the complexity that full redundancy introduces into our configurations and setup, we will not cover it in depth in this book. Failover, however, is both easier to set up and maintain than redundancy and we will explain how to implement it within Nagios following our short section on redundancy.

Redundancy

When we configured clustering, we were in essence setting up a redundant configuration of Nagios. If at any time the master server is lost in a clustered environment, an administrator can simply enable notifications on the remote system and that system will take over monitoring and alerting functions for all defined hosts and services. When setting up master server redundancy we make similar configuration changes to each server. We use scripts and cron jobs to periodically synchronize configuration files between the two master Nagios servers in a redundant configuration. With these cron jobs in place, we have two systems performing the same checks across all devices and services in our organization. While having two servers perform the same checks on every device does ensure that monitoring continues even if a monitoring server fails, it also doubles the amount of network traffic and the load placed on monitored servers by the monitoring hosts. For many organizations this additional load on the network and on managed hosts will not be worth the time and effort needed to properly implement this type of configuration, so be sure to speak with management and the staff that maintain network devices and servers at your organization before considering implementing full redundancy using Nagios.

Failover

In failover mode, the master server actively polls hosts and services. The master server also runs a periodic job (via cron) that pushes host and service check results and configuration settings from the master server to the secondary server. Should the primary server fail, an administrator will need to log into the secondary server to start Nagios; the secondary server will then take over where the primary server left off. Overall, it is easier to set up and maintain a pair of servers in failover mode than it is to maintain a pair of clustered servers. The transition time to switch from the primary server in failover mode to the secondary server is not instant as it would be in a clustered setup, but it is very short. The Nagios documentations describes how to configure Nagios for basic failover mode operation. We expand on that documentation in order to clarify and explain it to users who are not familiar with how failover mode works for applications in general and specifically for Nagios. We hope that by the end of this chapter you will have a clear understanding of how to implement failover mode for Nagios at your organization.

Establish Data Synchronization between Two Nagios Servers

1. Create a master IP address for Nagios. This master IP address will only be active on the active Nagios server. It will be used for the official host name of the Nagios host so Web users and administrators can reach the active Nagios server regardless of which server is active. It will also be used as the destination for SNMP traps or NSCA checks used by agents on managed devices. Finally, it will be used in the Web server configuration on each Nagios host so there is only one Apache configuration for Nagios between the two hosts.

2. Set up a primary Nagios server with two IP addresses. The primary IP will be used for systems management; all monitoring and passive checks will be done using the second IP address. The second IP address will be the master Nagios

IP address. It will be "moved" from the primary server to the secondary server when we need to make the secondary server the master server by de-activating it on the primary server and activating it on the secondary server.

3. Set up a secondary Nagios server with the same software and setup as your primary Nagios server, including two IP addresses:—one unique IP address for systems management that will be active, and a secondary IP address that is *the same* as the master Nagios IP address you configured on the primary system. *Be sure to leave the master Nagios IP address configuration disabled on the secondary server. Failure to do so will cause an IP address conflict on your network that will disable access to the primary Nagios server via the Nagios master IP address.*

4. Establish an encrypted communication channel between the two Nagios servers using rsync and SSH. Rsync (http://rsync.samba.org/) is a freely available application that keeps files and permissions synchronized between two systems. Rsync is very efficient; only changes in files and directories are copied between two systems when it runs. Rsync can synchronize files using its own TCP-based transport protocol, or it can use SSH as its transport. We highly recommend using SSH as the transport, as SSH encrypts all data sent between two systems. SSH also allows us to use cryptographically strong keys (Public Key Infrastructure) for authentication instead of passwords; by using SSH keys we can set up rsync to synchronize files between the two systems without requiring a user to be present to enter a password. Install rsync and ssh and set up SSH key-based authentication (use ssh-keygen to make the keys) between your primary server and secondary server; you should create a key on each server so rsync can run in either direction without user intervention. You can either choose to create SSH keys that have no passphrase for this purposes, or set up a passphrase for your SSH keys and use a combination of ssh-agent and Keychain (www.gentoo.org/proj/en/keychain/) to manage the passphrases. Which one you choose will depend on the security policies in your organization; if you choose to use ssh-agent and Keychain you will need to enter the passphrases for the SSH keys you set up one time on each server when the servers are rebooted.

5. Create a cron job on the primary server that runs the *rsync* command and pushes all changes to configuration files to the secondary server at regular intervals. Our recommendation is to have the synchronization job

run every 10 minutes. The cron job can be as simple as running the command `rsync -avz -e ssh /usr/local/nagios/ secondary:/usr/local/nagios/`. This will recursively copy any changes to files from the primary server to the secondary server while preserving file and directory permissions, links, and access times.

6. Set up a synchronization job from the secondary to the master server *but leave it disabled*. Should you need to switch from the primary to the secondary server and keep the two in sync, this secondary cron job can be activated to perform that function. (See Figure 3.9.)

Figure 3.9 Nagios in Failover Mode with Two Servers

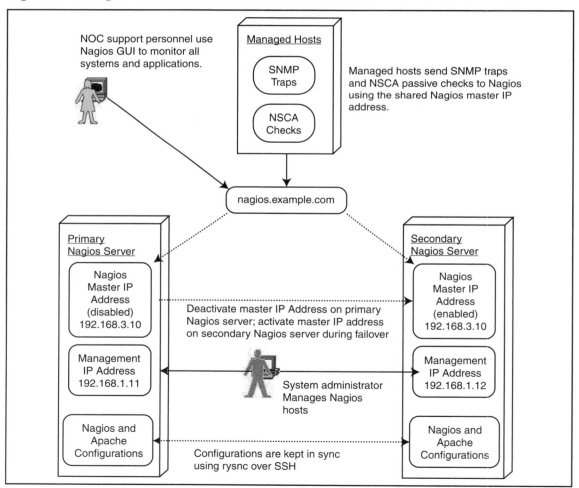

At this point, our failover scenario setup is complete. By using rsync over ssh, we have created a simple system to keep all configuration files, data files, and core program files synchronized between our primary and secondary servers. We can now test our failover configuration (it is very important to test failover *before* a real problem happens!). Perform the following steps to switch Nagios from the primary server to the secondary server:

1. Disable the master IP address on the primary server.
2. Activate the master IP address on the secondary server.
3. Stop Nagios and all related applications on the primary server.
4. Stop the rysnc job on the primary server by commenting out the cron job.
5. Start Nagios and other Nagios-related applications (SNMPTT, NSCA daemon, NDO, etc.) on the secondary server.
6. Start the sync job on the secondary server so data will be synchronized to the primary server (if the primary server is still able to accept data). (See Figure 3.10.)

Figure 3.10 Nagios Failover Sequence

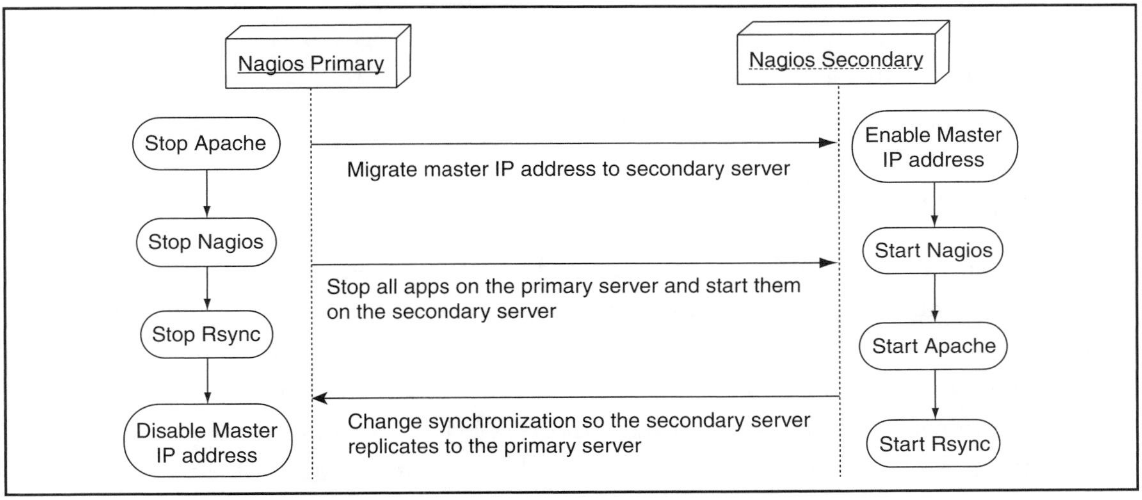

Remember to shut down Nagios on the primary server or at least make sure notifications are disabled on the primary server. In addition, you must remember to disable the rsync cron job on the primary server (if the primary is still up) to ensure it doesn't replicate bad old data to the secondary server once the secondary server becomes the master.

You can execute the check_nagios plug-in on the primary system to check the health of Nagios:

```
./check_nagios -F /usr/local/nagios/var/nagios.log -C nagios -e 10
NAGIOS OK: 5 processes, status log updated 454 seconds ago
```

This will tell us if the local system has failed. You can use this type of check to enable an automatic failover from the primary to the secondary. We normally recommend against this, as many times failures of the primary Nagios process have to do with configuration changes, and in those cases, a failover system will not resolve the issue. It is normally recommended that you avoid automatic failover and instead set a time limit. If the primary Nagios server is down for longer than your specified time, you should begin the process to move to the secondary server. Even in those cases where you do need to fail back to the master, you will be able to one-time reverse the rsync process and be ready to move back to your primary server.

This configuration also works well for upgrades. You can disable the cron job on the primary server, upgrade the secondary server, and then bring the secondary server online to test and validate the upgrade while having the safety net of being able to go back to the primary server if you encounter upgrade issues. As you work more with your Nagios server, you will identify more areas where the open configuration and easy scripting nature of the application make it so that any system can be easily measured and monitored including your Nagios server.

The Future

The future of Nagios is of keen interest to all of us. Members of our team (Derrick Bennet, Max Schubert) have been using Nagios since it was called Netsaint in a wide variety of locations. We have used it to monitor environments that are as small as four servers in a small office, to hundreds of servers across multiple data centers and through numerous firewalls and network filters. We have always found that keeping monitoring as simple as possible produces the best results. Nagios adheres to this philosophy and has been flexible enough to succeed in every environment in which we have used it. We have never found a service, application, or system that could not be monitored using Nagios. In many situations, we find that someone else in the large, enthusiastic Nagios community has already found a way to monitor devices we use. Several of us have spent time installing Nagios side by side with commercial products like Tivoli and HP Openview. In all cases, we find that the people who monitor and manage devices and networks on a daily basis time and time again choose Nagios over any other product.

So, what does that leave for the future? Quite a lot! Nagios is very flexible, which means much can be done to make it even better. Nagios 3.0 brought massive improvements in performance and large-scale configurations. Many of the features of Nagios we covered in this chapter were traditionally only available in large commercial packages as recently as a year ago. The improvements in Nagios as of version 3 are quite amazing and we can only imagine the functionality that will be added to Nagios with future releases.

Database Persistence

There has long been a cry for database support native in Nagios. NDOutils provides much of that functionality today. Having used several of the add-on database packages for Nagios we can provide some insight on why integrating a relational database into the Nagios life cycle is difficult. The biggest issue with using a database is keeping Nagios simple. When using templates stored in plain-text files you can configure hosts and services faster than is possible in any current database implementation due to the impedance mis-match between a traditional relational database model and an object-oriented, inheritence based model. There are two barriers to a native core database design:

- Having a database understand templates in a dynamic fashion is tricky. The traditional database design model does not easily map to an object-oriented model. Some databases (PostgresQL, for example) do implement object-oriented features, but we have yet to see anyone attempt to map the Nagios configuration object model to an object-oriented database like Postgres.

- Providing a user interface that allows for dynamic adjustments of database-level constraints without having to drop and re-create tables or alter table designs on the fly. The database-based Nagios configuration add-ons we have used have had us cursing by about the 23rd entry at the amount of duplicate data we had to enter because they do not fully implement the OO inheritance model Nagios supports.

CGI Front End

The only subject we have seen more debate about on than database persistence is the Nagios front-end CGI programs. Very few web applications in use today use a C-based front end. Many members of the Nagios community would really like to see the Nagios GUI ported to perl, python, or another very high-level scripted language. One of the major benefits of a C-based front end, however, is the speed and reliability the interface provides. No requirements for Java on the client, or large desktop packages to be installed; the CGIs all generate HTML and CSS. Alas, it seems that 3.0 will most likely be the last version to use C on the front end; the assumption is that PHP will be used as the front-end in version 4 of Nagios.

The biggest reason we see for a conversion from C to a very high-level language is not the functionality the CGIs provide, but rather the strong desire people have to change the look of the GUI or to integrate Nagios with other Web-based tools. We do look forward to the next version of the Nagios front end, but we will never complain about the C code in use today and how compatible Nagios output is with web browsers, from Links to Firefox. An additional benefit to having a PHP-based front end will be the ability to easily internationalize the Nagios GUI, which will allow Nagios to be used by a much broader audience.

Even More

We expect to see an even more flexible core Nagios distribution in the future. This includes additional event handlers and triggers within the Nagios Event Broker (NEB) and interpreters for high-level languages that will allow more types of plug-ins in more languages to be used with Nagios, similar to how an API-like mod_perl allows for Perl scripts and modules to act and react to Apache events throughout the life cycle of Apache. We expect this new core to allow for plug-ins written in high-level languages like PHP, ruby, Python, Perl, or Lua to register themselves as listeners for Nagios events, eliminating the constant need to work on Nagios data from outside Nagios. We hope to see this same change happen for check commands and notifications to allow more commands to be executed by Nagios directly from memory. Some people within the Nagios community really want to see Nagios moved into a Web application framework like Zend or Zope. It is our hope that Nagios does not follow this path, but rather remains its own self-hosting framework so it can continue to do what it does better than any other comparable application in its market. Overall, we expect that the largest changes will be in the areas of access control lists, authentication, and customization, but we leave the real decisions to Nagios' one true developer, Ethan Galstad. Always remember that if Nagios does not support a feature you would really like to see in place, there is always room for you to create it and contribute to the project!

A Pluggable Core

Unlike many open source projects and commercial software projects that are unwilling to change core features once a feature is stable, even if the reasons are valid and useful, Nagios dropped a piece of core functionality with version 2.*x* that many people found useful: built-in database persistence. Why was this done? Because the lead developers saw that the best way to keep Nagios an open, extensible framework was to move away from adding features to the core and develop a flexible, extensible plug-in framework. Nagios 2.*x* saw the introduction of this framework, called Nagios Event Broker (NEB). NEB allows third-party developers to write C extensions that register themselves to be notified when various events happen in the Nagios life cycle. This includes system startup, host and service check changes, and triggering of external events to name a few.

With the advent of Nagios 3, we see this framework becoming even more stable and we see a growing number of NEB modules available for Nagios. An important module in this evolution is Nagios Data Output Utils (NDO utils). This module replaces the Nagios 1.*x* database persistence model, allowing Nagios administrators to persist host and service configurations and host and service check results to a database. It was introduced in the 2.*x* series of Nagios and continues to receive major attention and use with version 3 of Nagios. A wildly popular add-on, NagVis, makes extensive use of NDO Utils. Community feedback on the NDO Utils module and community driven patches are quickly driving this module to a place of maturity and stability.

We expect the NEB framework to continue to grow in popularity and the number of plug-ins available for Nagios that make use of it to grow as well. It would not be surprising to see most noncore functionality (for example, the Web-based GUI) to eventually be removed from the core Nagios source code and re-implemented as NEB-based add-ons. The future is looking bright for Nagios as a monitoring framework, and we expect that NEB will be a major part of that future.

## Chapter 4

Plug-ins, Plug-ins, and More Plug-ins

Solutions in this chapter:

- **Plug-in Guidelines and Best Practices**
- **Software Services and Network Protocols**
- **Servers**
- **HTTP Scraping Plug-ins**
- **Testing Telnet-like interfaces (Telnet or SSH)**
- **Monitoring LDAP**
- **Monitoring Databases**
- **Specialized Hardware**
- **Anti-Virus Devices**
- **Environmental Probes**

☑ **Summary**

Introduction

One of the many advantages Nagios has over commercial/closed network and system monitoring systems is its terrific plug-in API. The Nagios plug-in API is open, easy to use, and well documented. You can develop your plug-ins in any language you want and you can monitor anything that is important to your users. C and Perl are currently the most popular languages used for plug-ins; C because it is fast, and Perl because Nagios comes with an embedded Perl interpreter that caches Perl scripts in memory, letting them execute much more quickly than other interpreted languages (much like mod_perl would).

In this section, we discuss plug-in development best practices and guidelines. We then show examples of monitoring using SNMP, as SNMP is typically in use at large organizations. From there we discuss how to monitor a variety of application-level protocols such as LDAP and HTTP. Finally, we show you examples of monitoring a variety of Enterprise-class hardware devices, from proxies to environmental monitoring systems. All the code presented in this chapter is available for download at no cost from the book's Web site.

Plug-in Guidelines and Best Practices

The official documentation for Nagios plug-in writing can be found at http://nagiosplug.sourceforge.net/developer-guidelines.html. It covers everything from command-line interface expectations to performance data output formats. Writing plug-ins is a lot of fun; just make sure your plug-ins conform to the standards so others can easily understand how they work and you can share them with the Nagios community if you choose to do so. Plug-ins should be written in simple, clear logic and defensive programming involved as they are designed to trap and report on error statuses. They should be documented well as they tend to not be changed often once they are working and deployed in a production environment.

Use Plug-ins from the Nagios Community

The Nagios community is diverse and enthusiastic. Thanks to the open nature of Nagios, you will find a plethora of service and host checking plug-ins. If you can, use community-written plug-ins rather than reinvent the wheel, as this helps lower the barriers to learning Nagios for people new to the framework. If you find you need to enhance existing code or write new plug-ins to meet your needs, contribute them to the Nagios community, as the community makes Nagios a terrific fault management framework!

Use Version Control

Your Nagios plug-ins are most likely not the star code at the company you work for. Most likely the output from them or the value they produce is also not visible to end users. This does not mean you should not follow software development best practices! Make your life easier by using version control to manage your plug-in code, be that with SVN, CVS, GIT, or your version control system of choice. The lower the risk of code change for yourself, the more likely you are to enhance, improve, and refine your plug-ins over time.

Output Performance Data

You should develop your plug-ins with performance data in mind. A variety of Nagios add-ons process this data in very useful ways. For example, PNP (PNP is not PerfParse) will take this data and produce RRD-based trending graphs. You can also use this output in Cacti or other trending tools already installed in your environment. Get in the habit of adding performance data to your plug-ins and you will increase the shelf life and interest your plug-in has to your users and the Nagios community as a whole. Please make sure to follow the Nagios performance data guidelines found at http://nagiosplug.sourceforge.net/developer-guidelines.html#AEN203.

Software Services and Network Protocols

Writing plug-ins is an area where integrators and IT professionals can really shine. Nagios' plug-in framework is very easy to code and lets you design just about any kind of service check you can imagine. In this chapter, we discuss a number of types of service checks that tend to be important for larger organizations. We start with SNMP and clusters, and then get into more protocol-specific checks for enterprise-important technologies such as databases, LDAP, and Web services.

SNMP Plug-ins

SNMP has a reputation for being insecure and a large security risk. This is too bad. It is a risk if the network it is used on is not designed properly and permissions are not set up properly. With the advent of SNMP v3, however, that risk is diminished, as SNMP v3 uses strong encryption and protects both the data and credentials of the server and client.

If you are fortunate enough to be allowed to use SNMP on your network, read on. SNMP agents expose a tremendous amount of useful information from a device, from configuration management related information to performance indicators to indications that faults are in progress or are about to occur on a device.

We assume in this chapter that you have used SNMP. The meanings of the terms *community string*, *MIB*, and *OID* should be familiar to you; if not, there are many sites on the Internet and many books you can read to learn about SNMP.

All the monitoring techniques in this section will work with any version of SNMP. We use a combination of both SNMP v2 and SNMP v3 in the examples; SNMP v2 for routers and network devices, and SNMP v3 for hosts. For each example, we also list the device model and name we used to test the techniques as well as the MIBs the device needs to support for the monitoring tests to work. This should allow you to determine whether devices not listed for the examples will work with the code examples/scripts in this chapter.

We start this section with a short description of the kinds of monitoring SNMP agents do well. We will cover the following types of devices in this section: network devices, servers, and specialized hardware (load balancers, proxies). We additionally cover software agent monitoring for specialized applications such as LDAP servers and Java Web application servers.

What SNMP Is Good For

SNMP is especially well suited for monitoring private services and indicators that are not accessible over a network. CPU usage, swap utilization, RAM usage, and disk partition utilization are common examples. SNMP is also very useful for monitoring process activity on a device; agents that support the HOST-MIB allow you to remotely query the complete process table of a device, which includes the memory and CPU utilization each process is using, and the command and arguments of the command line used to start the process. Using just the process information we can monitor and alert on useful measures of device and service health such as critical processes stopping, too much memory or CPU consumed over time for a process or group of processes and unusual numbers of processes running.

What SNMP Is Not Good For

It is preferable to monitor network-accessible services from outside the device itself, as remote tests experience conditions that are closer to what a real user or remote host would experience, including network latency, external network interface congestion, and problems due to firewall or network misconfiguration. SNMP is also a poor choice for Internet-exposed hosts unless you use SNMP v3 exclusively, as SNMP versions 1 and 2c are plain text protocols. SNMP requires senior developers if the development staff is to implement custom agents. Finally, SNMP can be a poor choice for monitoring devices that sit on low-bandwidth, high-latency networks, as the SNMP traffic for devices with many SNMP-accessible elements (like larger routers) can potentially use a significant portion of the bandwidth on a low-bandwidth link.

Nagios::Plug-in and Nagios::Plug-in::SNMP

Nagios::Plug-in is a Perl module created by Ton Voon <ton.voon@altinity.com>, now maintained by the Nagios Plug-in development team; source code and documentation for it can be found at http://nagios-plug.sourceforge.net. This Perl module provides a number of convenience routines to make it easier to write Nagios plug-ins, including routines to simplify adding, parsing, and reading command-line options, create performance data, check thresholds, and output properly formatted Nagios status lines and status codes. We recommend this module for your Perl-based plug-ins, as it significantly reduces the amount of time you spend doing basic plug-in infrastructure. As we write and publish this book, the Nagios plug-in developers are establishing standards for thresholds that are much richer than the currently documented standards. This new set of standards will allow for complex threshold specifications and should help to encourage plug-in developers to write code using the common argument parsing code, making it easier for users to quickly integrate plug-ins from a diverse development community.

Nagios::Plug-in::SNMP is a subclass of Nagios::Plug-in Max Schubert wrote to make it easier to create SNMP-based scripts. It includes code to handle common SNMP options and to perform SNMP GET and WALK requests. Nagios::Plug-in:: SNMP uses the Net-SNMP module to perform SNMP requests. While the developers of the Net-SNMP project recommend using the Perl SNMP classes that come with the Net-SNMP agent over the Net-SNMP module, we have found Net-SNMP to work very well for querying any SNMP device we have needed to query. The module can be downloaded from the book site or from CPAN.

Some of the scripts in this section also use a utility module Max Schubert wrote that makes parsing and checking thresholds that use a format of

```
'label,<op>,value:label2,<op>,value'
Where <op> is one of:
gte: >=
gt: >
lte: <=
lt: <
E.g. 'user,gt,90:system,gt,60'
```

It also includes a routine to convert metrics to Kb, kb, Mb, MB, GB, gb, and %, and a routine to output results for the results from the multiple threshold checks in an easy-to-read format. Here is the module; it is also available online from the book site. This module does not use the new style of threshold specifications the Nagios:: Plug-in developers are using, as that standard was not complete during the time this book was written.

```
package Nenm::Utils;
=pod
=head1 NAME
Nagios Enterprise Network Monitoring Utils
=head1 SYNOPSIS
A collection of routines that make multi-threshold parsing and checking
easier, these routines let us check warning and critical thresholds that
are in the format 'metric,<op>,value:metric2,<op>,value2', e.g. 'nice,gt,90:
user,lt,5'.
Valid operators are gt (>), lt (<), gte (>=), and lte (<=). Valid metrics
are passed into the parse and check functions as a hash ref where the keys
are the metrics and the values are hashes with at least a key called 'value'
that contains the value associated with the metric.
=cut
$Nenm::Utils::DEBUG = 1;
use strict;
use Nagios::Plugin;    # For error levels
=pod
=head2 parse_multi_threshold($conditions_ref, $valid_metrics);
Parse warning and critical condition strings passed in by the user; returns
a reference to an array of arrays containing thresholds that the function
check_multi_thresholds can check and an array of error messages from errors
that occurred during parsing..if no errors occur, the size of the error
array will be 0.
```

```perl
Example:
my %metrics = (
    'idle' => {'value' => 0},
    'nice' => {'value' => 0}
);
my ($wthr, $werrs) = Utils::parse_multi_threshold($plugin->opts->warning,
                                                \%metrics);
=cut
sub parse_multi_threshold {
    my $threshold_conditions =
        shift || die "Missing condition string to parse!";
    my $valid_metrics =
        shift || die "Missing hash ref of valid metrics";
    my @errors;
    my @thresholds;
    my @conditions = split(':', $threshold_conditions);
    for my $condition (@conditions) {
        my $has_error = 0;
        my ($metric, $op, $value) = split(',', $condition);
        if (! defined($metric)) {
            push(@errors, "$condition missing metric to check!");
        }
        if (! defined($op)) {
            push(@errors, "$condition missing operator to use for check!");
        }
        if (! defined($value)) {
            push(@errors, "$condition missing value to check!");
        }
        if (! exists $valid_metrics->{$metric}) {
            my $msg = "$metric is not a valid metric, valid metrics " .
                    "are " . join(', ', sort keys %$valid_metrics);
            push(@errors, $msg);
        }
        my $valid_ops = 'lt|gt|gte|lte';
        my $real_op = '';
        $op = lc($op);
        if ($op eq 'lt') {
            $real_op = '<';
        } elsif ($op eq 'gt') {
            $real_op = '>';
        } elsif ($op eq 'gte') {
            $real_op = '>=';
        } elsif ($op eq 'lte') {
            $real_op = '<=';
```

```perl
        } else {
            my $msg = "$op is not a valid operator, valid operators " .
                      "are $valid_ops";
            push(@errors, $msg);
        }
        next if scalar(@errors) > 0;
        debug("parse_multi_threshold: adding $metric $real_op ($op) $value");
        push(@thresholds, [$metric, $real_op, $value]);
    }
    return (\@thresholds, \@errors);
}
=pod
=head2 check_multi_thresholds($metrics, $warning_ref, $critical_ref, $type);
Checks all thresholds in $warning_ref and $critical_ref arrays (arrays
returned by parse_multi_thresholdc calls) and returns a hash of results
with the following keys:
* warning = reference to array of warning messages
* critical = reference to array of critical messages
* ok = reference to array of ok messages
* perfdata = string of perfdata, ready for output
$type is the threshold value type (%, K, M, B) and is added to perfdata
output to indicate the type of number in perfdata output. Use any valid
perfdata symbol that applies to your data.
Each key in metrics have a value that is a hash reference where there is
at least the key 'value' holding the real value for the metric.
Example:
my %metrics = (
    'idle' => {'value' => 80},
    'nice' => {'value' => 55}
);
my $results =
    Utils::check_multi_thresholds(\%metrics, $warn_ref, $crit_ref, '%');
=cut
sub check_multi_thresholds {
    my $metrics =
        shift || die "Missing hash ref of metrics to check!";
    my $warning =
        shift || die "Missing array ref of warning thresholds!";
    my $critical =
        shift || die "Missing array ref of critical thresholds!";
    my $type_label =
        shift || die "Missing type label (e.g. \%, K, M, B) for metrics!";
    my $results = {
        'critical' => [],
        'warning' => [],
```

```
        'ok' => [],
        'perfdata' => ''
};
my %checked;
for my $c (@$critical) {
    my ($metric, $op, $value) = (@{$c});
    debug("check_multi_thresholds: check critical $metric $op $value");
    my $real = $metrics->{$metric}->{'value'};
    my $result = eval_expr("$real $op $value");
    $checked{$metric}->{'critical'} = $value;
    if ($result == 1) {
        push(@{$results->{'critical'}},
            "$metric ($real$type_label $op $value$type_label)");
        $checked{$metric}->{'caught'} = 1;
    }
}
for my $w (@$warning) {
    my ($metric, $op, $value) = (@$w);
    my $real = $metrics->{$metric}->{'value'};
    $checked{$metric}->{'warning'} = $value;
    debug("check_multi_thresholds: check warning $metric $op $value");
    next if exists $checked{$metric}->{'caught'};
    my $result = eval_expr("$real $op $value");
    if ($result == 1) {
        push(@{$results->{'warning'}},
            "$metric ($real$type_label $op $value$type_label)");
        $checked{$metric}->{'caught'} = 1;
    }
}
my $perfdata;
for my $metric (sort keys %$metrics) {
    my $w = 0;
    $w = $checked{$metric}->{'warning'}
        if exists $checked{$metric}->{'warning'};
    my $c = 0;
    $c = $checked{$metric}->{'critical'}
        if exists $checked{$metric}->{'critical'};
    $perfdata .= " '$metric'=$metrics->{$metric}->{'value'}" .
                "$type_label;$w;$c";
    next if exists $checked{$metric}->{'caught'};
    my $value = $metrics->{$metric}->{'value'};
    push(@{$results->{'ok'}}, "$metric $value$type_label");
}
```

```perl
        $results->{'perfdata'} = $perfdata;

        return $results;

}

sub eval_expr {

    my $expr = shift;

    my $result = 0;

    eval {
        $result = eval "($expr);";
        die $@ if $@;
    };

    $result = 0 if ((! defined $result) or ($result eq ''));

    debug("eval_expr: $expr returned $result");

    return $result;

}

=pod

=head2 convert_to($type_symbol, $metrics_hash_ref)

    Convert all values in the 'value' keys of the hash passed in by reference
    to the type referenced by the $type_symbol passed in. Valid values for
    $type_symbol are: '%', 'K', 'k', 'G', 'g', 'T', 't', 'M', or 'm'. Large
    K, G, M, T all will be computed using powers of 1024, lower case versions
    will be multiplied by 1000 * N where K == 1, M == 2, G == 3, and T == 4.

    If percent is specified, the routine assumes that all passed in metrics
    added together make up the total for the type of metric they represent.
    Routine expects that 'raw' values will be in a key named 'raw' for
    every metric passed in, e.g.

    my $cpu_metrics = {
        'nice' => { 'raw' = 2390239, 'value' => 0
        'system' => { 'raw' = 23902390, 'value' => 0
        'user' => { 'raw' = 949348984, 'value' => 0
    };

        Nenm::Utils::convert_to('%', $cpu_metrics);

=cut

sub convert_to {

    my $convert_to = shift;
    my $metrics_ref = shift;

    my $valid_types = '\%|B|M|K|G';

    die "Invalid metric type $convert_to passed in!"
        unless $convert_to =~ m/^${valid_types}$/i;

    if ($convert_to eq '%') {

        my $total = 0;

        for my $metric (keys %{$metrics_ref}) {
            $total += $metrics_ref->{$metric}->{'raw'};
        }
```

```perl
        for my $m (keys %{$metrics_ref}) {
            $metrics_ref->{$m}->{'value'} =
                sprintf("%.2f", ($metrics_ref->{$m}->{'raw'} / $total) * 100);
        }
    } else {
        my $base = 1024;
        $base = 1000 if ($convert_to =~ /[a-z]/);
        my $power = 0;
        $convert_to = lc($convert_to);
        if ($convert_to eq 'b') {
            $power = 1;
        } elsif ($convert_to eq 'm') {
            $power = 2;
        } elsif ($convert_to eq 'g') {
            $power = 3;
        } elsif ($convert_to eq 't') {
            $power = 4;
        }
        my $multiplier = $base ** $power;
        for my $m (keys %{$metrics_ref}) {
            $metrics_ref->{$m}->{'value'} =
                $metrics_ref->{$m}->{'raw'} * $multiplier;
        }
    }
}
=pod
=head2 output_multi_levels($label, $results_hash_ref);
Takes a Nagios plugin label along with the results as returned by
check_multi_thresholds and outputs results text, including perfdata.
For every result passed in, the most critical result wins; list of
all thresholds breached and all values that are ok is output in a
comma separated list, divided by label. Example:

=cut
sub output_multi_results {
    my $label = shift;
    my $results = shift;
    my @critical = @{$results->{'critical'}};
    my @warning = @{$results->{'warning'}};
    my @ok = @{$results->{'ok'}};
    my $level = OK;
    print "$label ";
    if (scalar(@critical)) {
        print "CRITICAL - " . join(', ', @critical) . ' ';
        $level = CRITICAL;
    }
```

```perl
    if (scalar(@warning)) {
        print "WARNING - " . join(', ', @warning) . ' ';
        $level = WARNING unless $level == CRITICAL;
    }
    if (scalar(@ok)) {
        print "OK - " . join(', ', @ok) . ' ';
    }
    print " | $results->{'perfdata'}\n";
    return $level;
}
sub debug {
    return unless $Nenm::Utils::DEBUG == 1;
    my $msg = shift;
    warn scalar(localtime()) . ": $msg\n";
}
1;
```

ePN—The Embedded Nagios Interpreter

ePN is an embedded Perl interpreter that runs inside Nagios, as mod_perl does with Apache. For shops that heavily use Perl for plug-ins, it can dramatically decrease the load Nagios puts on a system. Please note that there are caveats to watch out for when using ePN; the most important is that once you start using ePN, you should not use the *reload* target of the Nagios init script (equivalent of sending a HUP signal to Nagios), as the reload does not properly clean up memory used by scripts run under ePN. For some this may be a deal-breaker; if it is not, please take advantage of this feature. When coding plug-ins to run under ePN you must be more careful with variable scoping and destruction than with normal scripts, because the scripts do persist in memory as they would with mod_perl. ePN, like the other parts of Nagios, has a very simple API scripts should conform to:

- Each script defines a single function; all variables should be scoped within this function.

- Each script calls the single function at the end of the script and exits with the return value of the function.

Example

```perl
#!/usr/bin/perl
# nagios: +epn
sub my_cool_check {
```

```
use strict;
my $helper = Helper->new();
my $output = $helper->do_stuff();
...
$helper = undef; # Make sure references are cleared
return 0;   # OK
}
exit my_cool_check();
```

Notice the line

```
# nagios: +epn
```

This tells Nagios that the script *wants* to be run under the embedded Perl interpreter. This line has to be put in the first 10 lines of your script; if you do not have the embedded Perl interpreter enabled in your configuration file this line will have no effect on the execution of the script.

The nice thing about the ePN coding style is that plug-ins written using it can be used with Nagios regardless of whether ePN is enabled. For more information on ePN, refer to the Nagios documentation. All plug-ins in this section use an ePN-compliant coding style.

Network Devices—Switches, Routers

Managed network devices offer a huge variety of information through SNMP, so it can be difficult to decide what is important to monitor. This section shows a number of scripts to help you monitor critical indicators of problems on network devices.

Assumptions made in this section:

- All network devices are Cisco devices
- SNMP version used is version 2
- Community string for the device is stored in a custom host variable named __snmp_community

CPU Utilization

MIB needed

CISCO-PROCESS-MIB
ENTITY-MIB

OIDs needed

CISCO-PROCESS-MIB

cpmCPUTotal5secRev: 1.3.6.1.4.1.9.9.109.1.1.1.1.6

cpmCPUTotal1minRev: 1.3.6.1.4.1.9.9.109.1.1.1.1.7

cpmCPUTotal5minRev: 1.3.6.1.4.1.9.9.109.1.1.1.1.8

cpmCPUTotalPhysicalIndex: 1.3.6.1.4.1.9.9.109.1.1.1.1.2

ENTITY-MIB

entPhysicalName: 1.3.6.1.2.1.47.1.1.1.1.7

As with servers, network device CPU over-utilization is a key indicator that a network device needs to be replaced or upgraded. According to Cisco documentation (see How to Collect CPU Utilization on Cisco IOS Devices Using SNMP— www.cisco.com/en/US/tech/tk648/tk362/technologies_tech_note09186a0080094a94. shtml), sustained CPU utilization of 90% or more can lead to degraded performance in 2500 series routers. For this reason, Cisco recommends a baseline CPU utilization threshold of 90%; they also recommend that only the five-minute CPU utilization metric should be used for alerting on CPU utilization; the one-minute-and-five-second metrics should be used for capacity planning purposes only.

This check follows those guidelines; the warning and critical threshold values are checked against the five-minute counter; one-second and one-minute metrics are not checked. All three counters are output as perfdata for use in trending. If the device has more than one CPU, all CPUs will be checked; the name of the CPU will be taken from the entPhysicalName OID if that OID exists for the CPU. If the CPU physical entity OID does not exist, the name "CPU N" will be used, where N starts at 0 and increments by one for each additional CPU found on the device.

Example Call to the Script

```
./check_snmp_cisco_cpu.pl --hostname rtr1.example.com --snmp-version 2c --
rocommunity mycommunity -w 90 -c 95
SNMP-CISCO-CPU CPU_0 0% | 'cpu_0_5sec'=1;0;0 'cpu_0_1min'=0;0;0
'cpu_0_5min'=0;90;95
```

The Script

```
#!/usr/bin/perl

=pod
=head1 NAME
check_snmp_cisco_cpu.pl - Check CPU utilization on a Cisco device.
=head1 SYNOPSIS
```

This script will check the 5 minute CPU % utilization on a Cisco device. Specify thresholds for utilization with the warning and critical switches. The thresholds will be checked for each CPU on the device if the device has multiple CPUs.

The script will output perfdata that also includes the 5 second and 1 minute CPU utilization metrics for the device.

```
=cut
# CISCO-PROCESS-MIB
# * cpmCPUTotal5secRev: 1.3.6.1.4.1.9.9.109.1.1.1.1.6
# * cpmCPUTotal1minRev: 1.3.6.1.4.1.9.9.109.1.1.1.1.7
# * cpmCPUTotal5minRev: 1.3.6.1.4.1.9.9.109.1.1.1.1.8
# * cpmCPUTotalPhysicalIndex: 1.3.6.1.4.1.9.9.109.1.1.1.1.2
#
# ENTITY-MIB (table)
# * entPhysicalName: 1.3.6.1.2.1.47.1.1.1.1.7
#
# Get 5 minute average, grab OID index for it, poll table
# .1.3.6.1.4.1.9.9.109.1.1.1.1.2.<INDEX>, if that OID has
# a non-zero value, save the index OID and poll
# .1.3.6.1.2.1.47.1.1.1.1.7.<INDEX> to get the human-readable
# description of the component the CPU is on.
#
# If .1.3.6.1.4.1.9.9.109.1.1.1.1.2.<INDEX> returns a zero value
# there is no mapping to a physical component description.
sub check_snmp_cisco_cpu {
    use strict;
    use FindBin;
    use lib "$FindBin::Bin/lib";
    use Nagios::Plugin::SNMP;
    use Nenm::Utils;

    my $LABEL = 'SNMP-CISCO-CPU';

    my $USAGE = <<EOF;
Usage: %s —warning % --critical %
EOF
    my $plugin = Nagios::Plugin::SNMP->new(
        'shortname'  => $LABEL,
        'usage'      => $USAGE
    );

    $plugin->getopts;
    $Nenm::Utils::DEBUG = $plugin->opts->get('snmp-debug');

    my $WARN = $plugin->opts->get('warning');
    $plugin->nagios_die("Missing warning threshold!") unless $WARN;

    my $CRIT = $plugin->opts->get('critical');
    $plugin->nagios_die("Missing critical threshold!") unless $CRIT;
```

```perl
my %OIDS = qw(
    cpmCPUTotalPhysicalIndex 1.3.6.1.4.1.9.9.109.1.1.1.1.2
    cpmCPUTotal5secRev 1.3.6.1.4.1.9.9.109.1.1.1.1.6
    cpmCPUTotal1minRev 1.3.6.1.4.1.9.9.109.1.1.1.1.7
    cpmCPUTotal5minRev 1.3.6.1.4.1.9.9.109.1.1.1.1.8
);
my %cpu;
my $phys_results = $plugin->walk($OIDS{'cpmCPUTotalPhysicalIndex'});
delete $OIDS{'cpmCPUTotalPhysicalIndex'};
my $phys_names = $phys_results->{$OIDS{'cpmCPUTotalPhysicalIndex'}};
my $cpu_counter = 0;
for my $row (keys %$phys_names) {
    my $idx = ($row =~ m/^.+\.(\d+)$/)[0];
    my $ent_name = "CPU_$cpu_counter";
    Nenm::Utils::debug(
        "CPU index $idx has physical entity index $phys_names->{$row}");
    if ($phys_names->{$row} > 0) {
        $ent_name = get_physical_name($plugin, $phys_names->{$row});
    }
    Nenm::Utils::debug("CPU index $idx now has cpuName $ent_name");
    $cpu_counter++;
    $cpu{$idx} = { 'cpuName' => $ent_name };
}
for my $oid (values %OIDS) {
    Nenm::Utils::debug("Walk OID $oid");
    my $results = $plugin->walk($oid);
    for my $base_oid (keys %$results) {
        my $idx = ($base_oid =~ m/^.+\.(\d+)$/)[0];
        my %table = %{$results->{$base_oid}};
        my $ent_name;
        for my $row (keys %table) {
            Nenm::Utils::debug("Received $row: $table{$row}");
            my ($base, $entity) = ($row =~ m/^(.+)?\.(\d+)$/)[0,1];
            for my $o (keys %OIDS) {
                my $v = $OIDS{$o};
                if ($v eq $base) {
                    Nenm::Utils::debug("Index $entity: $o = $table{$row}");
                    $cpu{$entity}->{$o} = $table{$row};
                }
            }
        }
    }
}
```

```perl
# Check 5 min CPu value for all CPUs
my $CRITICAL = $plugin->opts->get('critical');
my $WARNING = $plugin->opts->get('warning');

my @critical;
my @warning;
my @ok;

for my $cpu_idx (keys %cpu) {
    my $cpu5min = $cpu{$cpu_idx}->{'cpmCPUTotal5minRev'};
    my $name = $cpu{$cpu_idx}->{'cpuName'};

    Nenm::Utils::debug("$name 5 minute utilization is $cpu5min");

    if ($cpu5min > $CRITICAL) {
        push(@critical, "$name (${cpu5min}\% > ${CRITICAL}\%)");
    } elsif ($cpu5min > $WARNING) {
        push(@warning, "$name (${cpu5min}\% > ${WARNING}\%)");
    } else {
        push(@ok, "$name ${cpu5min}\%");
    }
}
my $output = "$LABEL ";
my $level = OK;
if (scalar(@critical) > 0) {
    $output .= 'CRITICAL - ' . join(', ', @critical) . ' ';
    $level = CRITICAL;
}
if (scalar(@warning) > 0) {
    $output .= ' WARNING - ' . join(', ', @warning) . ' ';
    $level = WARNING unless $level == CRITICAL;
}
if (scalar(@ok) > 0) {
    $output .= ' OK - ' . join(', ', @ok);
}
print "$output | " . make_perfdata(\%cpu) . "\n";
return $level;
sub get_physical_name {
    my $plugin = shift;
    my $idx = shift;

    my $oid = "1.3.6.1.2.1.47.1.1.1.1.7.$idx";
    Nenm::Utils::debug("Getting physical name OID $oid");

    my $result = $plugin->get($oid);
    my $name = $result->{$oid};
    Nenm::Utils::debug("Physical name for index $idx is $name");

    return $name;
}
```

```
sub make_perfdata {
    my $stats = shift;
    my $perfdata = "";
    for my $cpu (keys %$stats) {
        my $name = lc($stats->{$cpu}->{'cpuName'});
        $name =~ s/\s+/_/g;
        my $cpu5sec = $stats->{$cpu}->{'cpmCPUTotal5secRev'};
        my $cpu1min = $stats->{$cpu}->{'cpmCPUTotal1minRev'};
        my $cpu5min = $stats->{$cpu}->{'cpmCPUTotal5minRev'};
        $perfdata .= "'${name}_5sec'=$cpu5sec;0;0 " .
                     "'${name}_1min'=$cpu1min;0;0 " .
                     "'${name}_5min'=$cpu5min;$WARNING;$CRITICAL ";
    }
    return $perfdata;
}
}
exit check_snmp_cisco_cpu();
```

Memory Utilization

MIB needed

CISCO-MEMORY-POOL-MIB

OIDs needed

ciscoMemoryPoolName: 1.3.6.1.4.1.9.9.48.1.1.1.2
ciscoMemoryPoolUsed: 1.3.6.1.4.1.9.9.48.1.1.1.5
ciscoMemoryPoolFree: 1.3.6.1.4.1.9.9.48.1.1.1.6

Near 100% memory utilization for long periods of time indicates a device is overworked. This check looks at each memory pool on a Cisco device and will alert if one or more of the pools exceeds the % utilization warning and critical thresholds passed to the script.

Example Call

```
./check_snmp_cisco_mem_pool.pl --hostname rtr1.example.com --snmp-version 2c
--rocommunity mycommunity -w 90 -c 95
SNMP-CISCO-MEM-POOL OK - Processor 23.67%, I/O 40.10% |
'processor'=23.67%;90;95;0;100 'i/o'=40.10%;90;95;0;100
```

The Script

```perl
#!/usr/local/bin/perl

# nagios: +epn

=pod

=head1 NAME

check_snmp_cisco_mem_pool.pl - Check memory pool utilization
on a Cisco router or switch

=head1 SYNOPSIS

Check memory pool utilization on a Cisco device. This script will check each
memory pool available on a Cisco switch or router and alert if the % memory
utilized is greater than the warning and critical thresholds passed into
the script. Perfdata will be output for each pool found; the metrics will
be prefixed with the name of the pool as reported by the Cisco device.

=cut

sub check_snmp_cisco_mem_pool {

    use strict;
    use Nagios::Plugin::SNMP;
    use Nenm::Utils;

    my $USAGE = <<EOF;
Usage: %s --warning % --critical %
EOF

    my $LABEL = 'SNMP-CISCO-MEM-POOL';

    my $plugin = Nagios::Plugin::SNMP->new(
        'shortname'   => $LABEL,
        'usage'       => $USAGE
    );

    $plugin->getopts;

    $Nenm::Utils::DEBUG = $plugin->opts->get('snmp-debug');

    my $WARN = $plugin->opts->get('warning');
    $plugin->nagios_die("Missing warning threshold!") unless $WARN;

    my $CRIT = $plugin->opts->get('critical');
    $plugin->nagios_die("Missing critical threshold!") unless $CRIT;

    my %oids = qw(
        .1.3.6.1.4.1.9.9.48.1.1.1.2 ciscoMemoryPoolName
        .1.3.6.1.4.1.9.9.48.1.1.1.5 ciscoMemoryPoolUsed
        .1.3.6.1.4.1.9.9.48.1.1.1.6 ciscoMemoryPoolFree
    );

    my %mem;

    # Build our memory table, indexed by pool index, from
    # our metric tables.

    for my $oid (sort keys %oids) {

        Nenm::Utils::debug("Walking $oid");

        my $results = $plugin->walk($oid);
```

```perl
    for my $key (keys %{$results->{$oid}}) {
        my ($oid, $idx) = ($key =~ m/^(.+)\.(\d+)$/);
        Nenm::Utils::debug("Received $oid, $idx");

        $mem{$idx} = {} unless exists $mem{$idx};
        my $value = $results->{$oid}->{$key};
        $mem{$idx}->{$oids{$oid}} = $value;
        Nenm::Utils::debug("Pool index $idx - $oids{$oid} - $value");
    }
}

# How calculate % utilization based on free and used memory for
# each pool and check for threshold violations.
my @critical;
my @warn;
my @ok;

for my $pool (keys %mem) {
    my $name = $mem{$pool}->{'ciscoMemoryPoolName'};
    my $free = $mem{$pool}->{'ciscoMemoryPoolFree'};
    my $used = $mem{$pool}->{'ciscoMemoryPoolUsed'};
    my $util = sprintf("%.2f", ($used / ($used + $free)) * 100);

    $mem{$pool}->{'util'} = $util;

    Nenm::Utils::debug("$name - $util\% memory utilization");

    if ($util > $CRIT) {
        push(@critical, "$name ($util\% > $CRIT\%)");
    } elsif ($util > $WARN) {
        push(@warn, "$name ($util\% > $WARN\%)");
    } else {
        push(@ok, "$name $util\%");
    }
}

my $level = OK;

my $output = "$LABEL ";

if (scalar(@critical) > 0) {
    $output .= 'CRITICAL - ' . join(', ', @critical) . ' ';
    $level = CRITICAL;
}

if (scalar(@warn) > 0) {
    $output .= 'WARN - ' . join(', ', @warn) . ' ';
    $level = WARNING unless $level == CRITICAL;
}

if (scalar(@ok) > 0) {
    $output .= 'OK - ' . join(', ', @ok);
}

if (scalar(@critical) > 0) {
    $output .= 'CRITICAL - ' . join(', ', @critical) . ' ';
    $level = CRITICAL;
}
```

```
if (scalar(@warn) > 0) {
    $output .= 'WARN - ' . join(', ', @warn) . ' ';
    $level = WARNING unless $level == CRITICAL;
}
if (scalar(@ok) > 0) {
    $output .= 'OK - ' . join(', ', @ok);
}
$output .= make_perfdata(\%mem, $WARN, $CRIT);
print "$output\n";
return $level;
sub make_perfdata {
    my $mem_ref = shift;
    my $warn = shift;
    my $critical = shift;
    my $perfdata = ' | ';
    for my $pool (sort keys %$mem_ref) {
        my $name = lc($mem_ref->{$pool}->{'ciscoMemoryPoolName'});
        my $util = $mem_ref->{$pool}->{'util'};
        $perfdata .= "'$name'=$util\%;$warn;$critical;0;100 ";
    }
    return $perfdata;
}
}
exit check_snmp_cisco_mem_pool();
```

Component Temperature

MIB needed

ENTITY-MIB
CISCO-ENTITY-SENSOR-MIB

OIDs needed

ENTITY-MIB:

- entPhysicalDescr: 1.3.6.1.2.1.47.1.1.1.1.2

CISCO-ENTITY-SENSOR-MIB

- entSensorType: 1.3.6.1.4.1.9.9.91.1.1.1.1.1
- entSensorScale: 1.3.6.1.4.1.9.9.91.1.1.1.1.2

- entSensorValue: 1.3.6.1.4.1.9.9.91.1.1.1.1.4
- entSensorStatus: 1.3.6.1.4.1.9.9.91.1.1.1.1.5

Higher end Cisco devices include temperature sensors, and each has different temperature limits. The following check was written for 6500 series Cisco switches but should work with other Cisco devices that support temperature sensors. It will check each sensor that is available on the Cisco device and alert if any sensors exceed the temperature thresholds (Celsius) passed in to the script. The highest alert status for any sensor becomes the alert level of the check. The script will output perfdata metrics for each sensor the device supports for trending purposes.

Example Call to the Script

```
./check_snmp_cisco_temp.pl --hostname 192.168.3.1 --snmp-version 2c
--rocommunity mycommunity --warning 30 \
      --critical 36 --snmp-max-msg-size 50000 --sensor-regex inlet
WARNING - Inlet_1 (40c >= 30c), OK Inlet_2 28c | 'Inlet_1'=40c;30;36
'Inlet_2'=28;30;36
```

The Script

```
#!/usr/local/bin/perl
=cut
=head1 NAME
check_snmp_cisco_temp.pl - Check temperature sensors on Cisco devices
that support temperature sensors.
=head1 DESCRIPTION
This script will check the temperatures of all temperature sensors on
a Cisco device. Pass in warning and critical temperature thresholds
(in degrees Celsius)
and the script will alert if one or more temperature sensors on
the device exceed the thresholds supplied to the script; the highest
alert level becomes the alert level for the script.
If the device does not support temperature sensors, UNKNOWN will be returned.
You must specify which sensors to check by using the --sensor-regex switch.
If you pass the word 'all' to the switch, every sensor will be checked;
if you specify a regular expression, only sensors matching that expression
will be matched. For example, you could specify
—sensor-regex Inlet
to only check inlet sensors. Regular expression matching is case insensitive.
Please note that you may need to use the --snmp-max-msg-size switch to
increase the SNMP buffer size for devices with a large number of sensors.
50000 is a good place to start.
=pod
```

```
#
# Descriptions of sensors
# snmpwalk -c -read -v 2c 192.168.3.1 1.3.6.1.2.1.47.1.1.1.1.2
#
# Type - 8 == celsius, 12 == truth value
# snmpwalk -c -read -v 2c 192.168.3.1 1.3.6.1.4.1.9.9.91.1.1.1.1.1
#
# Scale (exponent) - 9 == units (10^0)
# snmpwalk -c -read -v 2c 192.168.3.1 1.3.6.1.4.1.9.9.91.1.1.1.1.2
#
# Most recent measurements
# snmpwalk -c -read -v 2c 192.168.3.1 1.3.6.1.4.1.9.9.91.1.1.1.1.4
#
# Status 1 == ok, 2 == cannot report, 3 == broken
# snmpwalk -c -read -v 2c 192.168.3.1 1.3.6.1.4.1.9.9.91.1.1.1.1.5
sub check_snmp_cisco_temp {
    use strict;
    use FindBin;
    use lib "$FindBin::Bin/lib";
    use Nagios::Plugin::SNMP;
    my $LABEL = 'SNMP-CISCO-TEMP';
    my $USAGE = <<EOF;
Usage: %s --sensor-regex 'Inlet' --warning 30 --critical 36
EOF
    my $plugin = Nagios::Plugin::SNMP->new(
        'shortname'  => $LABEL,
        'usage'      => $USAGE
    );
    $plugin->add_arg(
        'spec' => 'sensor-regex|S=s@',
        'help' => "-S, --sensor-regex\n" .
                    "   Regular expression to use to select sensors to\n" .
                    "   read. For example, -S 'Inlet' would select only\n" .
                    "   inlet sensors on a device. Use the word 'all' to\n" .
                    "   have the script check ALL sensors.",
        'required' => 1
    );
    $plugin->add_arg(
        'spec' => 'warning|w=i',
        'help' => "-w, --warning degrees-celsius\n" .
                    "   Upper warning threshold in degrees celsius for\n" .
                    "   the temperature of a sensor",
        'required' => 1
    );
    $plugin->add_arg(
        'spec' => 'critical|c=i',
```

```perl
        'help' => "-c, --critical degrees-celsius\n" .
                  " Upper critical threshold in degrees celsius for\n" .
                  " the temperature of a sensor",
        'required' => 1
    );
$plugin->getopts;
my $DEBUG = $plugin->opts->get('debug');
# Get the sensor index
my $sensor_oid = '1.3.6.1.2.1.47.1.1.1.1.2';
my $result = $plugin->walk($sensor_oid)->{$sensor_oid};
debug("Retrieved sensor list");
my %sensors;
debug("Retrieved " . keys(%$result) . "sensor descriptions");
my @idxs;
my $sensor_regexes = $plugin->opts->get('sensor-regex');
for my $var (keys %$result) {
    my $name = $result->{$var};
    if (lc($sensor_regexes->[0]) ne 'all') {
        # Choose just ones that match our regexes
        my $matched = 0;
        for my $expr (@$sensor_regexes) {
            if ($name =~ m/$expr/i) {
                debug("Matched sensor $name against $expr");
                $matched = 1;
                last;
            }
        }
        next unless $matched == 1;
    }
    $name =~ s/['"]//g;
    $name =~ s/temperature\s+sensor//ig;
    $name =~ s/\s+$//;
    $name =~ s/^\s+//;
    my $idx = ($var =~ m/(\d+)$/)[0];
    debug("Setting oid $var to name $name and index $idx");
    $sensors{$idx} = {
        'name'   => $name,
        'type'   => 0,
        'scale'  => 0,
        'temp'   => 0,
        'status' => 0
    };
}
```

```perl
debug("Checking " . keys(%sensors) . " sensors");
my $prefix = '.1.3.6.1.4.1.9.9.91.1.1.1.1';
# Check type, eliminate those that are not type 8 (celsius)
for my $idx (keys %sensors) {
    my @oids = (
             "${prefix}.1.$idx",# Type - 8 is temp
             "${prefix}.2.$idx",# Scale - 9 == 10^0
             "${prefix}.4.$idx",# Measurement
             "${prefix}.5.$idx" # Status - 1 ok, 2 cannot report, 3 broken
    );
    $result = $plugin->get(@oids);
    foreach my $p (keys %$result) {
        if ($p eq "${prefix}.1.$idx") {
            $sensors{$idx}->{'type'} = $result->{$p};
        }
        if ($p eq "${prefix}.2.$idx") {
            $sensors{$idx}->{'scale'} = $result->{$p};
        }
        if ($p eq "${prefix}.4.$idx") {
            $sensors{$idx}->{'temp'} = $result->{$p};
        }
        if ($p eq "${prefix}.5.$idx") {
            $sensors{$idx}->{'status'} = $result->{$p};
        }
    }
}
# Close and destroy session
$plugin->close();
# Now check sizes
my $w = $plugin->opts->get('warning');
my $c = $plugin->opts->get('critical');
my @ok;
my @warn;
my @crit;
my $level = OK;
my $has_temperature_sensors = 0;
my @perf_data;
for my $idx (keys %sensors) {
    my $s = $sensors{$idx};
    # Type 8 == temperature, ignore all others
    next if $s->{'type'} != 8;
    $has_temperature_sensors = 1;
    # Status of 2 is non-measurable, 3 is broken
    next if $s->{'status'} == 2;
    push(@perf_data, perf_data($s->{'name'}, $s->{'temp'}, $w, $c));
```

```perl
            if ($s->{'status'} == 3) {
                $level = CRITICAL;
                push(@crit, "$s->{name} offline");
                next;
            }
            if ($s->{'temp'} >= $c) {
                $level = CRITICAL;
                push(@crit, "$s->{'name'} ($s->{'temp'}c >= ${c}c)");
            } elsif ($s->{'temp'} >= $w) {
                $level = WARNING unless $level == CRITICAL;
                push(@warn, "$s->{'name'} ($s->{'temp'}c >= ${w}c)");
            } else {
                push(@ok, "$s->{'name'} $s->{'temp'}c");
            }
        }
    }
    if (! $has_temperature_sensors) {
        $plugin->nagios_die("Device does not have temperature sensors");
    }
    print "$LABEL ";
    if (scalar(@crit) > 0) {
        print "CRITICAL - " . join(', ', @crit) . ' ';
    }
    if (scalar(@warn) > 0) {
        print "WARNING - " . join(', ', @warn) . ' ';
    }
    if (scalar(@ok) > 0) {
        print "OK - " . join(', ', @ok) . ' ';
    }
    print "|" . join(' ', @perf_data) . "\n";
    return $level;
    sub perf_data {
        my $module = shift;
        my $temp   = shift;
        my $warn   = shift;
        my $crit   = shift;
        $module = ~ s/\s+/_/g;
        $module = ucfirst($module);
        return "'${module}'=$temp;$warn;$crit;;";
    }
    sub debug {
        return unless $DEBUG == 1;
        my $msg = shift;
        print STDERR scalar(localtime()) . ": $msg\n";
    }
}
exit check_snmp_cisco_temp();
```

Bandwidth Utilization

MIB needed

IF-MIB
ETHERLIKE-MIB

OIDs needed

IF-MIB

- ifDescr: 1.3.6.1.2.1.2.2.1.2
- ifSpeed: 1.3.6.1.2.1.2.2.1.5
- ifOperStatus: 1.3.6.1.2.1.2.2.1.8
- ifInOctets: 1.3.6.1.2.1.2.2.1.10
- ifOutOctets: 1.3.6.1.2.1.2.2.1.16

ETHERLIKE-MIB:

- dot3StatsIndex: 1.3.6.1.2.1.10.7.2.1.1
- dot3StatsDuplexStatus: 1.3.6.1.2.1.10.7.2.1.19

Bandwidth utilization is very important to organizations that pay for bandwidth. This check will monitor a specific interface on a Cisco device and report if traffic in or out of the interface exceeds the thresholds set for the script. The user can optionally specify the maximum bandwidth for the interface; this is useful for situations in which the port connects to an upstream device that is not manageable and has much less bandwidth capacity than the managed device. An example of this would be a core router whose uplink port connects to an ISP-owned router; both ports might have a maximum interface speed of 100 Mb/sec, but the ISP might only allow the customer to use 10 Mb/sec. Method for calculating bandwidth taken from Cisco documentation (How to Calculate Bandwidth Utilization Using SNMP—www.cisco.com/en/US/tech/tk648/tk362/technologies_tech_note09186a008009496e.shtml).

Example Call to the Script

In this case, we want to warn if there is more than 90% utilization inbound or outbound for the interface; alert with a critical status if the utilization is greater than 98% inbound or outbound, and have a maximum speed of 100 Mb/sec on the interface. Maximum speed specifications can be done as "g" for gigabits per second, "m" for megabits per second, or "k" for kilobits per second. If no suffix is present, bits per second is assumed.

> **NOTE**
>
> This script should work for hosts too when used with the *--no-duplex-check* switch, as most host-based agents implement the IF-MIB but do not support the ETHERLIKE-MIB.

```
./check_snmp_if_bw_util.pl --snmp-version 2c --hostname rtr1.example.com
--rocommunity mycommunity \
--warning 'in_util,gt,90:out_util,gt,90' --critical
'in_util,gt,98:out_util,gt,98' \
--interface FastEthernet0/1 --sleep-time 5 --max-speed 100m
SNMP-IF-BW-UTIL FastEthernet0/1 (Full Duplex) OK - in_util 2.31%, out_util
8.36% | 'in_util'=2.31%;90;98 'out_util'=8.36%;90;98
```

The Script

```perl
#!/usr/local/bin/perl
# nagios: +epn
=pod
=head1 NAME
check_snmp_if_bw_util.pl - Check bandwidth utilization for an interface on
a device that implements IF-MIB.
=head1 SYNOPSIS
```

Check bandwidth % utilization on an interface on a device that supports the IF-MIB. Bandwidth utilization is checked by both in bits/second and out bits/second. Maximum bandwidth will be taken from the IF-MIB::ifSpeed OID unless the maximum speed for the interface is specified using the --max-speed argument to the script. The name of the interface to check must be passed in using the --interface argument to the script.

This script expects the interface being checked to be up and in full duplex mode; if the interface is in half-duplex mode, use the --half-duplex switch to indicate that. If the interface is down or in the wrong mode, the script will exit with a CRITICAL level alert. If you wish to not have the script check duplex because the device you are querying does not support the ETHERLIKE-MIB, just pass in the --no-duplex-check switch.

Warning and critical thresholds can be specified using the following format:
metric,<op>,number:metric,<op>,number

```
Where metric is one of:
* in_util
* out_util
and <op> is one of
* lt - <
* lte - <=
* gt - >
* gte - >=
Example:
--warning 'in_util,gt,90:out_util,gt,90' --critical 'out_util,gt,95'
Multiple thresholds specified with ':' will be OR'd; if any of the
passed in threshold checks is true, the script will alert. The most
critical alert status becomes the alert level for the script.
The script will also output perfdata for in and out utilization.
Example call and output:
./check_snmp_if_bw.pl —hostname myrouter --interface FastEthernet0/1 --max-speed
10m --warn 'in_util,gt,90:out_util,gt,90' --critical 'out_util,gt,95'
--max-speed 10m
SNMP-IF-BW-UTIL WARN - IN UTIL (93% > 90%), OK - OUT UTIL 85% |
'in_util'=93%;90;95;
0;100 'out_util'=85%;90;95;0;100
=cut
sub check_snmp_if_bw {
    use strict;
    use Nagios::Plugin::SNMP;
    use Nenm::Utils;

    my $USAGE = <<EOF;
Usage: %s --warning 'spec' --critical 'spec' --interface NAME \
          [--max-speed SPEC] [--half-duplex | --no-check-duplex]
EOF
    my $LABEL = 'SNMP-IF-BW-UTIL';

    my $plugin = Nagios::Plugin::SNMP->new(
        'shortname' => $LABEL,
        'usage'     => $USAGE
    );

    $plugin->add_arg(
        'spec' => 'interface|i=s',
        'help' => "—interface, -i: Name of the interface to use; use the\n" .
                  "                description as returned by ifDescr.\n",
        'required' => 1
    );

    $plugin->add_arg(
        'spec' => 'sleep-time|S=i',
        'help' => "--sleep-time, -s: Time to sleep between samples; if not\n" .
                  "                 present, defaults to 10.\n",
        'required' => 0,
        'default' => 10
    );
```

```perl
$plugin->add_arg(
    'spec' => 'half-duplex',
    'help' => "--half-duplex: Interface should be in half-duplex,\n" .
              "               otherwise script expects interface\n" .
              "               to be in full duplex mode.",
    'required' => 0,
    'default' => 0
);
$plugin->add_arg(
    'spec' => 'no-duplex-check',
    'help' => "--no-duplex-check: DO not check duplex state on the\n" .
              "                   interface; useful for devices \n" .
              "                   that do not implement ETHERLIKE-MIB.\n",
    'required' => 0,
    'default' => 0
);
$plugin->add_arg(
    'spec' => 'max-speed|M=s',
    'help' => "--max-speed, -M: Maximum speed for the interface being\n" .
              "                 checked. Specify 'g', 'm', or 'k'\n" .
              "                 for Gigabits, megabits, or kilobits\n" .
              "                 per second. If no maximum speed is\n" .
              "                 specified, the script will use the \n" .
              "                 value from ifSpeed.\n",
        'required' => 0,
        'default' => ''
    );
$plugin->getopts;
$Nenm::Utils::DEBUG = $plugin->opts->get('snmp-debug');
my $SLEEP_TIME = $plugin->opts->get('sleep-time');
my $IFDESCR = $plugin->opts->get('interface');
$plugin->nagios_die("Missing interface to check!") unless $IFDESCR;
my $EXPECTED_DUPLEX = '';
if ($plugin->opts->get('no-duplex-check') == 0) {
    if ($plugin->opts->get('half-duplex') == 1) {
        $EXPECTED_DUPLEX = 'halfDuplex';
    } else {
        $EXPECTED_DUPLEX = 'fullDuplex';
    }
}
my %if_stats = (
    'in_util' => {qw(value 0)},
    'out_util' => {qw(value 0)}
);
my ($wthr, $werrs) = Nenm::Utils::parse_multi_threshold(
                        $plugin->opts->warning, \%if_stats);
```

```perl
if (scalar(@$werrs) > 0) {
    $plugin->nagios_die("Invalid warning threshold specified: " .
                    join(', ', @$werrs));
}
my ($cthr, $cerrs) = Nenm::Utils::parse_multi_threshold(
                        $plugin->opts->critical, \%if_stats);
if (scalar(@$cerrs) > 0) {
    $plugin->nagios_die("Invalid critical threshold specified: " .
                    join(', ', @$cerrs));
}
my $CRIT = $plugin->opts->get('critical');
$plugin->nagios_die("Missing critical threshold!") unless $CRIT;
# Optional .. if -1, use ifSpeed for the interface.
my $MAX_SPEED = $plugin->opts->get('max-speed');
# Get the index for this interface, return UNKNOWN if not found
my $IF_IDX = get_if_index($plugin, $IFDESCR);
if ($IF_IDX == -1) {
    $plugin->nagios_die("Could not find interface $IFDESCR in IF-MIB");
}
# Check to see if the interface is up (1), if not, exit with UNKNOWN
if (! if_is_up($plugin, $IF_IDX)) {
    $plugin->nagios_exit(CRITICAL,
                    "Interface $IFDESCR is not up, can't check!");
}
# Get the duplex for the interface from ETHERLIKE-MIB, exit with
# critical if it is not in the expected duplex state.

if ($plugin->opts->get('no-duplex-check') == 0) {
    my $DUPLEX = get_if_duplex($plugin, $IF_IDX);

    if ($DUPLEX ne $EXPECTED_DUPLEX) {

        $plugin->nagios_exit(CRITICAL,
                        "Interface $IFDESCR is in $DUPLEX mode, " .
                        "expected to see if in $EXPECTED_DUPLEX mode");
    }
}
# if the user specified a max speed, translate it into bits; if they
# did not specify a max speed, get the max speed from the ifSpeed
# OID for the interface.

my $MAX_BITS = 0;

if ($MAX_SPEED eq '') {
    $MAX_BITS = get_if_speed($plugin, $IF_IDX);
} else {
   $MAX_BITS = speed_spec_to_bps($plugin, $MAX_SPEED);
}
Nenm::Utils::debug("Retrieving traffic sample 1");
# Get octets in and out for the interface
my ($IN_OCT1, $OUT_OCT1) = get_if_octets($plugin, $IF_IDX);

# Sleep for sleep-time seconds, sample again
Nenm::Utils::debug("Sleep $SLEEP_TIME seconds between samples");
```

```perl
sleep($SLEEP_TIME);

Nenm::Utils::debug("Retrieving traffic sample 2");
# Get octets in and out for the interface
my ($IN_OCT2, $OUT_OCT2) = get_if_octets($plugin, $IF_IDX);

my $IN_OCT = $IN_OCT2 - $IN_OCT1;
my $OUT_OCT = $OUT_OCT2 - $OUT_OCT1;

# Calculate % utilization based on bits in/out and max speed
# http://www.cisco.com/en/US/tech/tk648/tk362/technologies_tech_
note09186a008009496e.shtml
Nenm::Utils::debug(
    "In utilization: ($IN_OCT * 800) / ($SLEEP_TIME * $MAX_BITS)");
$if_stats{'in_util'}->{'value'} = sprintf("%.2f",
    (($IN_OCT * 800) / ($SLEEP_TIME * $MAX_BITS)) * 100);

Nenm::Utils::debug(
    "Out utilization: ($OUT_OCT * 800) / ($SLEEP_TIME * $MAX_BITS)");
$if_stats{'out_util'}->{'value'} = sprintf("%.2f",
    (($OUT_OCT * 800) / ($SLEEP_TIME * $MAX_BITS)) * 100);

my $results = Nenm::Utils::check_multi_thresholds(\%if_stats,
                                                 $wthr, $cthr, '%');

my $output_label = "$LABEL $IFDESCR";

if ($EXPECTED_DUPLEX ne '') {
    $EXPECTED_DUPLEX =~ s/^(\w+[a-z])([A-Z]\w+)$/\u$1 $2/;
    $output_label .= " ($EXPECTED_DUPLEX)";
}

return Nenm::Utils::output_multi_results($output_label, $results);

# Search for SNMP index of specified interface; if found return
# the integer index of the interface. If not found, return -1.
sub get_if_index {

    my $snmp = shift;
    my $wanted_if = lc(shift());

    my $results = $snmp->walk('.1.3.6.1.2.1.2.2.1.2');
    my $iftable = $results->{'.1.3.6.1.2.1.2.2.1.2'};

    Nenm::Utils::debug("Checking for IF description $wanted_if");

    my $found_idx = -1;

    for my $oid (keys %$iftable) {

        my $descr = lc($iftable->{$oid});

        Nenm::Utils::debug("Retrieved IF description $descr");

        if ($descr eq $wanted_if) {
            my $idx = ($oid =~ m/^.+\.(\d+)$/)[0];
            Nenm::Utils::debug("Found IF $wanted_if - index $idx");
            $found_idx = $idx;
            last;
        }
    }

    return $found_idx;
}
```

```perl
sub if_is_up {
    my $snmp = shift;
    my $idx = shift;

    my %states = qw(
        1 up
        2 down
        3 testing
        4 unknown
        5 dormant
        6 notPresent
        7 lowerLayerDown
    );

    my $oid = ".1.3.6.1.2.1.2.2.1.8.$idx";
    my $results = $snmp->get($oid);
    my $status = $results->{$oid};

    Nenm::Utils::debug("Interface status is $states{$status}");

    return ($status == 1) ? 1 : 0;
}
sub get_if_duplex {
    my $snmp = shift;
    my $wanted_idx = shift;

    my %oids = qw(
        dot3StatsIndex        .1.3.6.1.2.1.10.7.2.1.1
        dot3StatsDuplexStatus .1.3.6.1.2.1.10.7.2.1.19
    );

    my %duplexes = qw(
        1 unknown
        2 halfDuplex
        3 fullDuplex
    );

    my $results = $snmp->walk($oids{'dot3StatsIndex'});
    my $ports = $results->{$oids{'dot3StatsIndex'}};

    my $duplex = '';

    for my $port (keys %$ports) {
        my $idx = $ports->{$port};
        if ("$idx" eq "$wanted_idx") {
            my $eidx = ($port =~ m/^.+\.(\d+)/)[0];
            Nenm::Utils::debug("Etherlike-MIB Index for $idx: $eidx");
            my $duplex_oid = "$oids{'dot3StatsDuplexStatus'}.$eidx";
            Nenm::Utils::debug("Etherlike-MIB duplex OID: $duplex_oid");
            my $d_results = $snmp->get($duplex_oid);
            my $didx = $d_results->{$duplex_oid};
            $duplex = $duplexes{$didx};
```

```perl
                Nenm::Utils::debug("Etherlike-MIB Duplex $didx: $duplex");
                last;
            }
        }
        return $duplex;
    }
sub get_if_speed {
    my $snmp = shift;
    my $idx = shift;

    my $bps = 0;
    my $oid = ".1.3.6.1.2.1.2.2.1.5.$idx";
    my $results = $snmp->get($oid);
    $bps = $results->{$oid};
    Nenm::Utils::debug("Interface speed is $bps");

    return $bps;
}
sub speed_spec_to_bps {
    my $helper = shift;
    my $spec = shift;

    my ($number, $mult) = ($spec =~ m/^(\d+)(\D*)$/)[0,1];

    if ($number eq '') {
        $helper->nagios_die("Invalid speed $spec!");
    }
    my $bps = 0;
    if ($mult eq '') {
        Nenm::Utils::debug("No multiplier, returning speed $number");
        $bps = $number;
    } else {
        if (length($mult) != 1) {
            $helper->nagios_die("Invalid speed $spec!");
        }
        $mult = lc($mult);
        if ($mult eq 'g') {
            $bps = $number * (1000 ** 3);
        } elsif ($mult eq 'm') {
            $bps = $number * (1000 ** 2);
        } elsif ($mult eq 'k') {
            $bps = $number * 1000;
        } else {
            $helper->nagios_die("Invalid multiplier in speed spec " .
                            "$spec, valid labels are g, k, and m");
        }
    }
```

```
    Nenm::Utils::debug("Returning max speed ${bps} bits per second");
    return $bps;
            $bps = $number * (1000 ** 3);
        } elsif ($mult eq 'm') {
            $bps = $number * (1000 ** 2);
        } elsif ($mult eq 'k') {
            $bps = $number * 1000;
        } else {
            $helper->nagios_die("Invalid multiplier in speed spec " .
                            "$spec, valid labels are g, k, and m");
        }
    }
    Nenm::Utils::debug("Returning max speed ${bps} bits per second");
    return $bps;
}
sub get_if_octets {
    my $snmp = shift;
    my $idx = shift;
    my %oids = (
        'ifInOctets'  => ".1.3.6.1.2.1.2.2.1.10.$idx",
        'ifOutOctets' => ".1.3.6.1.2.1.2.2.1.16.$idx"
    );
    my $results = $snmp->get(values %oids);
    my $in = $results->{$oids{'ifInOctets'}};
    my $out = $results->{$oids{'ifOutOctets'}};
    Nenm::Utils::debug("Interface $idx: in $in, out $out");
    return ($in, $out);
  }
}
exit check_snmp_if_bw();
```

Network Interface as Nagios Host?

In some cases this can be very useful. Many clients uses point-to-point VPNs to tunnel traffic from one office location to another. Many businesses also will not allow SNMP on DMZ devices like VPN concentrators. You can still visually show whether traffic is flowing between sites by creating a "virtual" host in Nagios that has as its host-alive check an SNMP check that ensures the interface on a managed router or switch that is attached to the VPN concentrator is enabled and active.

Host Definition Example

Note that the network device interface status check is used as the host alive check.

```
define host {
    use                     generic-host
    host_name               europe-vpn
    alias                   Europe VPN
    address                 192.168.3.1
    parents                 core_rtr
    check_command           check-snmp-if-oper-status!20
    contact_groups          admins
    notification_interval   120
    icon_image              cisco.png
    notes                   VPN to Europe via PIX
    statusmap_image         cisco.png
}
```

The command definition for the operational interface status check:

```
define command {
    command_name check-snmp-if-oper-status
    command_line $USER1$/check_ifoperstatus -k $ARG1$ -H $HOSTADDRESS$
    -C snmp-community
}
```

Servers

Servers, those lovely boxes with the fancy blinking lights. So many interesting metrics to monitor, so little time. Which metrics should you care about? It depends. While network and system monitoring products make it easy to monitor just about everything your host SNMP agent can offer, resist the temptation to monitoring everything right away. Why? To make each check meaningful, you have to understand what is normal for your servers. This takes time. Even a measure as simple as CPU utilization requires knowledge of how your servers normally behave, how they behave under stress, and how hard the applications on them work the CPU. If you want to establish a baseline, use a trending tool like Cacti to record multiple metrics (or PNP or another RRD graphing add-on to Nagios). After you establish a baseline and determine which metrics are the best indicators of health or problems on the host, write Nagios checks for those metrics using the knowledge you have gained over time about how hosts and applications in use at your organization work.

Assumptions made in this section:

- SNMP v3 is used

- SNMP auth protocol is md5

- SNMP auth username is stored in a custom host variable named __snmp_auth_username

- SNMP auth password is stored in a custom host variable named __snmp_auth_password

- All devices use the Net-SNMP agent (unless otherwise noted)

Basic System Checks

All of the following examples were built to work with Net::SNMP and the Net-SNMP agent. Porting them to other SNMP agents should be easy, as most use either standard MIBs or private extensions that any host-based agent should support (e.g., load average). All assume the use of the Nagios::Plug-in::SNMP module discussed at the beginning of this section.

CPU utilization

MIB needed:

UCD-SNMP-MIB

OIDs used:

Raw user ticks: .1.3.6.1.4.1.2021.11.50.0
Raw nice ticks: .1.3.6.1.4.1.2021.11.51.0
Raw system ticks: .1.3.6.1.4.1.2021.11.52.0
Raw idle ticks: .1.3.6.1.4.1.2021.11.53.0
Raw wait ticks: .1.3.6.1.4.1.2021.11.54.0
Raw kernel ticks: .1.3.6.1.4.1.2021.11.55.0
Raw interrupt ticks: .1.3.6.1.4.1.2021.11.56.0

CPU utilization, like many of the metrics we discuss in this section, varies from system to system. What indicates a problem in performance on one system may be completely acceptable on another. Bursts of 100% CPU utilization on most active systems are completely acceptable. The Net-SNMP agent exposes four CPU utilization metrics: idle time, user time, nice time, and system time. Excessive CPU user time over a period of time indicates the CPU is busy processing application logic; for some systems this will be expected, for others it may indicate problems. Excessive system time may indicate that hardware peripherals attached to the system are being over-utilized (disk arrays, other custom devices), or that hardware peripherals are too slow or experiencing failures. Excessive nice time can be an indication that the system is becoming over-utilized and system administrators are running a number of processes at lower or higher priority to balance system load.

This plug-in was a bit more challenging to write than some of the others in this chapter. First, only user, nice, system, and idle CPU metrics are standard across all of the Unix and Unix-like platforms Net-SNMP supports. Wait, kernel, and interrupt tick counters have always existed in Solaris, but for Linux they were not exposed to userland processes like the Net-SNMP agent until the 2.6.*x* family of kernel was introduced. On Solaris, system time is the sum of kernel and wait time, while on BSD-based operating systems, system is the sum of system and interrupt time. This script handles all of these operating system differences gracefully.

We recommend that you use the *first_notification_delay* service configuration directive to delay notification of CPU issues; delaying notification for at least 30 minutes is a good rule of thumb, as CPU utilization only becomes a problem over extended periods of time. Using first_notification_delay will allow you to capture when the CPU exceeds the thresholds you set without driving NOC and system administration staff crazy with meaningless notifications.

This plug-in lets you check one or more of the CPU metrics for both warning and critical levels. It also outputs all metrics in perfdata format so you can graph them using a perfdata parsing output plug-in like PNP (pnp4nagios.sf.net), which we use extensively in this section.

Example Call and Output

```
./check_net_snmp_cpu.pl --hostname host.example.com --snmp-version 3
--auth-username user \
--auth-password password --auth-protocol md5 -c 'user,gt,80:system,gt,80'
-w 'idle,gte,10'
NET-SNMP-CPU WARNING - idle (68.35% >= 10%) OK - system 4.44%, user 9.81%,
nice 17.41% | 'system'=4.44%;0;80 'user'=9.81%;0;80 'idle'=68.35%;10;0
'nice'=17.41%;0;0
```

The Script

```perl
#!/usr/local/bin/perl
# nagios: +epn
=pod
=head1 NAME
check_net_snmp_cpu.pl - Check CPU utilization on a Net-SNMP
enabled device.
=head1 SYNOPSIS
Check CPU idle, system, user, and nice % utilization on a Net-SNMP
enabled device.
e.g.
$0 [ .. options .. ] -w 'idle<5' -c 'system>98'
The plugin will output a list of all thresholds that have been breached and
all that are ok; the most critical status becomes the return status of the plugin.
For perfdata the plugin will output all metrics checked by the script. Output is
in % for all perfdata metrics.
e.g.
'system'=44%;0;0 'idle'=48%;0;0 'nice'=0%;0;0 'user'=8%;0;0
=cut
sub check_net_snmp_cpu {
  use strict;
  use FindBin;
  use lib "$FindBin::Bin/lib";
  use Nagios::Plugin::Threshold;
  use Nagios::Plugin::SNMP;
  use Nenm::Utils;
  my $USAGE = <<EOF;
Usage: %s [--warning 'metric,<op>,number:metric,<op>,number'] \\
         --critical 'metric,<op>,number:metric,<op>,number'
EOF
my $LABEL = 'NET-SNMP-CPU';
my $plugin = Nagios::Plugin::SNMP->new(
    'shortname' => $LABEL,
    'usage' => $USAGE
);
$plugin->add_arg(
    'spec' => 'sleep-time|S=i',
    'required' => 0,
    'help' => "-S, --sleep-time\n" .
              " Seconds to sleep between CPU samples (default 15s)",
    'default' => '15'
);
```

```perl
$plugin->getopts;
$Nenm::Utils::DEBUG = $plugin->opts->get('snmp-debug');
my %cpu = (
    'user' => {qw(oid .1.3.6.1.4.1.2021.11.50.0 raw 0 s0 0 s1 0 value 0)},
    'nice' => {qw(oid .1.3.6.1.4.1.2021.11.51.0 raw 0 s0 0 s1 0 value 0)},
    'system' => {qw(oid .1.3.6.1.4.1.2021.11.52.0 raw 0 s0 0 s1 0 value 0)},
    'idle' => {qw(oid .1.3.6.1.4.1.2021.11.53.0 raw 0 s0 0 s1 0 value 0)},
    'wait' => {qw(oid .1.3.6.1.4.1.2021.11.54.0 raw 0 s0 0 s1 0 value 0)},
    'kernel' => {qw(oid .1.3.6.1.4.1.2021.11.55.0 raw 0 s0 0 s1 0 value 0)},
    'interrupt' =>
        {qw(oid .1.3.6.1.4.1.2021.11.56.0 raw 0 s0 0 s1 0 value 0)}
);
my ($wthr, $werrs)= ([], []);
if (defined $plugin->opts->warning) {
    ($wthr, $werrs) =
        Nenm::Utils::parse_multi_threshold($plugin->opts->warning, \%cpu);
}
if (scalar(@$werrs) > 0) {
  $plugin->nagios_die("Errors found in warning thresholds specified:" .
                      "\n " . join("\n ", @$werrs));
}
my ($cthr, $cerrs) =
    Nenm::Utils::parse_multi_threshold($plugin->opts->critical, \%cpu);
if (scalar(@$cerrs) > 0) {
    $plugin->nagios_die("Errors found in critical thresholds specified:" .
                        "\n " . join("\n ", @$cerrs));
}
my @oids;
for my $metric (keys %cpu) {
  push(@oids, $cpu{$metric}->{'oid'});
}
my $snmp_results = $plugin->get(@oids);
Nenm::Utils::debug("First sample of CPU metrics taken");
# Sample once
$cpu{'user'}->{'s0'} = $snmp_results->{$cpu{'user'}->{'oid'}};
$cpu{'nice'}->{'s0'} = $snmp_results->{$cpu{'nice'}->{'oid'}};
$cpu{'system'}->{'s0'} = $snmp_results->{$cpu{'system'}->{'oid'}};
$cpu{'idle'}->{'s0'} = $snmp_results->{$cpu{'idle'}->{'oid'}};
$cpu{'wait'}->{'s0'} = $snmp_results->{$cpu{'wait'}->{'oid'}};
$cpu{'kernel'}->{'s0'} = $snmp_results->{$cpu{'kernel'}->{'oid'}};
$cpu{'interrupt'}->{'s0'} = $snmp_results->{$cpu{'interrupt'}->{'oid'}};
# Various metrics of the seven in this script are not present on all
# OSes so check for each; if they are not present, delete them.
```

```perl
for my $might_have (sort keys %cpu) {
    if ($cpu{$might_have}->{'s0'} eq 'noSuchObject') {
        Nenm::Utils::debug("Agent does not support $might_have");
        delete $cpu{$might_have};
    }
}
# Rebuild OIDs list as it might have changed.
@oids = ();
for my $metric (sort keys %cpu) {
  push(@oids, $cpu{$metric}->{'oid'});
}
sleep $plugin->opts->get('sleep-time');
# Sample again to get values to use for % change
$snmp_results = $plugin->get(@oids);
Nenm::Utils::debug("Second sample of CPU metrics taken");
$plugin->close();
# Save results of second query in s1
for my $metric (sort keys %cpu) {
    $cpu{$metric}->{'s1'} = $snmp_results->{$cpu{$metric}->{'oid'}};
}
my ($ostype, $sysdescr) = $plugin->get_sys_info();
Nenm::Utils::debug("OS type is $ostype, sysDescr is $sysdescr");
for my $metric (keys %cpu) {
  my $s0 = $cpu{$metric}->{'s0'};
  my $s1 = $cpu{$metric}->{'s1'};
  my $diff = $s1 - $s0;
  Nenm::Utils::debug("CPU: $metric; $s1 - $s0 = $diff ticks");
  $cpu{$metric}->{'raw'} = $diff;
}
# Net-SNMP platform differences
#
# There may be differences for other platforms, but for
# now just covering Linux, BSD, and Solaris.
if (($ostype =~ /bsd/i) || ($ostype eq 'solaris')) {
    my $system = $cpu{'system'}->{'raw'};
    my $wait = (exists $cpu{'wait'}) ? $cpu{'wait'}->{'raw'} : 0;
    my $kernel = (exists $cpu{'kernel'}) ? $cpu{'kernel'}->{'raw'} : 0;
    my $interrupt =
            (exists $cpu{'interrupt'}) ? $cpu{'interrupt'}->{'raw'} : 0;
    Nenm::Utils::debug('Performing platform-specific % calculations');
    # On Solaris, system == wait + kernel
    # On BSD, system == system + interrupts
    #
    # We skip system in calculating % and calculate
    # it after the rest so we don't throw off the metrics
```

```
        # and the end user can use this script without having
        # to worry about platform differences. Thanks to David
        # Shield for pointing me to where the CPU specific Net-SNMP
        # code lives in the Net-SNMP source.

        my $total;

        # Sum all but OS-specific metrics
        for my $metric (sort keys %cpu) {
            next if (($ostype =~ /bsd/) && ($metric eq 'interrupt'));
            next if (($ostype eq 'solaris') && ($metric =~ /wait|kernel/));
            $total += $cpu{$metric}->{'raw'};
    }

    # Calculate all but system
    for my $metric (sort keys %cpu) {
        next if (($ostype =~ /bsd/) && ($metric eq 'interrupt'));
        next if (($ostype eq 'solaris') && ($metric =~ /wait|kernel/));
        my $raw = $cpu{$metric}->{'raw'};
        $cpu{$metric}->{'value'} = sprintf("%.2f", ($raw / $total) * 100);
    }

    # Now subtract system ticks diff so we can get % utilization
    # for the platform-specific metrics that comprise it
    $total -= $cpu{'system'}->{'raw'};

    if ($ostype =~ /bsd/i) {

      # For BSD we have to add back interrupt ticks as system
      # system on BSD is CPU_SYS + CPU_INTR.
      $total += $cpu{'interrupt'}->{'raw'};

      $cpu{'interrupt'}->{'value'} =
          sprintf("%.2f", ($cpu{'interrupt'}->{'raw'} / $total) * 100);

    } elsif ($ostype eq 'solaris') {

        # For Solaris we have to add interrupt and kernel to the
        # total to get an accurate % utilization for system as system
        # is the sum of kernel and interrupt.
        $total += ($cpu{'interrupt'}->{'raw'} + $cpu{'kernel'}->{'raw'});
        $cpu{'wait'}->{'value'} =
            sprintf("%.2f", ($cpu{'wait'}->{'raw'} / $total) * 100);
        $cpu{'kernel'}->{'value'} =
            sprintf("%.2f", ($cpu{'kernel'}->{'raw'} / $total) * 100);
    }

    } else {

      Nenm::Utils::convert_to('%', \%cpu);

    }

    my $results = Nenm::Utils::check_multi_thresholds(\%cpu,
                                                $wthr, $cthr, '%');

    return Nenm::Utils::output_multi_results($LABEL, $results);

    }

    exit check_net_snmp_cpu();
```

RAM utilization

MIB needed

UCD-SNMP-MIB

OIDS used

Memory free: .1.3.6.1.4.1.2021.4.11.0
Memory shared: .1.3.6.1.4.1.2021.4.13.0
Memory buffered: .1.3.6.1.4.1.2021.4.14.0
Memory cached: .1.3.6.1.4.1.2021.4.15.0

Like CPU utilization, RAM utilization on servers will peak at times and for some servers will stay near 100% while the server is active. The Net-SNMP agent allows us to see RAM utilization broken out into free memory, cached memory, memory buffered, and shared memory. High percentages of cached and shared memory indicate the kernel is caching files and kernel objects to speed disk access and the server is not experiencing memory stress; the kernel will decrease the amount of memory used for caching frequently used files and kernel objects as the demands on the system for RAM increase. Do not ever expect to see a large percentage of memory in the free category for a Unix or Unix-like system, as the kernel will use as much free memory as it can for caching files and objects.

The Script

```
#!/usr/local/bin/perl
# nagios: +epn
=pod
=head1 NAME
check_net_snmp_mem.pl - Check memory utilization on a Net-SNMP
                        enabled device.
=head1 SYNOPSIS
Check memory used, free, shared, buffered, and cached. Specify
warning thresholds by metric type using either bytes or %.
e.g.
$0 [ .. options .. ] -w 'free,lt,900k' -c 'used,gt,99%'
You can use the suffixes K, M, or G to indicate kilobytes, megabytes,
or gigabytes. If you specify no suffix, bytes is assumed.

The plugin will output a list of all thresholds that have been breached and all
that are ok; the most critical status becomes the return status of the plugin. For
perfdata the plugin will output all metrics checked by the script. Output is in
bytes for all perfdata metrics.
```

```
e.g.

'used'=230230239;0;0 'free'=50000032;0;0 'shared'=1G;0;0 'buffered'=23023094;0;0
'cached'=3029499;0;0
=cut
sub check_net_snmp_mem {
    use strict;
    use FindBin;
    use lib "$FindBin::Bin/lib";
    use Nagios::Plugin::Threshold;
    use Nagios::Plugin::SNMP;
    use Nenm::Utils;

    my $USAGE = <<EOF;
Usage: %s [--warning
'metric[%|k|m|g]?,<op>,number:metric[%|k|m|g]?,<op>,number'] \\
        --critical
'metric[%|k|m|g]?,<op>,number:metric[%|k|m|g]?,<op>,number' \\
        [—convert-to \%|K|G|M]
EOF
    my $LABEL = 'NET-SNMP-MEM';

    my $plugin = Nagios::Plugin::SNMP->new(
        'shortname' => $LABEL,
        'usage' => $USAGE
    );

    $plugin->add_arg(
        'spec' => 'convert-to|T=s',
        'required' => 0,
        'help' => "-T, --convert-to\n" .
                  " Specify how to convert returned agent memory metrics\n" .
                  " (%, b, K, M, or G). Values from agent will be " .
                  " converted\n" .
                  " to this type, threshold values will be considered to\n" .
                  " be of this type, and perfdata values will use this \n" .
                  " type. Default conversion type is bytes if option is \n" .
                  " not present",
        'default' => 'b'
    );

    $plugin->getopts;

    $Nenm::Utils::DEBUG = $plugin->opts->get('snmp-debug');

    my %mem = (
        'free' => {qw(oid .1.3.6.1.4.1.2021.4.11.0 raw 0 value 0)},
        'shared' => {qw(oid .1.3.6.1.4.1.2021.4.13.0 raw 0 value 0)},
        'buffered' => {qw(oid .1.3.6.1.4.1.2021.4.14.0 raw 0 value 0)},
        'cached' => {qw(oid .1.3.6.1.4.1.2021.4.15.0 raw 0 value 0)}
    );
```

```perl
    my ($wthr, $werrs)= ([], []);
    if (defined $plugin->opts->warning) {
        ($wthr, $werrs) =
          Nenm::Utils::parse_multi_threshold($plugin->opts->warning, \%mem);
    }
    if (scalar(@$werrs) > 0) {
        $plugin->nagios_die("Errors found in warning thresholds specified:" .
                            "\n " . join("\n ", @$werrs));
    }
    my ($cthr, $cerrs) = Nenm::Utils::parse_multi_threshold(
                                      $plugin->opts->critical, \%mem);
    if (scalar(@$cerrs) > 0) {
        $plugin->nagios_die("Errors found in critical thresholds specified:" .
                            "\n " . join("\n ", @$cerrs));
    }
    my @oids;
    for my $metric (keys %mem) {
        push(@oids, $mem{$metric}->{'oid'});
    }
    my $snmp_results = $plugin->get(@oids);
    $plugin->close();
    $mem{'free'}->{'raw'} = $snmp_results->{$mem{'free'}->{'oid'}};
    $mem{'shared'}->{'raw'} = $snmp_results->{$mem{'shared'}->{'oid'}};
    $mem{'buffered'}->{'raw'} = $snmp_results->{$mem{'buffered'}->{'oid'}};
    $mem{'cached'}->{'raw'} = $snmp_results->{$mem{'cached'}->{'oid'}};
    my $CONVERT_TO = $plugin->opts->get('convert-to');
    Nenm::Utils::convert_to($CONVERT_TO, \%mem);
    my $results = Nenm::Utils::check_multi_thresholds(\%mem, $wthr, $cthr,
                                              $CONVERT_TO);
    return Nenm::Utils::output_multi_results($LABEL, $results);
}
    exit check_net_snmp_mem();
```

Swap utilization

MIB needed

UCD-SNMP-MIB

OIDs used

Total swap space: .1.3.6.1.4.1.2021.4.3.0
Swap space available: .1.3.6.1.4.1.2021.4.4.0

Check the percentage of swap in use. This one has simple thresholds that let us make use of all of the convenience methods Nagios::Plug-in has to offer. Code for the plug-in:

```perl
#!/usr/local/bin/perl
# nagios: +epn
=pod
=head1 NAME
check_net_snmp_swap.pl - Check the swap space % in use
=head1 SYNOPSIS
Check the % swap space in used on a server, warning
and critical thresholds are upper acceptable limits for
swap space utilization.
This plugin will output the percent swap space in use as perfdata.
=cut
sub check_net_snmp_swap {
    use strict;
    use FindBin;
    use lib "$FindBin::Bin/lib";
    use Nagios::Plugin::SNMP;
    my $USAGE = <<EOF;
Usage: %s [--warning %] --critical %
EOF
    my $LABEL = 'NET-SNMP-SWAP';
    my $plugin = Nagios::Plugin::SNMP->new(
        'shortname' => $LABEL,
        'usage' => $USAGE
    );
    $plugin->getopts;
    $plugin->set_thresholds(
        'warning' => $plugin->opts->warning,
        'critical' => $plugin->opts->critical,
    );
    use constant TOTAL => '.1.3.6.1.4.1.2021.4.3.0';
    use constant AVAIL => '.1.3.6.1.4.1.2021.4.4.0';
    my @oids = (TOTAL(), AVAIL());
    my $results = $plugin->get(@oids);
    $plugin->close();
    my @warning;
    my @critical;
    my @ok;
    my $total = $results->{TOTAL()};
    my $avail = $results->{AVAIL()};
    my $pct_used = sprintf("%5.2f", (($total - $avail) / $total) * 100);
    my $code = $plugin->check_threshold(check => $pct_used);
```

```
my $msg;
if ($code == CRITICAL) {
    $msg = "${pct_used}% > " . $plugin->opts->critical . "%";
} elsif ($code == WARNING) {
    $msg = "${pct_used}% > " . $plugin->opts->warning . "%";
} else {
    $msg = "${pct_used}% swap in use";
}
$plugin->add_perfdata(
    'label' => "'pct_used",
    'value' => $pct_used,
    'uom' => "%"
);
$plugin->nagios_exit($code, $msg);
}

check_net_snmp_swap();
```

Here is a command definition for this plug-in. Since swap thresholds will be pretty standard across Net-SNMP hosts, in this case we will hard-code the thresholds in the command definition.

```
define command {
    command_name check_net_snmp_swap
    command_line $USER2$/check_net_snmp_swap.pl --hostname $HOSTADDRESS$ --port
161 --snmp-version 3 --auth-protocol md5 --auth-username '$_HOST_SNMP_AUTH_
USERNAME$' —auth-password '$_HOST_SNMP_AUTH_PASSWORD$' --warning 70 --critical 85
}
```

Partition Utilization
MIB needed

HOST-RESOURCES-MIB

OIDs needed

hrFSMountPoint: 1.3.6.1.2.1.25.3.8.1.2
hrFSIndex: 1.3.6.1.2.1.25.3.8.1.1
hrFSStorageIndex: 1.3.6.1.2.1.25.3.8.1.7 -> link to hrStorageEntry for this device
hrFSType: 1.3.6.1.2.1.25.3.8.1.4 -> FS type from hrFSTypes
HR FS Types: 1.3.6.1.2.1.25.3.9
hrStorageDescr: .1.3.6.1.2.1.25.2.3.1.3.1
hrStorageAllocationUnits: 1.3.6.1.2.1.25.2.3.1.4
hrStorageSize: 1.3.6.1.2.1.25.2.3.1.5
hrStorageUsed: 1.3.6.1.2.1.25.2.3.1.6

hrStorageAllocationFailures: 1.3.6.1.2.1.25.2.3.1.7

hrStorageType: 1.3.6.1.2.1.25.2.1—type of storage device; e.g., (hrStorageFixed Disk, hrStorageRemovableDisk)

Device Type Index: – .1.3.6.1.2.1.25.3.2.1.2

Trending software packages typically make partition trending a two-step process. First, you run a "discovery" process on the target agent that retrieves the names of all partitions on a host. Next, you choose which partitions you wish to monitor, and from that point on the agent checks only those partitions. With Nagios, it is customary to use a service check per important partition. While both of these models work, we prefer to have the flexibility of both in one tool and the ability to also have a plug-in that checks every partition on a host without us caring about what their names are ahead of time.

check_snmp_storage.pl does just that. You can tell it to check all partitions or a defined set of partitions in one pass. Thresholds for the script are in % free space or bytes free, selected by the *--measure* switch. If you pass the *all* argument to the *--partition* selector or pass a list of partitions to the script, the thresholds are applied to all partitions. Finally, the script will output perfdata for the partitions you tell it to check, giving you output for trending as well.

A nice feature of this disk utilization check script is that it uses an industry standard MIB; the following code should work for any SNMP agent that supports the HOST-RESOURCES-MIB. Here is an example call:

```
/check_snmp_hr_storage.pl --hostname 192.168.3.1 --snmp-version 3 --auth-username
my_user --auth-password my_pass -w 90 -c 95 -U % -P all
```

Example output

Everything is ok

```
SNMP-HR-STORAGE OK - /backup = 88.38%, / = 82.82%, /home2 = 36.93%, /tmp = 1.77%,
/boot = 14.72%, \
/home3 = 10.97% |'/backup'=88.38%;90;95;0;100 '/'=82.82%;90;95;0;100
'/home2'=36.93%;90;95;0;100 \
'/tmp'=1.77%;90;95;0;100 '/boot'=14.72%;90;95;0;100 '/home3'=10.97%;90;95;0;100
Here is the code:
#!/usr/local/bin/perl
# nagios: +epn
=pod
=head1 NAME
```

```
check_snmp_hr_storage.pl - Check storage devices using the
                        HOST-RESOURCES-MIB
```

=head1 SYNOPSIS

Check partition utilization on a device by percent space used or minimum free space available; you can filter partitions based on mount point (-P), file system type (-T), or storage device type (-F).

In addition to thresholds, script will output performance data, percent used if -U % is selected, free bytes if -U [KMG] is selected.

Examples:

* By percent, SNMP v3, all partitions. Warn at 90% used, critical at 95% used.

```
./check_snmp_hr_storage.pl --hostname 192.168.3.1 --snmp-version 3 --auth-username
my_user --auth-password my_pass -w 90 -c 95 -U % -P all
SNMP-HR-STORAGE OK - /backup = 88.38%, / = 82.82%, /home2 = 36.93%, /tmp = 1.77%,
/boot = 14.72%, /home3 = 10.97% | '/backup'=88.38%;90;95;0;100
'/'=82.82%;90;95;0;100 '/home2'=36.93%;90;95;0;100 '/tmp'=1.77%;90;95;0;100
'/boot'=14.72%;90;95;0;100 '/home3'=10.97%;90;95;0;100
```

* By minimum space free, SNMP v2c, /tmp and /boot, in Megabytes. Warn at 50M left available, critical at 20M available

```
./check_snmp_hr_storage.pl --hostname 192.168.3.1 --snmp-version 2c --rocommunity
-w 50 -c 20 -U M -P /tmp -P /boot
SNMP-HR-STORAGE OK - /tmp - 932.82M, /boot - 84.19M | '/tmp'=978128896;52428800;
20971520;0;995774464 '/boot'=88274944;52428800;20971520;0;103515136
```

=cut

```perl
sub check_snmp_hr_storage {
    use strict;
    use FindBin;
    use lib "$FindBin::Bin/lib";

    use Nagios::Plugin::SNMP;
    use Nagios::Plugin::Threshold;

    my $USAGE = <<EOF;
Usage: check_snmp_hr_storage.pl \
    {-P all | -P NAME0 ... -P NAMEN }
    [-F FStype] [ -T storage_type ]
    [ -U threshold_unit_type ]
    [ -X volatile_partition1 ... -X volatile_partitionN ]
EOF
    my $LABEL = 'SNMP-HR-STORAGE';
    my $plugin = Nagios::Plugin::SNMP->new(
       'shortname' => $LABEL,
       'usage' => $USAGE
);
```

```
$plugin->add_arg(
    'spec' => 'partition|P=s@',
    'help' => "-P, --partition NAME\n" .
              " Partition(s) to check, use switch multiple times\n" .
              " to specify multiple partitions or use 'all' to \n" .
              " check all partitions [required]",
    'required' => 1
);
$plugin->add_arg(
    'spec' => 'fs-type-expr|F=s',
    'help' => "-F, --fs-type-expr\n" .
              " String or regular expression to use to determine\n" .
              " which file systems to include in disk checks.\n" .
              " Use fs-type-opt to select the operator to use\n" .
              " for the check. [optional, default 'any']",
    'default' => 'any'
);
$plugin->add_arg(
    'spec' => 'fs-type-op|O=s',
    'help' => "-O, --fs-type-op\n" .
              " Operator to use when checking to see if a file\n" .
              " system should be included in checks this plugin\n" .
              " performs. Valid operators are 'eq', 'ne', '=~'\n" .
              " and '~!'. [optional, default '']",
    'default' => ''
);
$plugin->add_arg(
    'spec' => 'storage-type|T=s',
    'help' => "-T, --storage-type\n" .
              " Type of storage (e.g. 'hrStorageFixedDisk')\n" .
              " [optional, default 'any']",
    'default' => 'any'
);
$plugin->add_arg(
  'spec' => 'unit-type|U=s',
  'help' => "-U, --unit-type\n" .
            " type of unit to use for check:\n" .
            " (B: bytes, M: Megabytes, G: Gigabytes, %: percent)\n" .
            " If a byte measurement is specified, thresholds are\n" .
            " low bounds. If % is specified thresholds are high\n" .
            " bounds (e.g. use > 90%) [optional, default '%']",
  'default' => '%'
);
$plugin->add_arg(
  'spec' => 'volatile-partition|X=s@',
  'help' => "-X, --volatile-partition\n" .
            " Names of partitions that may not always be present\n" .
            " on the system when disks are checked; this will\n" .
            " cause the script to output 0s for perf_data for\n" .
```

```
            " any partition listed to keep trending data in good\n" .
            " shape.\n",
    'required' => 0,
    'default' => []
);
$plugin->add_arg(
    'spec' => 'no-fsafc|N',
    'help' => "--N, —no-fsafc\n" .
              " Do not check for storage allocation failures; \n" .
              " provided for use with buggy HOST-RESOURCES MIB\n" .
              " implementations.",
    'required' => 1,
    'default' => '0'
);
$plugin->getopts;
my $WARNING = $plugin->opts->get('warning');
my $CRITICAL = $plugin->opts->get('critical');
my $UNIT_TYPE = uc($plugin->opts->get('unit-type'));
if ($UNIT_TYPE !~ m/^[%MKG]$/) {
die <<EOF;
Invalid unit type specified ($UNIT_TYPE), valid types are
* % - percent utilization
* K - Kilobytes
* M - Megabytes
* G - Gigabytes
EOF
}
if ($plugin->opts->get('fs-type-op') ne '') {
    my $expr = $plugin->opts->get('fs-type-expr');
    my $op = $plugin->opts->get('fs-type-op');
    if ($op !~ m/^(?:=~|!~|eq|ne)$/) {
        die <<EOF;
Invalid fs-type-op value '$expr' provided, valid values are:
    * eq - Type of filesystem equals string provided in fs-type-expr.
    * ne - Type of filesystem does not equal string provided in fs-type-expr.
    * =~ - Type of filesystem matches regular expression in fs-type-expr.
        * !~ - Type of filesystem does not match regular expression
               in fs-type-expr.
EOF
    }
    # Call will die if the expression is invalid
    fs_type_check('test', $op, $expr);
}
if ($plugin->opts->get('fs-type-expr') ne 'any') {
    die "fs-type-op is required if fs-type-expr is provided!"
        if $plugin->opts->get('fs-type-op') eq '';
}
```

```perl
my @partitions = @{$plugin->opts->partition};

my %wanted;

#
# Filter on mount point
#

my %mount_names =
    filter_on_mount_point($plugin, \%wanted, @partitions);
# Add volatile partitions in if not present so trending data
# stays constant for partitions not always present
my $volatile_partitions = $plugin->opts->get('volatile-partition');
if (ref($volatile_partitions) eq 'ARRAY') {
    my @volatile = @$volatile_partitions;
    for my $vp (@volatile) {
        next if exists $mount_names{$vp};
        $mount_names{$vp} = -1;
    }
}
#
# Filter on FS type
#
filter_on_fs_type($plugin, \%wanted, \%mount_names,
                  $plugin->opts->get('fs-type-op'),
                  $plugin->opts->get('fs-type-expr'));

#
# Get storage indexes - table at 1.3.6.1.2.1.25.3.8.1.7
#
{
    local $_;
    my @oids = map { ".1.3.6.1.2.1.25.3.8.1.7.$_"; } keys %wanted;
    my $results = $plugin->get(@oids);
    for my $sindex (keys %$results) {
        my $idx = ($sindex =~ m/.+\.(\d+)$/)[0];
        debug("$wanted{$idx}->{'mount'} - IDX $idx - SIDX $sindex");
        $wanted{$idx}->{'storage_index'} = $results->{$sindex};
    }
}
#
# Filter out based on storage type if user requested we filter
# based on type.
#
# hrStorageType table at 1.3.6.1.2.1.25.2.3.1.2
#
my $storage_type = $plugin->opts->get('storage-type');
filter_on_storage_type($plugin, \%wanted, \%mount_names, $storage_type);
```

```perl
#
# Get storage units, storage size, description, storage used,
# and storage failures for each device we have left
#
add_hr_storage_metrics($plugin, \%wanted);
#
# Check for storage failures and utilization problems
#
dump_wanted(\%wanted) if ($plugin->opts->get('snmp-debug') == 1);
my @ok;
my @warn;
my @crit;
for my $name (sort keys %mount_names) {
    my $idx = $mount_names{$name};
    # Volatile partition, just add dummy perfdata to keep trending
    # straight
    if ($idx == -1) {
        $plugin->add_perfdata(
            'label' => "'${name}'",
            'value' => 0,
            'uom'   => '',
            'min'   => 0,
            'max'   => 0,
            'threshold' => make_threshold(0, 0)
        );
        next;
    }
    debug("$name [$idx]: checking utilization");
    my %part = %{$wanted{$idx}};
    my $mount = $part{'mount'};
    $mount_names{$mount} = 1;
    if ($plugin->opts->get('no-fsafc') == 0) {
        my $sf = $part{'storage_allocation_failures'};
        if (($sf ne 'noSuchInstance') && ($sf > 0)) {
            push(@crit, "$mount - $sf storage allocation failures");
        }
    }
    my $units = $part{'storage_allocation_units'};
    my $size = $part{'storage_size'};
    my $used = $part{'storage_used'};
    # Only on Solaris does this happen with Net-SNMP. Thank you!
    if ($size == 0) {
        debug("$mount - agent returned 0 bytes as size. Is this " .
              "a Solaris zone or other VPS?");
        next;
    }
```

```perl
    # If % was specified, we are checking utilization to see if
    # partition is more utilized than thresholds
    if ($UNIT_TYPE eq '%') {
        my $pct_used = sprintf("%.2f", ($used / $size) * 100);
        if ($pct_used >= $CRITICAL) {
            push(@crit, "$mount (${pct_used}% >= ${CRITICAL}%)");
        } elsif ($pct_used >= $WARNING) {
            push(@warn, "$mount (${pct_used}% >= ${WARNING}%)");
        } else {
            push(@ok, "$mount = ${pct_used}%");
        }
    }
    $plugin->add_perfdata(
        'label' => "'${mount}'",
        'value' => $pct_used,
        'uom' => '%',
        'min' => 0,
        'max' => 100,
        'threshold' => make_threshold($WARNING, $CRITICAL)
        );
    } else {
      # Otherwise we are checking for space remaining
      my $warn_bytes = $WARNING;
      my $crit_bytes = $CRITICAL;
      my $size_bytes = $size * $units;
      my $used_bytes = $used * $units;
      my $free_bytes = $size_bytes - $used_bytes;
      my $free_label;
      if ($UNIT_TYPE eq 'K') {
          $warn_bytes *= 1024;
          $crit_bytes *= 1024;
          $free_label = $free_bytes / 1024;
      } elsif ($UNIT_TYPE eq 'M') {
          $warn_bytes *= (1024 ** 2);
          $crit_bytes *= (1024 ** 2);
          $free_label = $free_bytes / (1024 ** 2);
      } elsif ($UNIT_TYPE eq 'G') {
          $warn_bytes *= (1024 ** 3);
          $crit_bytes *= (1024 ** 3);
          $free_label = $free_bytes / (1024 ** 3);
      }
      if ($free_bytes <= $crit_bytes) {
          push(@crit, "$mount <= ${CRITICAL}${UNIT_TYPE} free");
      } elsif ($free_bytes <= $warn_bytes) {
          push(@warn, "$mount <= ${WARNING}${UNIT_TYPE} free");
```

```
        } else {
          my $free_label = sprintf("%.2f", $free_label);
          $free_label =~ s/\.00//;
          push(@ok, "$mount - $free_label$UNIT_TYPE");
        }
        $plugin->add_perfdata(
            'label' => "'${mount}'",
            'value' => $free_bytes,
            'uom' => '',
            'min' => 0,
            'max' => $size_bytes,
            'threshold' => make_threshold($warn_bytes, $crit_bytes)
        );
    }
}
my $level = OK;
my $msg = "";
if (scalar(@crit) > 0) {
    $msg = join(', ', @crit);
    $level = CRITICAL;
}
if (scalar(@warn) > 0) {
    if ($level == CRITICAL) {
        $msg .= "; WARNING ";
    } else {
        $level = WARNING;
    }
    $msg .= join(', ', @warn);
}
if (scalar(@ok) > 0) {
    if ($level != OK) {
        $msg .= "; OK ";
    }
    $msg .= join(', ', @ok);
}
$plugin->nagios_exit($level, $msg);
########
# SUBS #
########
sub dump_wanted {
    my $wanted = shift;
    for my $idx (keys %$wanted) {
        warn "Index $idx\n";
    my %info = %{$wanted->{$idx}};
```

```perl
        for my $key (keys %info) {
            warn "- $key: $info{$key}\n";
        }
    }
}
sub filter_on_mount_point {
    my $agent = shift;
    my $wanted = shift;
    my @partitions = @_;
    my $hr_fs_mount_point = '.1.3.6.1.2.1.25.3.8.1.2';
    my $results = $agent->walk($hr_fs_mount_point);
    my %mounts = %{$results->{$hr_fs_mount_point}};
    my %mount_names = ();
    for my $mount (keys %mounts) {
        my $index = $mount;
        $index =~ s/$hr_fs_mount_point\.//;
        if ($partitions[0] ne 'all') {
            next unless grep(/^$mounts{$mount}$/, @partitions);
        }
        $wanted->{$index} = {'mount' => $mounts{$mount}};
        # Index mounts by mount name too (for volatile processing)
        $mount_names{$mounts{$mount}} = $index;
    }
    if (scalar(keys %$wanted) == 0) {
        die "No partitions found matching @partitions!";
    }
    return %mount_names;
}
sub filter_on_fs_type {
    my $agent = shift;
    my $wanted = shift;
    my $mount_names = shift;
    my $fs_filter_op = shift;
    my $fs_filter_expr = shift;
    # Indexed at 1.3.6.1.2.1.25.3.9.X
    my @hr_fs_types = qw(
        StartOfTable
        hrFSOther
        hrFSUnknown
        hrFSBerkeleyFFS
        hrFSSys5FS
        hrFSFat
        hrFSHPFS
        hrFSHFS
```

```
            hrFSMFS
            hrFSNTFS
            hrFSVNode
            hrFSJournaled
            hrFSiso9660
            hrFSRockRidge
            hrFSNFS
            hrFSNetware
            hrFSAFS
            hrFSDFS
            hrFSAppleshare
            hrFSRFS
            hrFSDGCFS
            hrFSBFS
            hrFSFAT32
            hrFSLinuxExt2
        );
        # hrFSType Table .1.3.6.1.2.1.25.3.8.1.4
        my @oids;
        {
            local $_; @oids = map { ".1.3.6.1.2.1.25.3.8.1.4.$_"; }
                        keys %$wanted;
        }
        my $results = $agent->get(@oids);
        for my $type (keys %{$results}) {
            my $idx = ($type =~ m/.+\.(\d+)$/)[0];
            my $fsidx = ($results->{$type} =~ m/.+\.(\d+)$/)[0];
            my $fs = $hr_fs_types[$fsidx];
            if (fs_type_check($fs, $fs_filter_op, $fs_filter_expr)) {
                # Add the FS type to the wanted entry
                $wanted->{$idx}->{'fstype'} = $fs;
            } else {
                # Not an FS type we are about, remove the entry
                delete $mount_names->{$wanted->{$idx}->{'mount'}};
                delete $wanted->{$idx};
                next;
            }
        }
    }
    if (scalar(keys %$wanted) == 0) {
    die "No partitions found that $fs_filter_op $fs_filter_expr!";
    }
}
sub filter_on_storage_type {
    my $agent = shift;
    my $wanted = shift;
```

```perl
my $mount_names = shift;
my $storage_type = shift;
# Indexed at 1.3.6.1.2.1.25.2.1.X
my @hr_storage_types = qw(
    StartOfTable
    hrStorageOther
    hrStorageRam
    hrStorageVirtualMemory
    hrStorageFixedDisk
    hrStorageRemovableDisk
    hrStorageFloppyDisk
    hrStorageCompactDisc
    hrStorageRamDisk
);
# hrStorageType Table 1.3.6.1.2.1.25.2.3.1.2
my @oids;
my %idx_storage_idx;
for my $idx (keys %$wanted) {
    my $sidx = $wanted->{$idx}->{'storage_index'};
    push(@oids, ".1.3.6.1.2.1.25.2.3.1.2.$sidx");
    $idx_storage_idx{$sidx} = $idx;
}
my $results = $agent->get(@oids);
for my $type (keys %{$results}) {
    my $sidx = ($type =~ m/.+?\.(\d+)$/)[0];
    my $i = $idx_storage_idx{$sidx};

    if ($results->{$type} eq 'noSuchInstance') {
        my $m = $wanted->{$i}->{'mount'};
        debug("$m - agent returned noSuchInstance for " .
            "storage type index - deleting. Is this a " .
            "Solaris zone or other VPS?");
        delete $mount_names->{$wanted->{$i}->{'mount'}};
        delete $wanted->{$i};
        next;
    }
    my $stidx = ($results->{$type} =~ m/.+?\.(\d+)$/)[0];
    my $stype = $hr_storage_types[$stidx];
    if (($storage_type ne 'any') && ($stype !~ /$storage_type/i)) {
        # Not an storage type we care about, remove the entry
        delete $mount_names->{$wanted->{$i}->{'mount'}};
        delete $wanted->{$i};
        next;
    }
    $wanted->{$i}->{'storage_type'} = $stype;
}
```

```perl
    if (scalar(keys %$wanted) == 0) {
        die "No partitions found matching storage type $storage_type!";
    }
}
sub add_hr_storage_metrics {
    my $agent = shift;
    my $wanted = shift;
    my %stoids = qw(
        .1.3.6.1.2.1.25.2.3.1.3 storage_descr
        .1.3.6.1.2.1.25.2.3.1.4 storage_allocation_units
        .1.3.6.1.2.1.25.2.3.1.5 storage_size
        .1.3.6.1.2.1.25.2.3.1.6 storage_used
    );
    # Check for storage allocation failures unless user
    # requests we do not check for them.
    if ($plugin->opts->get('no-fsafc') == 0) {
        $stoids{'.1.3.6.1.2.1.25.2.3.1.7'} =
            'storage_allocation_failures';
    }
    for my $mount (keys %wanted) {
        my @oids;
        my $sidx = $wanted->{$mount}->{'storage_index'};
        for my $oid (keys %stoids) {
            push(@oids, "${oid}.$sidx");
        }
        my $result = $agent->get(@oids);
        debug("$mount - populating info");
        for my $i (keys %$result) {
            my ($base, $idx) = ($i =~ m/^(.+)\.(\d+)$/);
            my $key = $stoids{$base};
            $wanted->{$mount}->{$key} = $result->{$i};
        }
    }
}
sub make_threshold {
    my $w = shift;
    my $c = shift;
    return
        Nagios::Plugin::Threshold->set_thresholds('warning' => $w,
                                                  'critical' => $c);
}
sub fs_type_check {
    my $value = shift;
```

```
        my $op = shift;
        my $expr = shift;
        my $code = "";
        # If user wants custom FS type filter
        if (($expr eq 'any') || ($expr eq '')) {
            return 1;
        }
        if ($op =~ m/~/) {
            $code = "('$value' $op m{$expr}i);";
        } else {
            $code = "('$value' $op q{$expr});";
        }
        my $result = 0;
        eval {
            $result = eval $code;
            die $@ if $@;
        };
        die "Invalid fs type operator / expression: $@" if $@;
            debug("fs_type_check: evaled $code, result $result");
        return $result;
    }
    sub debug {
        return unless $plugin->opts->get('snmp-debug') == 1;
        my $msg = shift;
        warn scalar(localtime()) . ": $msg\n";
    }
}
exit check_snmp_hr_storage();
```

Load Averages

MIB needed

UCD-SNMP-MIB

OIDs used

1-minute load average: .1.3.6.1.4.1.2021.10.1.3.1
5-minute load average: .1.3.6.1.4.1.2021.10.1.3.2
15 minute load average: .1.3.6.1.4.1.2021.10.1.3.3

Load average is a relative measurement; over time, you will learn what thresholds mean trouble for your servers. The following plug-in checks the 1-minute, 5-minute, and 15-minute load averages in one check; the script also provides performance data so you can create trending graphs from the output as well. You can specify warning and critical thresholds by passing a colon-separated list of values to the warning or critical options in the format:

```
[--warning | --critical ] 1min:5min:15min
```

The Nagios::Plug-in module comes with convenience methods to set and check thresholds and to output a status line to Nagios and an exit code. We are overloading the meanings of the warning and critical switches in this case, so we will not be able to use the built-in methods. If we were to rewrite this plug-in so it checked just one load average at a time, we could use the convenience methods, but then we lose efficiency as Nagios would run the check three separate times to get the three averages; we also lose the ability to get all performance statistics at once for trending (we use PNP for graphing).

Example call and output

```
./check_net_snmp_load.pl -H hostname --snmp-version 3 --auth-username joesmith
--auth-password mypassword -w 20:15:10 -c 40:30:20
NET-SNMP-LA OK - 1min: 0.03, 5min: 0.14, 15min: 0.13 | '1min'=0.03;20;40
'5min'=0.14;15;30 '15min'=0.13;10;20
```

And here is the code for the plug-in

```perl
#!/usr/local/bin/perl
# nagios: +epn
=pod
=head1 NAME
check_net_snmp_load.pl - Check the load averages on a server
=head1 SYNOPSIS
Check the 1 minute, 5 minute, and 15 minute loads on a Net-SNMP device using SNMP.
specify warning and critical thresholds as comma-separated lists in the format
1 minute : 5 minute : 15 minute
e.g.
$0 [ .. options .. ] -w 20:15:5 40:30:10
The plugin will output a list of all thresholds that have been breached and all
averages that are ok; the most critical status becomes the return status of the
plugin.
=cut
sub check_net_snmp_la {
    use strict;
    use FindBin;
    use lib "$FindBin::Bin/lib";
```

```perl
use Nagios::Plugin::Threshold;
use Nagios::Plugin::SNMP;

my $USAGE = <<EOF;

Usage: %s [--warning 1min:5min:15min] --critical 1min:5min:15min

EOF

my $LABEL = 'NET-SNMP-LA';

my $plugin = Nagios::Plugin::SNMP->new(
    'shortname' => $LABEL,
    'usage' => $USAGE
);

$plugin->getopts;

use constant LOAD1 => '.1.3.6.1.4.1.2021.10.1.3.1';
use constant LOAD5 => '.1.3.6.1.4.1.2021.10.1.3.2';
use constant LOAD15 => '.1.3.6.1.4.1.2021.10.1.3.3';

my @oids = (LOAD1, LOAD5, LOAD15);

my $results = $plugin->get(@oids);

$plugin->close();

my %la = (
    '1min' => $results->{LOAD1()},
    '5min' => $results->{LOAD5()},
    '15min' => $results->{LOAD15()}
);

my $index = 0;

my @warning;
my @critical;
my @ok;

my @wthresh = split(':', $plugin->opts->warning);
my @cthresh = split(':', $plugin->opts->critical);

my $i = 0;

for my $avg (qw(1min 5min 15min)) {

    my %t;

    $t{'warning'} = $wthresh[$i] if defined($wthresh[$i]);

    $t{'critical'} = $cthresh[$i] if defined($cthresh[$i]);

    if ((defined $t{'critical'}) && ($la{$avg} > $t{'critical'})) {
        push(@critical, "${avg}: $la{$avg} > $cthresh[$i]");
    } elsif ((defined $t{'warning'}) && ($la{$avg} > $t{'warning'})) {
        push(@warning, "${avg}: $la{$avg} > $wthresh[$i]");
    } else {
        push(@ok, "${avg}: $la{$avg}");
    }
```

```
        my $threshold = Nagios::Plugin::Threshold->set_thresholds(%t);
        $plugin->add_perfdata(
            'label' => "'${avg}'",
            'value' => $la{$avg},
            'uom' => "",
            'threshold' => $threshold
        );
        $i++;
    }
    my $level = OK;
    print "$LABEL ";
    if (scalar(@critical)) {
        print "CRITICAL - " . join(', ', @critical) . ' ';
        $level = CRITICAL;
    }
    if (scalar(@warning)) {
        print "WARNING - " . join(', ', @warning) . ' ';
        $level = WARNING unless $level == CRITICAL;
    }
    if (scalar(@ok)) {
        print "OK - " . join(', ', @ok) . ' ';
    }
    print ' | ' . $plugin->all_perfoutput . "\n";
        return $level;
}
    exit check_net_snmp_la();
```

Now we can make a command to go along with our check. Here is a command definition for it based on the assumptions made at the beginning of this section. With this command definition, you associate the authentication information and thresholds with the host definition itself, making it very easy to see the host limits in the configuration.

```
define command {
    command_name check_net_snmp_la
    command_line $USER1$/check_net_snmp.la --hostname $HOSTADDRESS$ --port 161
--snmp-version 3 --auth-protocol md5 --auth-username '$_HOST_SNMP_AUTH_
USERNAME$' --auth-password '$_HOST_SNMP_AUTH_PASSWORD$' --warning '$_HOST_LA_
WARNING$' --critical '$_HOST_LA_CRITICAL$'
}
```

Process Behavior Checks

While it is very useful to know how a host is performing overall, it can also be very useful to know how specific mission-critical processes or groups of processes on your system are performing or behaving. For example, on a Web server, there is certainly value in knowing how many instances of the Apache daemon are running or receiving alerts should the number of process in zombie state suddenly start to grow. In this section, we cover a number of plug-ins that allow you to get insight on how processes are behaving and performing on your systems.

Number of Processes by State and Number of Processes By Process Type

MIB Needed

HOST-RESOURCES MIB

OIDs used

hrSWRunName: 1.3.6.1.2.1.25.4.2.1.2
hrSWRunPath: 1.3.6.1.2.1.25.4.2.1.4
hrSWRunParameters: 1.3.6.1.2.1.25.4.2.1.5
hrSWRunStatus: 1.3.6.1.2.1.25.4.2.1.7

The HOST-RESOURCES-MIB defines four states for processes: running, runnable, not runnable, and invalid. Running processes are being actively serviced by the CPU; runnable processes are waiting for a system resource (CPU cycles, memory, disk I/O) or have been explicitly stopped by a signal (suspended, for example). "Not runnable" processes are loaded into memory but not waiting for resources or running (uninterruptible sleep, for example). The invalid state with Net-SNMP exists as an SNMP SET state and as an SNMP GET state; if a user sets a process into the invalid state (requires write access to the agent), the Net-SNMP agent will stop the process from running. When used as an SNMP GET state, invalid indicates the process is either idle, a zombie, or in another state not described by running, runnable, or not runnable.

Another useful indicator of break-ins, bugs, runaway processes, or other process problems is to look at the number of processes that run on your system by process type. For example, you probably know how many Apache processes are normal for an Apache Web server in your organization because that limit is set in the Apache configuration file. If suddenly the number of processes drops to zero or climbs to twice the maximum limit specified, you know something is very wrong. This script allows you to check numbers of critical processes by process type and graph the numbers of critical processes by process type. Thresholds are set on a process-by-process basis; each process can have a high limit and a low limit. Figure 4.1 is a screenshot showing the output of this script on a host on which it is used to track the number of Tomcat and Apache processes; note that the graph shows the upper limits for both processes.

Figure 4.1 Apache and Tomcat Processes on a Server

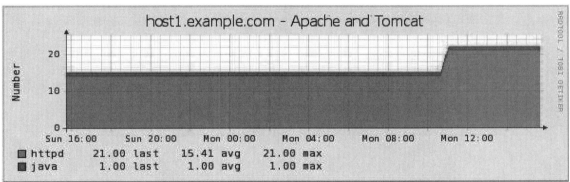

Note that for best performance you might have to adjust the SNMP maximum message size as the SNMP process table can be big; in the two example calls below we set it to 50000 bytes.

Script call in process count mode. In this example we are watching for MySQL and Apache processes, we want critical alerts if either process is not running, if the number of MySQL processes is greater than 20, or if the number of Apache processes is graeter than 150:

```
./check_snmp_procs.pl --hostname host1.example.com --snmp-version 3 --auth-username
myuser --auth-password mypass \
                          --auth-protocol md5 ./check_snmp_procs.pl --mode
count --match /bin/httpd:apache \
                          --match 'mysqld.+basedir:mysql' \
                          --critical apache,lt,1:apache,gt,150:mysql,lt,1:
mysql,gt,20 \
                          --snmp-max-msg-size 50000
SNMP-PROCS OK - apache 14, mysql 15 | 'apache'=14;0;150 'mysql'=15;0;20
```

Script call in process state mode. In this case we warn a warning if the number of runnable processes is greater than 30 and we want a critical alert if the total number of processes is greater than 100.

```
./check_snmp_procs.pl --hostname host1.example.com --snmp-version 3 --auth-username
myuser --auth-password mypass \
                               --auth-protocol md5
./check_snmp_procs.pl --mode state \
                               --match 'mysqld.+basedir:mysql' \
                               --warning runnable,gt,30 --critical total,gt,100 \
                               --snmp-max-msg-size 50000
SNMP-PROCS WARNING - runnable (97 > 30) OK - invalid 0, notRunnable 0, running 1,
total 98 | 'invalid'=0;0;0 'notRunnable'=0;0;0 'runnable'=97;30;0 'running'=1;0;0
'total'=98;0;100
```

And the code for the script:

```perl
#!/usr/local/bin/perl
=pod
=head1 NAME
```

check_snmp_procs.pl - check process numbers by process state or by number of
processes by process name

```
=head1 DESCRIPTION
```

This script allows you to check the process table on an SNMP agent that implements
the HOST-RESOURCES-MIB. This script lets you monitor processes by process state or
by number of processes running by process name and number of matching processes.

Activate the state check mode by passing

```
-m state
```

to the script. Activate process number checking by passing in

```
-m count
```

to the script.

You can specify warning and critical thresholds for each mode in the
following format:

```
metric,op,number
```

Where op is one of:

```
=over 4
=item *
gt - >
=item *
lt - <
=item *
lte - <=
=item *
gte - >=
=item *
ne - !=
=item *
eq - ==
```

=back

You can create a string of OR'd conditions by separating each additional warning or critical threshold by colons. Example:

--warning 'runnable,gt,50:invalid,gt,50' -c 'invalid,gt,100'

You must specify a critical threshold for at least one metric; specifying a warning threshold is optional.

=head2 Process State Mode

To activate process state check mode, pass -m state to the script.

The HOST-RESOURCES-MIB defines four process states and we define an additional metric (total) that you can use in 'state' mode. Total holds the total number of processes in the process table.

=over 4

=item *

Running - processes actively being serviced by the CPU

=item *

Runnable - processes waiting for system resources

=item *

Not runnable - processes that are in memory but not waiting to run

=item *

Invalid - process is idle, a zombie, or other state

=item *

Total - total number of processes in the process table

=back

Example threshold specification:

--warning 'runnable,gt,50:invalid,gt,50' -c 'invalid,gt,100'

In state mode, perfdata will be output with counts of the number of processes in each state and the total numbers of processes as well as warning and critical threshold numbers. Example:

'runnable'=4;50;0 'running'=100;0;0 'not_runnable'=1;0;0 'invalid'=50;0;100

=head2 Process Count Mode

To activate process count check mode, pass -m 'count' to the script. In this mode you pass process match specifications to the script that indicate:

=over 4

=item *

The perl regular expression to use to match processes from the process table.

=item *

The friendly name to output for this process type in script output

=back

These process patterns should be passed to the script by appending one or more -M <specifier> argument/value pairs to the script in the following format:

-M 'perl-regular-expression:friendly name'

Example:

```
-M 'java.+-Xmx:tomcat' -M 'httpd:apache' -M 'sshd:ssh'
```

Warning and critical thresholds can then be specified; for example, if we want to define the rules "Between 1 and 20 Apache processes, exactly 1 java process, and more than 0 MySQL processes" we would pass in this argument list to the script:

```
-M 'java:tomcat' -M 'httpd:apache' -M 'mysqld:mysql -c 'apache,gt,20:apache,lt,1:
tomcat,ne,1:mysql,gt,0'
```

The script will output perfdata for every process definition passed into the script, regardless of whether you define a process count threshold for the process or not. Example:

```
'tomcat'=1;0;0 'httpd'=15;0;0 'mysqld'=4;0;0
=cut
sub check_snmp_procs {
    use strict;
    use FindBin;
    use lib "$FindBin::Bin/lib";
    use Nagios::Plugin::SNMP;
    use Nenm::Utils;
    my $LABEL = 'SNMP-PROCS';
    my $USAGE = <<EOF;
USAGE: %s -m state|count \
        -M 'process-regex:friendly name' [-m spec1 ... -m specN ]
EOF
    my $plugin = Nagios::Plugin::SNMP->new(
        'shortname' => $LABEL,
        'usage' => $USAGE
    );
    $plugin->add_arg(
        'spec' => 'mode|m=s',
        'help' => "-m, --mode state|count\n" .
                " Specify the mode of operation for the script; in \n" .
                " 'state' mode the script will check the states of\n" .
                " all processes on the server; in 'count' mode the\n" .
                " script will check for numbers of critical processes.\n" .
                " See perldoc in this script for more information.",
        'required' => 1
);
$plugin->add_arg(
    'spec' => 'match|M=s@',
    'help' => "-M, —match regex:friendly\n" .
            " Specify a perl regular expression to match against\n" .
            " the process table of the remote host, then a colon,\n" .
            " then the friendly name for the matched processes,\n" .
            " e.g. 'java.+-server|weblogic'",
```

```perl
        'required' => 0,
        'default' => []
);

$plugin->getopts;

$Nenm::Utils::DEBUG = $plugin->opts->get('snmp-debug');

my $MODE = $plugin->opts->get('mode');

$plugin->nagios_die(
    "Invalid mode selected, valid modes are 'state' or 'count'")
    unless $MODE =~ m/^(?:state|count)$/;

$plugin->nagios_die("Critical threshold required!")
    unless defined($plugin->opts->get('critical'));

if ($MODE eq 'state') {
    # Check states of all processes on the remote host
    my %oids = qw(
        hrSWRunStatus .1.3.6.1.2.1.25.4.2.1.7
    );

    my %states = (
        'running'     => {qw(value 0)},
        'runnable'    => {qw(value 0)},
        'notRunnable' => {qw(value 0)},
        'invalid'     => {qw(value 0)},
        'total'       => {qw(value 0)}
    );

    my %states_map = qw(
        1 running
        2 runnable
        3 notRunnable
        4 invalid
    );

    my ($wthr, $werrs)= ([], []);

    if (defined $plugin->opts->warning) {
        ($wthr, $werrs) = Nenm::Utils::parse_multi_threshold(
                            $plugin->opts->warning, \%states);
    }

    if (scalar(@$werrs) > 0) {
        $plugin->nagios_die("Errors found in warning thresholds " .
                            "specified:\n " .
                            join("\n ", @$werrs));
    }

    my ($cthr, $cerrs) =
        Nenm::Utils::parse_multi_threshold($plugin->opts->critical,
                                           \%states);
    if (scalar(@$cerrs) > 0) {
        $plugin->nagios_die("Errors found in critical thresholds " .
                            "specified:\n " .
                            join("\n ", @$cerrs));
    }
```

```
    my $snmp_results = $plugin->walk(values %oids);

    my $procs = $snmp_results->{$oids{'hrSWRunStatus'}};

    for my $state (keys %$procs) {
        $states{$states_map{$procs->{$state}}}->{'value'}++;
        $states{'total'}->{'value'}++;
        Nenm::Utils::debug("Process is $states_map{$procs->{$state}}");

    }

    my $results = Nenm::Utils::check_multi_thresholds(\%states,
                                                $wthr, $cthr, '');

    return Nenm::Utils::output_multi_results($LABEL, $results);

} else {
    # Check for numbers of critical processes running on the
    # remote server by process name regular expression.
    my %matchers;

    $plugin->nagios_die("Need at least one --match specification!")
        unless scalar(@{$plugin->opts->get('match')}) > 0;

    my @MATCH_SPECS = @{$plugin->opts->get('match')};

    for my $spec (@MATCH_SPECS) {
        Nenm::Utils::debug("Parsing $spec");

        $plugin->nagios_die("Invalid format for matcher! Valid format " .
                        "perl-regular-expression:friendly-name")

        unless ($spec =~ m/^(.+):(.+)$/);

    my ($regex, $friendly) = ($1, $2);

    $matchers{$friendly} = {
        'value' => 0,
        'regex' => $regex
    };

    Nenm::Utils::debug("Set $friendly to $regex");

}

my ($wthr, $werrs)= ([], []);

if (defined $plugin->opts->warning) {
    ($wthr, $werrs) = Nenm::Utils::parse_multi_threshold(
                        $plugin->opts->warning, \%matchers);

}

if (scalar(@$werrs) > 0) {
    $plugin->nagios_die("Errors found in warning thresholds " .
                        "specified:\n " .
                        join("\n ", @$werrs));

}

my ($cthr, $cerrs) =
    Nenm::Utils::parse_multi_threshold($plugin->opts->critical,
                                    \%matchers);
```

```perl
if (scalar(@$cerrs) > 0) {
    $plugin->nagios_die("Errors found in critical thresholds " .
                        "specified:\n " .
                        join("\n ", @$cerrs));
}
my %oids = qw(
    hrSWRunPath         1.3.6.1.2.1.25.4.2.1.4
    hrSWRunParameters   1.3.6.1.2.1.25.4.2.1.5
);
my $snmp_results = $plugin->walk(values %oids);
my %processes;
my %run_paths = %{$snmp_results->{$oids{'hrSWRunPath'}}};
for my $oid (keys %run_paths) {
    my $idx = ($oid =~ m/^.+\.(\d+)$/)[0];
    $processes{$idx} = $run_paths{$oid};
    Nenm::Utils::debug("Process $idx has path $run_paths{$oid}");
}
my %run_params = %{$snmp_results->{$oids{'hrSWRunParameters'}}};
for my $oid (keys %run_params) {
    my $idx = ($oid =~ m/^.+\.(\d+)$/)[0];
    next unless defined $run_params{$oid};
    $processes{$idx} .= " $run_params{$oid}";
    Nenm::Utils::debug("Process $idx has params $run_params{$oid}");
}
# Now check each process against our regexes to determine if we match
# them or not; if we match, increment the counter for the matcher.
for my $proc (sort keys %processes) {
    my $cmd_line = $processes{$proc};
    for my $matcher (keys %matchers) {
        my $regex = $matchers{$matcher}->{'regex'};
        if ($cmd_line =~ m{$regex}i) {
            Nenm::Utils::debug("$matcher: $cmd_line =~ $regex");
            $matchers{$matcher}->{'value'}++;
        }
    }
}
  my $results = Nenm::Utils::check_multi_thresholds(\%matchers,
                                        $wthr, $cthr, '');
  return Nenm::Utils::output_multi_results($LABEL, $results);
  }
}
exit check_snmp_procs();
```

Critical Services by Number of Processes

MIB needed

TCP-MIB

OIDS used

TCP connection state: .1.3.6.1.2.1.6.13.1.1

There are three types of TCP connection metric tests and collections we find useful. The first is numbers of connections inbound and outbound along with unique source and destination IP addresses. The second is TCP connections states. The third is connections to the server by service, where a service is defined as a set of one or more ports (for example, "mail" might comprise ports 25, 26, 465, and 587. For all of these checks/metric collections we also want to be able to filter by server port. As with the other SNMP performance-based scripts in this section, use the first_notification_delay_period option with the service or host group the service is a part of to keep Nagios from sending out notifications until the performance issue requires human intervention.

Figure 4.2 is a graph showing the output from the TCP connection count script over 24 hours (using the PNP plug-in for Nagios).

Figure 4.2 TCP Connections Count Graph

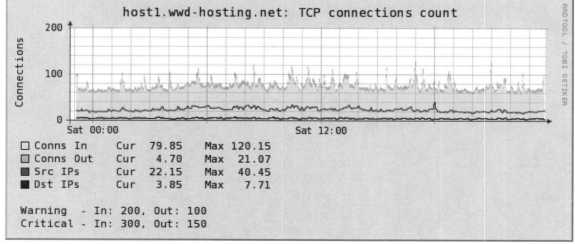

Figure 4.3 is a graph showing the output from the TCP connection state script over 24 hours for a server with a misconfigured service (using the PNP plug-in for Nagios); a high number of connections in FIN_WAIT2 state relative to the total number of connections is a sure sign of a TCP service problem.

Figure 4.3 TCP Connection States Graph

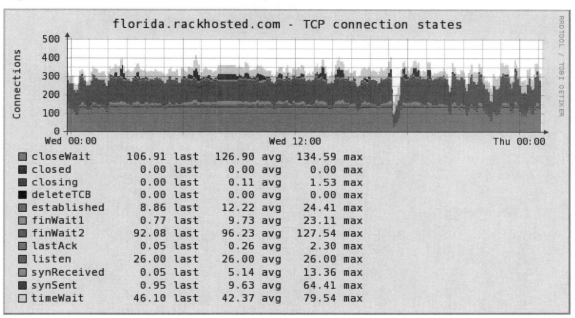

Finally, Figure 4.4 is a graph showing the output from the TCP service mode of this script over 24 hours (using the PNP plug-in for Nagios). This is a Web server, so the warning and critical thresholds are set to alert if HTTP/HTTPS exceed normal counts for the server (although you can see from the graph that IMAP is by far the most popular TCP-based service on the server). In service mode, each graph item can represent one or more ports; for example, in Figure 4.4, "mail" represents TCP ports 25, 26, 465, and 587.

Figure 4.4 TCP Connections by Service Graph

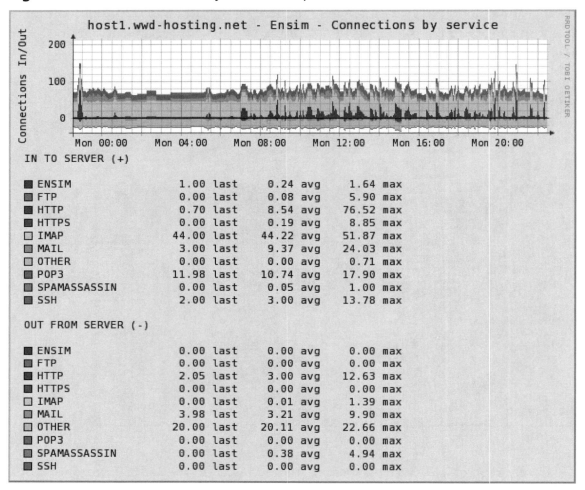

The Code for the Script

```
#!/usr/local/bin/perl
# nagios: +epn
=pod
=head1 NAME
check_snmp_tcpconns.pl - Check TCP connection states, numbers, and
                         port distributions.
=head1 SYNOPSIS
This plugin uses the TCP-MIB tcpConnState table to check the following metrics:
=over
=item *
```

How many TCP connections are present in and out of a device and how many unique source and destination IP addresses are present?

=item *

What is the connection state distribution (open, established, timWait, etc) for the device being checked?

=item *

How many connections TO or FROM the device are there by user-specified protocol (e.g. Web (80/443/8080), SMTP (25/587/465) etc.

=back

=head1 THRESHOLDS

In all cases where multiple thresholds are specified, conditions are OR'd; if any of the conditions present are true, the threshold will be considered breached.

For 'conn' mode thresholds are colon-separated lists of high limits for connections inbound and connections outbound.

Example: -w 40:20 -c 90:30

This would request 'warn if there are more than 40 connections inbound or 20 connections outbound; return critical if there are more than 90 connections inbound or 30 connections outbound.'

For 'state' mode this is a colon-separated list of list of conditionals to test against one or more of the TCP states

Example: -w 'timeWait,gt,5:established,gt,100' -c 'timeWait,gt,15: established,gt,500'

Where gt == >, lt == <, lte == <=, and gte == >=

This would request 'warn if there are more than 5 connections in time wait state or more than 100 established connections; return critical if there are more than 5 established connections or more than 15 connections in time wait state.'

For 'service' mode this is a colon separated list of conditionals to test against the service groupings you specified by passing them to the script using one or more -S arguments. For each service you define, you can also specify direction for tests by appending "_in" or "_out" to your service definition, e.g. "http_in,gt,5" would match only if the number of connections to the http service as you define it is greater than 5.

Note: passing the special token 'other' in as an -S argument will let you test against a special bucket that holds connections that don't match any service definitions you provide, you can then use other, other_in, or other_out in your warning and critical threshold check specifications if you wish as well.

Examples:

1. Check mail and FTP services, define mail as ports 25, 465, and 587 and define FTP and ports 20 and 21

   -S 'mail,25,465,587' -S 'ftp,20,21' -w 'mail,gt,5:ftp,gt,10' -c 'mail,gt,20'

2. Check web vs other.

   -S 'web,80,443,8080,8443' -S other -w 'web,gt,50' -c 'web,gt,100:other,gt,100'

In 'service' mode perfdata will include data for each service as a whole along with _in and _out broken out as well, example:

```
./check_snmp_tcpconns.pl --hostname my.example.com --snmp-version 3 \
                         --auth-username myusername \
                         --auth-password pass \
                         -M service \
                         -S other:mail,25,465,26,587 \
                         -S http,80:https,443 \
                         -S ftp,20,21:ssh,22:ensim,19638:imap,143,993 \
                         -S pop3,110,995 -w 'mail,gt,50' -c 'mail,gt,100'
SNMP-TCP-CONNS OK - mail (12)| 'ensim'=0;0;0 'ensim_in'=0;0;0 'ensim_out'=0;0;0
'ftp'=0;0;0 'ftp_in'=0;0;0 'ftp_out'=0;0;0 'http'=4;0;0 'http_in'=2;0;0
'http_out'=2;0;0 'https'=0;0;0 'https_in'=0;0;0 'https_out'=0;0;0 'imap'=44;0;0
'imap_in'=44;0;0 'imap_out'=0;0;0 'mail'=12;0;0 'mail_in'=8;0;0 'mail_out'=4;0;0
'other'=20;0;0 'other_in'=0;0;0 'other_out'=20;0;0 'pop3'=11;0;0 'pop3_in'=11;0;0
'pop3_out'=0;0;0 'ssh'=1;0;0 'ssh_in'=1;0;0 'ssh_out'=0;0;0
=head1 USAGE

Type ./check_snmp_tcpconns.pl --help

=cut

sub check_snmp_tcp_conns {

    use strict;
    use FindBin;
    use lib "$FindBin::Bin/lib";
    use Nagios::Plugin::SNMP;

    my $USAGE = <<EOF;
USAGE: %s [-M conn | state ] [ -p portN .. -p port1 ]
      [-P port1 .. -P portN]

      {
        # mode 'conn'
        -w 'conns_in:conns_out' -c 'conns_in:conns_out' |
        # mode 'state' where <op> is one of 'lt' (<),
        # 'gt' (>), 'gte' (>=), or 'lte' (<=)
        -w 'state,<op>,N:state,<op>,N:state,<op>,N'
        -c 'state,<op>,N:state,<op>,N:state,<op>,N'
        # mode 'service' where <op> is one of 'lt', 'gt', 'gte', or 'lte'
        -S service_def1 ... -S service_defN [ -S other ]
        -w 'service_name,gte,5:service_two,gte,10'
        -c 'web,gte,50:pop3,gte,15:imap4,gte,15:cpanel,gte,5'
      }
EOF
    my $LABEL = 'SNMP-TCP-CONNS';

    my @CONN_STATES = qw(
        startOfTable
        closed
        listen
        synSent
        synReceived
        established
```

```
            finWait1
            finWait2
            closeWait
            lastAck
            closing
            timeWait
            deleteTCB
);
my $plugin = Nagios::Plugin::SNMP->new(
     'shortname'  => $LABEL,
     'usage'      => $USAGE
);
$plugin->add_arg(
     'spec' => 'mode|M=s',
     'help' => "-M, --mode\n" .
               " Check mode (conn, states, or services), defaults\n" .
               " to 'conn'.\n" .
               " In 'conn' mode, the plugin checks the number\n" .
               " of inbound and outbound connections and outputs\n" .
               " connections in, connections out, unique destination\n" .
               " IP addresses and unique source IP addresses\n\n" .
               " In 'state' mode the script will check the states\n" .
               " of TCP connections to and from the server.\n\n" .
               " In 'service' mode the script will check the numbers\n" .
               " of connections to or from the server based on\n" .
               " service groups you specify by passing definitions\n" .
               " to the script using the '-S' switch",
     'default' => 'conn'
);
$plugin->add_arg(
     'spec' => 'include-port|P=i@',
     'help' => "-P, --include-port\n" .
               " Limit results to just connections that have a \n" .
               " client OR remote port matching the ports passed\n" .
               " in as options.",
     'required' => 0,
     'default'  => []
);
$plugin->add_arg(
     'spec' => 'service|S=s@',
     'help' => "-S, --service\n" .
               " Specify service groupings to use for service mode\n" .
               " (-M 'service') check calls. Pass in one or more \n" .
               " service group definition to the script, separated by\n" .
               "  colons, in the following format:\n" .
               " 'service_name,port1,port2,range1-range4'\n" .
               " Example: -S 'mail,25-26,465,587:www,80,443,8080,8443'.",
     'required' => 0,
     'default'  => []
);
```

```perl
$plugin->getopts;
my $DEBUG = $plugin->opts->get('snmp-debug');
my $MODE = $plugin->opts->get('mode');
if ($MODE !~ m/^(conn|state|service)$/) {
    $plugin->nagios_die("Invalid check mode '$MODE', " .
                        "must be 'conn', 'service', or 'state'!");
}
my $WARN = $plugin->opts->get('warning');
my $CRIT = $plugin->opts->get('critical');
my %SERVICES;
if ($MODE eq 'conn') {
    my @w = split(':', $WARN);
    my @c = split(':', $CRIT);
    if (scalar(@w) != 2) {
        $plugin->nagios_die("Warning option must contain 2 thresholds: " .
                            "conns_in:conns_out");
    }
if (scalar(@c) != 2) {
    $plugin->nagios_die("Critical option must contain 2 thresholds: " .
                        "conns_in:conns_out");
}
} elsif ($MODE eq 'state') {
    my @w = split(':', $WARN);
    my @c = split(':', $CRIT);
    my @cs = @CONN_STATES;
    shift @cs;
my $format_help = "Format: state,<op>,number where state is one of " .
                    join(', ', sort @cs) . " and op is one of " .
                    "'gt', 'gte', 'lt', or 'lte'";
if (scalar(@w) < 1) {
    $plugin->nagios_die("Warning option must contain at least\n" .
                        "one state check, e.g. 'timeWait,gte,44'\n" .
                        $format_help);
}
for my $w (@w) {
    my ($lv, $op, $rv) = parse_cond_threshold($w, \@cs);
    if (!(defined($lv) && defined($op) && defined($rv))) {
        $plugin->nagios_die("Invalid warning threshold $w.\n" .
                            $format_help);
    }
}
    if (scalar(@c) < 1) {
        $plugin->nagios_die("Critical option must contain at " .
                            "least one state check, e.g. 'timeWait,gt,44'");
}
```

```
        for my $c (@c) {
            my ($lv, $op, $rv) = parse_cond_threshold($c, \@cs);
            if (!(defined($lv) && defined($op) && defined($rv))) {
                $plugin->nagios_die("Invalid critical threshold $c.\n" .
                                    "$format_help");
            }
        }
    }
} elsif ($MODE eq 'service') {
    my $format_help = <<EOF;
            Format: service<op>number where 'service' is one of
            the services you specified to the script (-S switch)
            and op is one of 'gt', 'gte', 'lt', or 'lte'
EOF
    my @w = split(':', $WARN);
    my @c = split(':', $CRIT);
    my @svc_rules = @{$plugin->opts->get('service')};

    if (scalar(@svc_rules) < 1) {
        $plugin->nagios_die(<<EOF);
Must provide at least one service definition in
                  'service' mode!
$format_help
EOF
    }
    %SERVICES = parse_service_rules(join(':', @svc_rules));

    $format_help = <<EOF;
            Format: service<op>number where 'service' is one of
            @{[join(', ', keys %SERVICES)]}
            and op is one of 'gt', 'gte', 'lt', or 'lte'
EOF
    if (scalar(@w) < 1) {
        $plugin->nagios_die("Warning option must contain at least\n" .
                            "one service check, e.g. 'mail,gt,22'\n" .
                            $format_help);
    }
    if (scalar(@c) < 1) {
        $plugin->nagios_die("Critical option must contain at least\n" .
                            "one service check, e.g. 'mail,gt,22'\n" .
                            $format_help);
    }
    for my $w (@w) {
        my ($lv, $op, $rv) =
            parse_cond_threshold($w, [keys %SERVICES]);
        if (!(defined($lv) && defined($op) && defined($rv))) {
            $plugin->nagios_die("Invalid warning threshold $w.\n" .
                                $format_help);
        }
    }
}
```

```
        for my $c (@c) {
            my ($lv, $op, $rv) =
                parse_cond_threshold($c, [keys %SERVICES]);
            if (!(defined($lv) && defined($op) && defined($rv))) {
                $plugin->nagios_die("Invalid critical threshold $c.\n" .
                                    $format_help);
            }
        }
    }
} else {
    # Should not happen
    $plugin->nagios_die("Invalid mode $MODE!");
}
my @PORTS = @{$plugin->opts->get('include-port')};
my %wanted_ports;
{
    local $_;
    %wanted_ports = map { $_ => 1 } @PORTS;
}
if (scalar(@PORTS) > 0) {
    debug("Limit to ports: " . join(', ', (sort keys %wanted_ports)));
}
# Walk the TCP conn table
# RFC1213-MIB::tcpConnState .1.3.6.1.2.1.6.13.1.1
my $base_oid = '.1.3.6.1.2.1.6.13.1.1';
my $result = $plugin->walk($base_oid);
debug("Retrieved TCP connection table");
# Close and destroy session
$plugin->close();
my %conns;
my %states = map { $_ => 0; } @CONN_STATES;
delete $states{'startOfTable'};
foreach my $idx (keys %{$result->{$base_oid}}) {
        my ($local_ip, $local_port, $remote_ip, $remote_port) =
            ($idx =~ m/^
                    ${base_oid}
                    \.
                    (\d+\.\d+\.\d+\.\d+)
                    \.
                    (\d+)
                    \.
                    (\d+\.\d+\.\d+\.\d+)
                    \.
                    (\d+)
                    /ix);
```

```
    # If user requested filtering, only count connections
    # For ports they requested
    if (scalar(@PORTS) > 0) {
        next unless ((exists $wanted_ports{$remote_port}) ||
                     (exists $wanted_ports{$local_port}));
    }
    # Skip listening sockets if in conn mode as conn mode is just
    # interested in incoming and outgoing connections, not listeners
    if ($MODE eq 'conn') {
        next if ($local_ip eq '0.0.0.0' && $remote_ip eq '0.0.0.0');
        next if ($local_ip eq '0.0.0.0' && $local_port eq '0');
        next if ($remote_ip eq '0.0.0.0' && $remote_port eq '0');
    }
    $conns{"$idx"} = {} if ! exists $conns{"$idx"};
    my $state_idx = $result->{$base_oid}->{$idx};
    my $state = $CONN_STATES[$state_idx];
    $conns{"$idx"}->{'state'} = $state;
    $states{$state}++;
    $conns{"$idx"}->{'localip'} = $local_ip;
    $conns{"$idx"}->{'localport'} = $local_port;
    $conns{"$idx"}->{'remoteip'} = $remote_ip;
    $conns{"$idx"}->{'remoteport'} = $remote_port;
    my $dir = "";
    if ($local_port < $remote_port) {
        $conns{"$idx"}->{'direction'} = 'in';
        $dir = "<-";
    } else {
        $conns{"$idx"}->{'direction'} = 'out';
        $dir = "->";
    }
    debug("$local_ip:$local_port $dir $remote_ip:$remote_port")
      if $MODE eq 'conn';
}
if ($DEBUG == 1) {
    dump_conns(\%conns) if $MODE eq 'conn';
    dump_states(\%states) if $MODE eq 'state';
    print "\n";
}
my %results = (
    'ok' => [],
    'warn' => [],
    'crit' => [],
    'perf_data' => [],
);
```

```perl
my $ret = OK;
if ($MODE eq 'conn') {
    check_conn_counts(\%conns, $WARN, $CRIT, \%results);
} elsif ($MODE eq 'state') {
    my @cs = @CONN_STATES;
    shift @cs;
    check_conn_states(\%states, $WARN, $CRIT, \@cs, \%results);
} elsif ($MODE eq 'service') {
    check_services(\%conns, $WARN, $CRIT, \%SERVICES, \%results);
}
print "$LABEL ";
if (scalar(@{$results{'crit'}}) > 0) {
    print "CRITICAL - " . join(', ', @{$results{'crit'}});
    $ret = CRITICAL;
}

if (scalar(@{$results{'warn'}}) > 0) {
    print ', ' if scalar(@{$results{'crit'}}) > 0;
    print "WARNING - " . join(', ', @{$results{'warn'}});
    $ret = WARNING unless $ret == CRITICAL;
}

if (scalar(@{$results{'ok'}}) > 0) {
    print ', ' if ((scalar(@{$results{'crit'}}) > 0) ||
                   (scalar(@{$results{'warn'}}) > 0));
    print "OK - " . join(', ', @{$results{'ok'}});
}
print "| " . join(' ', @{$results{'perf_data'}}) . "\n";
exit($ret);
sub perf_data {
    my $label = shift;
    my $count = shift;
    my $warn = shift;
    my $crit = shift;
    return "'$label'=$count;$warn;$crit";
}

sub dump_conns {
    my $conns = shift;
    for my $idx (sort {$a cmp $b} keys %$conns) {
        my %info = %{$conns->{$idx}};
        for my $key (sort keys %info) {
            print STDERR "$key:$info{$key} ";
        }
        print STDERR "\n";
    }
}
```

```perl
sub dump_states {
    my $states = shift;
    for my $state (sort keys %$states) {
        print STDERR "'$state'=$states->{$state} ";
    }
}
sub dump_services {
    my $service_counts = shift;
    for my $svc (sort keys %$service_counts) {
        print STDERR "$svc: $service_counts->{$svc}\n";
    }
}
sub get_conn_stats {
    my $conns = shift;
    my $in = 0;
    my $out = 0;
    # Local connections - XXX - either side is 127.0.0.N
    my %unique_ips = ( 'in' => {}, 'out' => {} );
    for my $conn (keys %$conns) {
        my $ip = $conns->{"$conn"}->{'remoteip'};
        next unless exists $conns->{"$conn"}->{'direction'};
        if ($conns->{"$conn"->{'direction'} eq 'in'){
            $unique_ips{'in'}->{$ip} = 1;
            $in++;
        } else {
          $unique_ips{'out'}->{$ip} = 1;
          $out++;
        }
    }
    return ($in, $out,
    scalar(keys %{$unique_ips{'in'}}),
    scalar(keys %{$unique_ips{'out'}}));
}
sub debug {
    return unless $DEBUG == 1;
    my $msg = shift;
    print STDERR scalar(localtime()) . ": $msg\n";
}
sub check_conn_counts {
    my $conns = shift;
    my $warn_spec = shift;
    my $crit_spec = shift;
    my $info = shift;
```

```perl
    my ($conns_in, $conns_out, $unique_src, $unique_dst) =
        get_conn_stats($conns);

    my ($wci, $wco) = split(':', $warn_spec);
    my ($cci, $cco) = split(':', $crit_spec);

    if ($conns_in > $cci) {
        push(@{$info->{'crit'}}, "Connections in ($conns_in > $cci)");
    } elsif ($conns_in > $wci) {
        push(@{$info->{'warn'}}, "Connections in ($conns_in > $wci)");
    } else {
        push(@{$info->{'ok'}}, "Connections in ok ($conns_in < $wci)");

    }

    if ($conns_out > $cco) {
        push(@{$info->{'crit'}}, "Connections out ($conns_out > $cco)");
    } elsif ($conns_out > $wco) {
        push(@{$info->{'warn'}}, "Connections out ($conns_out > $wco)");
    } else {
        push(@{$info->{'ok'}}, "Connections out ok ($conns_out < $wco)");

    }

    push(@{$info->{'perf_data'}},
            perf_data('conns_in', $conns_in, $wci, $cci));
    push(@{$info->{'perf_data'}},
            perf_data('conns_out', $conns_out, $wco, $cco));
    push(@{$info->{'perf_data'}},
            perf_data('unique_src', $unique_src, 0, 0));
    push(@{$info->{'perf_data'}},
            perf_data('unique_dst', $unique_dst, 0, 0));
    return 1;
}

sub check_services {

    my $conns = shift;
    my $warn_spec = shift;
    my $crit_spec = shift;
    my $service_defs = shift;
    my $info = shift;

    my %conn_info = get_ports($conns);

    my %service_counts;
    my %checked;

    if (exists $service_defs->{'other'}) {

        $service_counts{'other'} = 0;
        $service_counts{'other_in'} = 0;
        $service_counts{'other_out'} = 0;

        $checked{'other'} = 1;
        $checked{'other_in'} = 1;
        $checked{'other_out'} = 1;

    }
```

```perl
for my $def (keys %$service_defs) {
    $service_counts{$def} = 0;
}

# Total up all 'services' counts
for my $conn (keys %conns) {
    # Port only counts in services totals if it is a server
    # port; for incoming connections that is the local
    # port, for outgoing connections that is the remote port
    my $direction = $conns{$conn}->{'direction'};

    my $port;

    if ($direction eq 'in') {
        $port = $conns{$conn}->{'localport'};
    } else {
        $port = $conns{$conn}->{'remoteport'};
    }
    # See if it matches any services; if so
    # increment the general service bucket and
    # the bucket for the service_<dir> bucket where
    # <dir> is in or out.
    my $matched = 0;
    for my $svc (keys %$service_defs) {
        my $check = $service_defs->{$svc};
        $check =~ s#\$port#$port#g;
        $check =~ s#\$direction#$direction#g;

        my $result = eval_expr($check);
        debug("$port vs $svc: $check returned $result");

        if ($result == 1) {

            $matched = 1;

            if (($svc =~ m/_in$/) && ($direction eq 'in') ||
                ($svc =~ m/_out$/) && ($direction eq 'out')) {
                $service_counts{$svc}++;
                $matched = 2;

            }

            if ($matched != 2) {
                $service_counts{$svc}++;
            }
        }
    }

    # Magical 'other' bucket catches anything not
    # matched by a user-provided service rule
    if (($matched == 0) && (exists $service_counts{'other'})) {
        debug("Port $port - no matches, incrementing 'other'");
        $service_counts{"other"}++;
        $service_counts{"other_$direction"}++;
    }
}
```

```perl
dump_services(\%service_counts) if $DEBUG == 1;
# Now check thresholds against the warning and critical rules
my @w = split(':', $warn_spec);
my @c = split(':', $crit_spec);
my %caught;
for my $c (@c) {
    my ($service, $op, $value) =
    parse_cond_threshold($c, [keys %$service_defs]);
    my $count = $service_counts{$service};
    my $result = eval_expr("$count $op $value");
    $checked{$service} = 1;
    if ($result == 1) {
        debug("Service CRIT: $service ($count $op $value)");
        push(@{$info->{'crit'}}, "$service ($count $op $value)");
        $caught{$service} = 1;
    }
}
for my $w (@w) {
    my ($service, $op, $value) =
        parse_cond_threshold($w, [keys %$service_defs]);
    $checked{$service} = 1;
    next if exists $caught{$service};
    my $count = $service_counts{$service};
    my $result = eval_expr("$count $op $value");
    if ($result == 1) {
      debug("Service WARN: $service ($count $op $value)");
      push(@{$info->{'warn'}}, "$service ($count $op $value)");
      $caught{$service} = 1;
    }
}
for my $key (sort keys %$service_defs) {
    next if exists $caught{$key};
    next unless ((grep(/${key}\b/, @w)) || (grep(/${key}\b/, @c)));
    push(@{$info->{'ok'}}, "$key ($service_counts{$key})");
}
# Create performance data
for my $key (sort keys %$service_defs) {
    push(@{$info->{'perf_data'}},
        perf_data($key, $service_counts{$key}, 0, 0));
    }
    return $info;
}
```

```perl
sub get_ports {
    my $connections = shift;
    my %ports = ('in' => {}, 'out' => {});
    for my $index (keys %$connections) {
        my $conn = $connections->{$index};
        my $direction = $conn->{'direction'};
        my $port;
        if ($direction eq 'in') {
            $port = $conn->{'localport'};
        } else {
            $port = $conn->{'remoteport'};
        }
        $ports{$direction}->{$port} = 0
            unless exists $ports{$direction}->{$port};
        $ports{$direction}->{$port}++;
    }
    return %ports;
}
sub parse_cond_threshold {
    my $expr = shift;
    my $valid_label_ref = shift;
    my $label_expr = join('|', @$valid_label_ref);
    my $ops = 'gt|gte|lte|lt';
    my ($lv, $op, $rv) = split(',', $expr);
    my $real_op = '';
    if (defined($lv) && defined($op) && defined($rv)) {
        if ($lv !~ m/^(?:$label_expr)$/i) {
            $lv = undef;
        }
        $op = lc($op);
        if ($op eq 'gt') {
            $real_op = '>';
        } elsif ($op eq 'gte') {
            $real_op = '>=';
        } elsif ($op eq 'lt') {
            $real_op = '<';
        } elsif ($op eq 'lte') {
            $real_op = '<=';
        } else {
            $real_op = undef;
        }
        if ($rv !~ m/^\d+$/) {
            $rv = undef;
        }
    }
```

```perl
        return ($lv, $real_op, $rv);
    }
sub parse_service_rules {
    my $expr = shift;
    my %services;
    my @rules = split(':', $expr);
    for my $rule (@rules) {
        my ($label, @port_specs) = split(',', $rule);
        if (exists $services{$label}) {
            die "Service label '$label' specified twice!";
        }
        die "Service specs: Invalid label '$label'"
            unless $label =~ m/\w+/;
        my @svc_tests;
        for my $spec (@port_specs) {
        if ($spec =~ m/^(\d+)$/) {
            push(@svc_tests, "(\$port == $1)");
        } elsif ($spec =~ m/^(\d+)\-(\d+)$/) {
            push(@svc_tests,
                "((\$port >= $1) && (\$port <= $2))");
        } else {
            die "Service specs: '$spec' is not a single port " .
                "or a range of ports!";
          }
        }
        my $cond = join(' || ', @svc_tests);
        $services{$label} = $cond;
        $services{"${label}_in"} = "($cond) && (\$direction' eq 'in')";
        $services{"${label}_out"} = "($cond) && (\$direction' eq 'out')";
        debug("Service rule $label: $cond");
    }
    return %services;
}
sub check_conn_states {
    my $states = shift;
    my $warn_spec = shift;
    my $crit_spec = shift;
    my $cs_ref = shift;
    my $info = shift;
    my %caught;
    for my $cspec (split(':', $crit_spec)) {
        my ($state, $op, $limit) = parse_cond_threshold($cspec, $cs_ref);
        my $actual = $states->{$state};
        my $expr = "$actual $op $limit";
```

```
        my $result = eval_expr($expr);
        debug("Critical $cspec: $expr returns $result");

        if ($result == 1) {
        push(@{$info->{'crit'}}, "$state $op $limit ($expr)");
        $caught{$state} = 1;

        }
    }
    for my $wspec (split(':', $warn_spec)) {
        my ($state, $op, $limit) = parse_cond_threshold($wspec, $cs_ref);
        next if exists $caught{$state};
        my $actual = $states->{$state};
        my $expr = "$actual $op $limit";
        my $result = eval_expr($expr);
        debug("Warn $wspec: $expr returns $result");
        if ($result == 1) {
            push(@{$info->{'warn'}}, "$state $op $limit ($expr)");
        } else {
            push(@{$info->{'ok'}}, "$state = $actual");
        }
    }
    for my $state (sort keys %$states) {
        push(@{$info->{'perf_data'}}, "'$state'=$states->{$state}");
    }
    return 1;
}
sub eval_expr {
    my $expr = shift;
    my $result = 0;
    eval {
        $result = eval "($expr);";
        die $@ if $@;
    };
    $result = 0 if ((! defined $result) or ($result eq ''));
    return $result;
    }
}
exit check_snmp_tcp_conns();
```

HTTP Scraping Plug-ins

HTTP: we love it—well-defined error codes, simple interface, a real gem of a protocol. HTML, we sometimes love it, sometimes hate it. Why? If you did not know already, the lack of XHTML conformance on the Web and the obvious emphasis on content meant for people not programs means that HTTP scraping can be fraught with peril: unmatched tags, unmatched or missing quotes for attribute values, standalone tags that are not terminated with a slash, pages with content rendered via JavaScript—all of which can make for parsing nightmares.

So, why do we have a section devoted to HTTP scraping? Often, it is the only way to monitor a device! Many older or lower end devices do not support SNMP or other network-accessible monitoring protocols; much like our predecessors in the 1970s and 1980s who had to resort to screen scraping, we must resort to HTTP scraping. Fear not; many good language-specific libraries make HTTP scraping more fun than pain, libraries that let us focus on what we want to monitor and not spend all our time in the weeds wondering how to write code to correct for poorly formed HTML (which is exactly what a sizable portion of code in Web browsers does).

In this section, we cover HTTP scraping as it pertains to information gathering from administrative interfaces. A later section in this chapter covers Web scraping as a technique to automate tests of sites that are designed to be automated. We will show you how you can make the most of this technique to get information out of important devices like UPSs, switches, and Web-based applications to ensure they are running and behaving as expected.

Robotic Network-Based Tests

"Nagios is a fault management tool," you say. "What does it have to do with robotic tests?" Nagios is an excellent tool to use for ensuring your applications run and react and respond to your users' requests in the manner you expect them to. In this section, we cover creating and integrating robotic tests into Nagios.

Testing HTTP-based Applications

A growing number of large organizations make use of Web applications to sell their products and services to customers or provide information about themselves to their customers. Knowing whether an application is performing as expected and that response meets customer requirements is very important. While most people think of Nagios as more of a base service checking platform, you can use it to drive continual checks of Web-based applications for your customers and users. In this section, we will use Perl to show examples of scripts that check the status of Web-based applications.

Ensuring the Home Page Performs Well and Has the Content We Expect

The first part of validating a Web-based application is checking response time for the home page of the application and validating that the content on the home page is the content the owner of the application expects to see. Fortunately for us, Nagios comes with a plug-in that does this out of the box—check_http—that allows for checking return status, MIME type, and content; it even allows for passing in credentials to ensure HTTP authentication is functioning as expected.

Here is an example call to the plug-in, making use of some of the more common options. In this case, we are checking a Web site with the string Featured Ultimate Domains, we want a 200 HTTP return code, and we want to receive the content back within three seconds.

```
./check_http -Hwww.ultimatedomains.com -u / -w 2 -c 3 -e 200 -s 'Featured
Ultimate Domains'
HTTP OK HTTP/1.1 200 OK - 0.320 second response time |time=0.319673s;2.000000;
3.000000;0.000000 size=48778B;;;0
```

Ensuring a Search Page Performs as Expected and Meets SLAs

Often, Web-based applications include search functionality. Especially with commercial applications, having the search page return results within a reasonable amount of time is critical to keeping customers' interests. A wonderful Perl module for use with this kind of check is WWW::Mechanize. It allows a Perl developer to quickly develop applications that interact with Web sites in the same fashion a user would from his Web browser. While a test like this does not simulate the delays involved with fully rendering pages and waiting for images to download the way a full-blown automation test can (using Win32::OLE for instance or by adding code to download every element on every page retrieved), it does simulate the path the user takes and, in this case, does properly measure the time the search takes and lets the Nagios administrator trend on search response and alert when time becomes unacceptable. The following script was written for a client of Max Schubert, who explicitly gave his permission for it to be used in the book. The script is run against his beta site so as not to disrupt statistics collected from his production Web site.

Definition of the check command:

```
define command {
    command_name check_ud_keyword_search
    command_line $_SERVICE_UD_BASE$/check_keyword_search.pl -s
    $_SERVICE_UD_KEYWORD_SEARCH_TERM$ -e $_SERVICE_UD_KEYWORD_SEARCH_ENV$ \
    -w $_SERVICE_UD_KEYWORD_SEARCH_WARN$ -c $_SERVICE_UD_KEYWORD_SEARCH_CRIT$
}
```

and the service definition showing the custom variables used in the command:

```
define service {
    use                         ud-base
    check_command              check_ud_keyword_search
    service_description        Ultimate Domains - Beta - Robotic keyword search
    __ud_keyword_search_term   Test
    __ud_keyword_search_env    example
    __ud_keyword_search_warn   15
    __ud_keyword_search_crit   20
    ... more definition ....
}
```

Example Call to the Script

```
./check_keyword_search.pl -s Test -e example -w 15 -c 20
KEYWORD_SEARCH OK - 1614 results in 8.345963 seconds | search=8.345963s;15;20
```

For this script, we also created a custom library that can be used to add helper routines as needed to extend the workflow test for this script or reuse common functions on additional application performance testing scripts we create. Special thanks to Jarred Cohen, the owner of ultimatedomains.com, for allowing us to use code developed for his site in this book.

The Library (WWW::UltimateDomains)

```
package WWW::UltimateDomains;
$WWW::UltimateDomains::VERSION =
'# $Id: UltimateDomains.pm 17 2008-01-06 05:28:48Z max $';
use strict;
use warnings;
use WWW::Mechanize;
use Time::HiRes qw(gettimeofday tv_interval);
=pod
```

```
=head1 SYNOPSIS
WWW::UltimateDomains - utilities for automation of tests of the
ultimatedomains.com site
=cut
=pod
=item new ('Timeout' => 60)

    Instantiate WWW::UltimateDomains class. Parameters:
    SubDomain - Sub-domain of ultimatedomains.com to test against [optional]
    Timeout - Maximum seconds any operation should take
    UserAgent - User-Agent header value [optional]

    my $ud = WWW::UltimateDomains->new(
        'Timeout' => 60,
        # The HTTP User-agent to use (optional)
        'UserAgent' => "Query Agent",
    );

    my ($results, $time) = $ud->keyword_search('cards');
=cut
sub new {
    my $class = shift;
    my $self = {
        'Timeout' => undef,
        'SubDomain' => 'www',
        'UserAgent' => 'UltimateDomainsTester/1.0'
    };
    my %args = @_;
    if (scalar(@_) == 0) {
        die <<EOF;
Missing options to new:
    Timeout - Maximum timeout in seconds for any called method [required]
    SubDomain - sub-domain to test against (e.g. www, dev, beta) [optional]
    UserAgent - Textual string to use for User-Agent header [optional]
Defaults:
    SubDomain: ${self}->{SubDomain}
    UserAgent: ${self}->{Useragent}
EOF
    }
    $self->{'Timeout'} = $args{'Timeout'} ||
        die "Missing required parameter 'Timeout'!";
    $self->{'SubDomain'} = $args{'SubDomain'} if defined($args{'SubDomain'});
    $self->{'UserAgent'} = $args{'UserAgent'} if defined($args{'UserAgent'});
    $self->{'_base_url'} = "http://$args{'SubDomain'}.ultimatedomains.com";
```

```perl
    # XXX - need error handling at some point
    $self->{'_agent'} = WWW::Mechanize->new('agent' => $self->{'UserAgent'});
    $self->{'_agent'}->timeout($self->{'Timeout'});

    return bless $self, $class;

}

=item keyword_search
```

Performs a HTTP request on keyword_search.php with a given search term.
It returns the number domains found by keyword_search.php, the time
it took to perform the HTTP request, and an error message if a catchable
error occurred.

Usage:

```perl
    my $ud = WWW::UltimateDomains->new('Timeout' => 60);
    my ($found, $time, $error) = $ud->keyword_search("search_term");
    die "Search failed: $error!" if defined $error;
```

```perl
=cut
sub keyword_search {
    my $self = shift;
    my $term = shift || die "Missing term to search for!";
    my $url = $self->{'_base_url'} . '/keyword_search.php';
    my $agent = $self->{'_agent'};

    # Encode non-alphanumeric characters in the search term.
    $term =~ s/([^A-Za-z0-9 ])/sprintf("%%02X", ord($1))/seg;
    $term =~ s/ /+/g;

    # Do the page fetch and time it
    my $start_time_ref = [gettimeofday];
    eval {
        $agent->get("${url}?search=${term}");
    };

    my $err = $@;

    my $search_time = tv_interval($start_time_ref);

    # Parse the content and look for the "Total Domains" string
    my $domains_found = 'No';

    my $content = $agent->content();

    my $err_msg = "";

    if ($err ne '') {
        $err_msg = "Search failed: $@";
    } elsif ($content =~ m/Total Domains\D+(\d+)/i) {
        $domains_found = $1;
    } elsif ( $content =~ m/No domains were found/ ) {
        $domains_found = 0;
    } elsif ( $content =~ m/500 read timeout/ ) {
        $err_msg = "Error: search timed out (${search_time}s > " .
            $self->{'Timeout'} . "s)";
    } else {
        $err_msg = "Expected 'Total Domains\\D+\\d+', received $content";
    }
```

```perl
    # Return number of domains found and search time
    return ($domains_found, $search_time, $err_msg);
}
1;
```

And then the check script:

```perl
#!/usr/local/bin/perl
=pod

=head1 DESCRIPTION

Search ultimatedomains.com for the passed in keyword and return an OK status if
    * The number of terms for the search is greater than 0
    * The search completes without exceeding the maximum execution time
      specified on the command line.

=cut

use strict;
use warnings;

use FindBin;
use lib "$FindBin::Bin/lib";

use Nagios::Plugin;
use WWW::UltimateDomains;

my $USAGE = <<EOF;
Usage: %s -s|--search=<keyword> [-e|--env]
          [-w|--warning=<threshold>] [-c|--critical=<threshold>]
          [-v|--verbose]
EOF
my @ENVS = qw(www beta jarred rich vince max);

    my $np = Nagios::Plugin->new(
    'version' => '$Id: check_keyword_search.pl 18 2008-01-06 14:54:07Z max $',
    'shortname' => "KEYWORD_SEARCH",
    'usage' => $USAGE,
    'timeout' => 60 # Default timeout
);
$np->add_arg(spec => 'env|e=s',
        help => "-e, --env=ENVIRONMENT\n " .
                "Env to search (" . join(',', @ENVS) .
                ") - [default $ENVS[0]\]",
        default => $ENVS[0]);
$np->add_arg(spec => 'warning|w=s',
        default => 5,
        help => "-w, --warning=INTEGER:INTEGER\n" .
                    " Warning threshold for search time [default 5]");
$np->add_arg(spec => 'critical|c=s',
        default => 10,
        help => "-c, --critical=INTEGER:INTEGER\n" .
                    " Critical threshold for search time [default 10]");
```

```perl
$np->add_arg(spec => 'search|s=s',
                    help => "-s, --search=KEYWORD\n Keyword to search",
                    required => 1);

$np->getopts;

my $env = $np->opts->env;

if (! grep(/$env/, @ENVS)) {
    die ("Invalid env argument " . $np->opts->env . "\n" .
        "    Valid envs are " . join(',', @ENVS) . "\n");
}

$np->set_thresholds('warning' => $np->opts->warning,
                    'critical' => $np->opts->critical);
# Variables for the results of the keyword search
my ($found, $time, $err_msg) = (undef, undef);

eval {
    my $agent = WWW::UltimateDomains->new(
                    'Timeout' => $np->opts->critical,
                    'SubDomain' => $np->opts->env
                );
    ($found, $time, $err_msg) = $agent->keyword_search($np->opts->search);
};

my $search_failed = $@;

$np->add_perfdata(
    label => "search",
    value => $time,
    uom => "s",
    threshold => $np->threshold()
);

# Module threw a die()
if ($search_failed) {
    $np->nagios_exit(UNKNOWN, $search_failed);
}

# Error during retrieval, known by WWW::UltimateDomains
if ($err_msg ne '') {
    $np->nagios_exit(CRITICAL, $err_msg);
}

if ($found < 1) {
    $np->nagios_exit(CRITICAL, "No domains found for keyword '" .
                    $np->opts->search .
                    "' ($time seconds)" )
}

# At this point, a positive number of domains were found, so let's make sure
# the http response was received in a timely manner.
my $code = $np->check_threshold(check => $time);
```

```
if ($code == WARNING) {
    $np->nagios_exit($code, "$found results in $time seconds (> " .
                            $np->opts->warning . "s)");
} elsif ($code == CRITICAL) {
    $np->nagios_exit($code, "$found results in $time seconds (> " .
                            $np->opts->critical . "s)");
} elsif ($code == OK) {
    $np->nagios_exit($code, "$found results in $time seconds");
} else {
# This should never happen
    $np->nagios_exit(UNKNOWN, "$found results in $time " .
                             "seconds, but threshold check failed.");
}
```

Testing Telnet-like Interfaces (Telnet or SSH)

Network Devices

This check can help determine if core network/management network paths have been disrupted. We have even seen cases where the telnet/ssh server on a network device failed due to high memory and CPU utilization; the administrative server failed before our CPU and memory alarms went off for the device, which has an OS image with a memory leak problem. No custom code for this one; just use the check_telnet or check_ssh programs that come with the Nagios plug-ins package.

Monitoring LDAP

LDAP continues to gain popularity in large organizations. It is easy to maintain, easy to integrate, and scales well. There are a large number of LDAP servers on the market. In this section, we focus on monitoring Sun One LDAP; the techniques we explain here can be applied to other LDAP servers as well. Sun One LDAP comes with a software SNMP agent, which makes it especially easy to monitor.

Testing Replication

This script tests simple replication between two LDAP instances. To do this, it expects both instances to have a single user who is allowed to make changes to the same portion of the LDAP tree being tested. The script will do the following:

1. Take a user-supplied LDIF (--ldif /path/to/ldif) and create the object specified in the LDIF on the master server.

2. Ensure the newly created object can be found by searching for it by the DN field in the LDIF supplied to the script (--ldif /path/to/ldif) on the master LDAP server.

3. Sleep a user-supplied number of seconds to allow replication to occur (--replication-wait).

4. Query for the record in the second master (or slave) LDAP server to ensure it made it to the replicant.

5. Delete the record from the second master (in master–master mode) or the only master (in master–slave) mode.

6. Sleep a user-supplied number of seconds to allow the deletion to propagate to both servers (--replication-wait).

7. Query for the record on the slave (in master–slave mode) or the primary master (in master–master mode) to make sure the record was properly deleted.

The script will alert at a CRITICAL level if any of the steps mentioned fail. It will output the following perfdata: time in seconds it took to BIND to each LDAP server, time in seconds used to add the record specified in the –ldif argument, and time in seconds used to search for the record on the second LDAP server. The scripts uses LDAP version 3 and was written to work with the SunONE LDAP server; it should work with other LDAP v3 compliant servers as well.

Example Call to This Script

```
/usr/local/bin/perl -w ./check_ldap_replication.pl --first-ldap-server
ldap01.example.com:4389 \
  --second-ldap-server ldap02.example.com:5389 --ldif
/home/testuser/src/replication.ldif \
--search-base ou=People,dc=test,dc=com --bind-dn 'cn=Directory Manager' \
--bind-password mypassword --replication-wait 1 --master-master-mode
LDAP-REPLICATION OK - Replicated one record in mode master-master in 1.08 seconds |
'1st_bind_time'=0.01s;0;0 '2nd_bind_time'=0.00s;0;0 'search_time'=0.02s;0;0 'total_
time'=1.08s;0;0
```

The Script

```
#!/usr/local/bin/perl
# nagios: +epn
=pod
=head1 NAME
```

```
check_ldap_replication.pl
=head1 SYNOPSIS
```

Verify that LDAP replication between two
LDAP v3 compliant master-master or master-slave mode servers is
working properly.

`=head1 DESCRIPTION`

This script will do the following:

`=over 4`

`=item *`

Take a user-supplied object creation LDIF and create the object in the master
server.

`=item *`

Ensure the newly created object can be found using a search for it by DN in
the master LDAP server.

`=item *`

Sleep a user-supplied number of seconds to allow replication to occur.

`=item *`

Query for the record in the second master (or slave) LDAP server to ensure it
made it to the replicant.

`=item *`

Delete the record from the second master (in master-master mode) or the only
master (in master-slave) mode.

`=item *`

Query for the record on the slave (in master-slave mode) or the primary
master (in master-master mode) to make sure the record was properly deleted.

`=back`

If any step of the process fails, the script will return a CRITICAL alert
status to Nagios along with a descriptive error message.

This script will also output performance data for the following metrics:

`=over 4`

`=item *`

Time it took to bind to each LDAP server

`=item *`

Total time used for the add

`=item *`

Total time required to search

`=back`

The script accepts the following arguments:

`=over 4`

`=item *`

`--bind-dn LDAP DN`

```
=item *
--bind-password password
=item *
--search-base string
=item *
--first-ldap-server host[:port]
=item *
--second-ldap-server host[:port]
=item *
--ldif /path/to/ldif
=item *
--master-master-mode or --master-slave-mode
=item *
--replication-wait SECONDS
=back
All arguments are required.
Example call:
./check_ldap_replication \
--ldif /home/nagios/etc/replication.ldif \
--first-ldap-server ldap01.example.com \
--second-ldap-server ldap02.example.com:2389 \
--master-master-mode
--replication-wait 2 \
--search-base ou=people,,dc=example,dc=com \
--bind-dn myusername \
--bind-password mypassword
LDAP-REPLICATION OK: 2 seconds to replicate 1 record | '1st_bind'=0.2s;0;0
'2nd_bind'=0.09s;0;0 'add'=0.5s;0;0 'search'=0.01s;0;0
=head1 Master-Master and Master-Slave Mode Differences
```

This test will operate slightly differently when testing master-master mode
LDAP replication then it will in master-slave mode.

The differences are as follows:

```
=over 4
=item *
```

In master-master mode, the replication record will be deleted from the second
LDAP server. In master-slave mode, the replication record will be deleted
from the master server.

```
=item *
```

In master-master mode, the script will then query to ensure the deleted
record doesn't exist on the first LDAP server; in master-slave mode, the
script will query the second (slave) LDAP server to ensure the replication
record deletion worked properly.

```
=back
=head1 Replication LDIF Format
```

LDIF file must have DN and uid attributes that can be searched on, all other
attributes depend on your schema. The record in this file will be added to the
server given in the --first-ldap-server argument. Replication will be
considered successful if all attributes in the LDIF exist on the server
given in --second-ldap-server. Here is an example LDIF used based on test
data that comes with the Sun One LDAP server:

```
dn: uid=reptest1,ou=People,dc=test,dc=com
uid: reptest1
objectClass: top
objectClass: person
objectClass: organizationalPerson
objectClass: inetOrgPerson
givenName: Reppie
sn: Test
cn: Replication Test
initials: RT
mail: reptest@example.com
telephoneNumber: 555-1212
description: This is record is for testing purposes only
=cut
sub check_ldap_replication {
    use strict;
    use Net::LDAP::Express;
    use Net::LDAP::LDIF;
    use Nagios::Plugin;
    use Time::HiRes qw(time);

    my $USAGE = <<EOF;
USAGE: check_ldap_replication.pl --ldif not -replicaiton-record /path/to/ldif \\
            --bind-dn uid=myid,ou=mygroup,dc=example,dc=com \\
            --bind-password mypassword \\
        --search-base ldap-search-base \\
        --first-ldap-server server[:port] \\
        --second-ldap-server server[:port] \\
        { --master-master-mode | --master-slave-mode } \\
        --replication-wait SECONDS \\
        [--debug]
EOF
    my $LABEL = 'LDAP-REPLICATION';
    my $plugin = Nagios::Plugin->new(
        'shortname' => $LABEL,
        'usage'     => $USAGE
    );
```

```
$plugin->add_arg(
    'spec' => 'bind-dn|U=s',
    'help' => "-U, --bind-dn LDAP DN\n" .
              " LDAP DN to use for the replication test. This user\n" .
              " must be able to add, search, and delete records from\n" .
              " both LDAP servers.",
    'required' => 1
);
$plugin->add_arg(
    'spec' => 'bind-password|P=s',
    'help' => "-P, --bind-password password\n" .
              " Password to use to authenticate against both LDAP\n" .
              " servers.",
    'required' => 1
);
$plugin->add_arg(
    'spec' => 'search-base|B=s',
    'help' => "-B, --search-base search-base\n" .
              " LDAP search base to use when searching for the\n" .
              " record added by the script",
    'required' => 1
);
$plugin->add_arg(
    'spec' => 'first-ldap-server|F=s',
    'help' => "-F, --first-ldap-server SERVER[:PORT]\n" .
              " First LDAP server to connect to, replication\n" .
              " record will be added to this server. Port is \n" .
              " optional, defaults to 389.",
    'required' => 1
);
$plugin->add_arg(
    'spec' => 'second-ldap-server|S=s',
    'help' => "-S, --first-ldap-server SERVER[:PORT]\n" .
              " Second LDAP server to connect to, replication\n" .
              " record will be searched for on this server. Port is \n" .
              " optional, defaults to 389.",
    'required' => 1
);
$plugin->add_arg(
    'spec' => 'ldif|L=s',
    'help' => "-L, --ldif /path/to/ldif\n" .
              " Full path and file name of LDIF file. LDIF file\n" .
              " must have a DN attribute that can be searched on,\n" .
              " all other attributes are optional. The record in\n" .
              " this file will be added to the server given in the\n" .
              " --first-ldap-server argument. Replication will\n" .
              " be considered successful if all attributes in the\n" .
              " LDIF exist on the server given in --second-ldap-server",
    'required' => 1
);
```

```perl
$plugin->add_arg(
    'spec' => 'master-master-mode',
    'help' => "--master-master-mode\n" .
              "  Replication is in master-master mode. See perldoc\n" .
              "  for details on how this affects the test.",
    'required' => 0
);
$plugin->add_arg(
    'spec' => 'master-slave-mode',
    'help' => "--master-slave-mode\n" .
              "  Replication is in master-slave mode. See perldoc\n" .
              "  for details on how this affects the test.",
    'required' => 0
);
$plugin->add_arg(
    'spec' => 'replication-wait|W=i',
    'help' => "-W, --replication-wait SECONDS\n" .
              "  How long (in seconds) to wait between adding the\n" .
              "  replication record and searching for it.",
    'required' => 1
);
$plugin->add_arg(
    'spec' => 'debug|D',
    'help' => "-D, --debug\n Enable debug mode",
    'required' => 0,
    'default' => 0
);
$plugin->getopts();
my %CFG = (
    'opts' => $plugin->opts,
    'mode' => 0,
    'ldif' => undef,
    'stats' => {
        '1st_bind_time' => 0,
        '2nd_bind_time' => 0,
        'search_time' => 0,
        'total_time' => 0
    },
    'first_conn' => undef,
    'second_conn' => undef
);
use constant MASTER_MASTER_MODE => 'master-master';
use constant MASTER_SLAVE_MODE => 'master-slave';
if ((! $plugin->opts->get('master-master-mode')) &&
    (! $plugin->opts->get('master-slave-mode'))) {
    $plugin->nagios_die("Must specify --master-master-mode or " .
                        "--master-slave-mode");
}
```

```perl
if ($plugin->opts->get('master-master-mode')) {
    $CFG{'mode'} = MASTER_MASTER_MODE;
} else {
    $CFG{'mode'} = MASTER_SLAVE_MODE;
}
debug("Running in $CFG{'mode'} mode");
# Ensure the specified LDIF exists and is valid.
debug("Parsing replication LDIF file " . $CFG{'opts'}->get('ldif'));
$CFG{'ldif'} = parse_ldif_file($plugin, $CFG{'opts'}->get('ldif'));
# Connect to the first server, time how long it takes to bind.
debug("Connecting to 1st LDAP server " .
    $CFG{'opts'}->get('first-ldap-server'));
my $start_time = time();
my ($first_ldap, $first_bind_time) = connect_to_ldap_server(
    $plugin,
    $CFG{'opts'}->get('first-ldap-server'),
    $CFG{'opts'}->get('bind-dn'),
    $CFG{'opts'}->get('bind-password'),
    $CFG{'opts'}->get('search-base')
);
$CFG{'1st_conn'} = $first_ldap;
$CFG{'stats'}->{'1st_bind_time'} = $first_bind_time;
# Add the LDIF to the first server.
if ($CFG{'opts'}->get('debug')) {
    debug("Adding LDIF to " . $CFG{'opts'}->get('first-ldap-server') .
        ": " . $CFG{'ldif'}->current_entry()->dump());
}
add_ldif_to_ldap($plugin, $CFG{'1st_conn'}, $CFG{'ldif'});
# Sleep --replication-wait seconds for replication to occur.
my $wait = $CFG{'opts'}->get('replication-wait');
debug("Sleeping $wait seconds to allow replication to occur");
sleep($wait);
debug("Connecting to 2nd LDAP server " .
    $CFG{'opts'}->get('second-ldap-server'));
# Search for the record on the second server.
my ($second_ldap, $second_bind_time) = connect_to_ldap_server(
    $plugin,
    $CFG{'opts'}->get('second-ldap-server'),
    $CFG{'opts'}->get('bind-dn'),
    $CFG{'opts'}->get('bind-password'),
    $CFG{'opts'}->get('search-base')
);
$CFG{'2nd_conn'} = $first_ldap;
$CFG{'stats'}->{'2nd_bind_time'} = $second_bind_time;
debug("Ensuring LDAP record was created on secondary server");
my ($found, $search_time) = search_for_record($plugin,
                                        $CFG{'2nd_conn'},
                                        $CFG{'ldif'}, 1);
```

```perl
$CFG{'stats'}->{'search_time'} = $search_time;

if ($found == 0) {
    $CFG{'stats'}->{'total_time'} = 0;
    $plugin->nagios_exit(CRITICAL,
        "Replication failed, record not found on replicant!" .
        make_perfdata($CFG{'stats'}));
    return CRITICAL;
}
# Delete the record from the secondary master in master-master mode
# or the slave in master-slave mode.
if ($CFG{'mode'} eq MASTER_MASTER_MODE) {
    debug("Deleting LDAP record from secondary master server");
    delete_record($plugin, $CFG{'2nd_conn'}, $CFG{'ldif'});
} else {
    debug("Deleting LDAP record from master server");
    delete_record($plugin, $CFG{'1st_conn'}, $CFG{'ldif'});
}
# Search for the record on the primary master in master-master mode
# or the slave in master-slave mode to ensure the deletion worked.
my $not_found = 0;

if ($CFG{'mode'} eq MASTER_MASTER_MODE) {
    debug("Ensuring LDAP record was deleted from secondary master server");
    my @results = search_for_record($plugin, $CFG{'2nd_conn'},
                                    $CFG{'ldif'}, 0);
    $not_found = ! $results[0];
} else {
    debug("Ensuring LDAP record was deleted from master server");
    my @results = search_for_record($plugin, $CFG{'1st_conn'},
                                    $CFG{'ldif'}, 0);
    $not_found = ! $results[0];
}

if ($not_found == 0) {
    $CFG{'stats'}->{'total_time'} = 0;
    $plugin->nagios_exit(CRITICAL, "Replication record deletion failed!" .
                        make_perfdata($CFG{'stats'}));
}
my $total_time = sprintf("%0.2f", time() - $start_time);
$CFG{'stats'}->{'total_time'} = $total_time;

my $message = "$LABEL OK - Replicated one record in mode $CFG{'mode'} in " .
              "$total_time seconds";
print "$message | " . make_perfdata($CFG{'stats'}) . "\n";

return OK;

sub parse_ldif_file {
    my $plugin = shift;
    my $file = shift;
    my $ldif = undef;
```

```perl
    eval {
        $ldif = Net::LDAP::LDIF->new($file, 'r', 'onerror' => 'die');
        my $entry = $ldif->read_entry();
    };
    if ($@) {
        $plugin->nagios_die("Can't parse LDIF $file: $@");
    }
    if ($CFG{'opts'}->get('debug')) {
        my $entry = $ldif->current_entry();
        my @attrs;
        foreach my $attr ($entry->attributes) {
            push(@attrs, join('=', $attr, $entry->get_value($attr)));
        }
        debug("Parsed LDIF: " . join(', ', @attrs));
        }
        return $ldif;
    }
sub connect_to_ldap_server {
    my $plugin = shift;
    my $server_spec = shift;
    my $dn = shift;
    my $pass = shift;
    my $search_base = shift;
    my ($host, $port) = split(':', $server_spec, 2);
    $port = 389 if ! defined $port;
    my $ldap = undef;
    my $start = time();
    my $debug = 0;
    if ($CFG{'opts'}->get('debug') == 1) {
        $debug = 1 | 2;
    }
    eval {
        $ldap = Net::LDAP::Express->new(
                    'host' => $host,
                    'port' => $port,
                    'bindDN' => $dn,
                    'bindpw' => $pass,
                    'base' => $search_base,
                    'debug' => $debug,
                    'searchattrs' => [qw(uid)]
                );
    } ;
    my $connect_time = time() - $start;
    if ($@) {
        $plugin->nagios_die("Can't connect to ldap server $host: $@");
    }
```

```perl
        return ($ldap, $connect_time);
}
sub add_ldif_to_ldap {
    my $plugin = shift;
    my $conn = shift;
    my $ldif = shift;

    debug("Adding new entry to replication master");
    my $new_entry = $ldif->current_entry();
    my $result = $conn->add($new_entry);

    if ($result->code) {
        my $msg = "Could not add record to LDAP: " . $result->error;
        $plugin->nagios_exit(CRITICAL, $msg);
    }
}
sub search_for_record {
    my $plugin = shift;
    my $conn = shift;
    my $ldif = shift;
    my $expect = shift;

    my $entry = $ldif->current_entry();
    my $filter = "(uid=" . $entry->get_value('uid') . ")";
    my $base = $CFG{'opts'}->get('search-base');

    debug("Searching for record with search base $base and filter $filter");

    my $start = time();
    my $results = $conn->search('filter' => $filter) ;
    my $total = time() - $start;

    my $count = $results->count();
    debug("Search return $count records");

    if ($count != $expect) {
        my $msg = "Expected 1 entry for $filter, base $base, found $count!";
        $plugin->nagios_exit(CRITICAL, $msg);
    }
    return($count, $total);
}
sub delete_record {
    my $plugin = shift;
    my $conn = shift;
    my $ldif = shift;

    my $result = $conn->delete($ldif->current_entry());

    if ($result->code) {
        my $msg = "Could not delete record: " . $result->error;
        $plugin->nagios_exit(CRITICAL, $msg);
    }
}
```

```
sub debug {
    return unless $CFG{'opts'}->get('debug') == 1;
    my $msg = shift;
    print STDERR scalar(localtime(time())) . ": $msg\n";
}
sub make_perfdata {
    my $stats = shift;
    my $output = "";
    for my $stat (sort keys %$stats) {
        $output .= sprintf("'$stat'=%0.2fs;0;0 ", $stats->{$stat});
    }
    return $output;
}
}
exit check_ldap_replication();
```

Monitoring Databases

Most applications in today use a database. As the backbone of most applications, the database can be as important to the application as switches are to networks. Nagios ships with several database plugins: check_mysql, check_mysql_query, and check_oracle to name a few. You can also use other core plugins to check the availability of databases. For example we can use check_tcp to make sure the network listener of the database system we are using is actually listening. If there is not a plugin for your database , it is generally easy to create scripts from scratch that will watch your database for signs of failure with Nagios. The difficult part of monitoring databases is that they usually do not fail in an obvious way. Most likely staff will find that a database on the edge of failure will first have issues with performance, for example: problems committing writes to disk, table locks not being released, or general slow downs in database performance. We recommend that the Nagios administrator work with their local database administrator to define situations to watch for and critical performance thresholds. A few key points to keep in mind when setting up database monitoring with Nagios:

- Set up a table on each production database server that will be used just for monitoring; the table should have a single timestamp field. From Nagios, periodically run a check script that inserts a row into the table, then runs a SELECT to ensure the row just inserted made it into the database, then deletes the row just inserted, and finally runs a final SELECT to ensure the row was deleted. This check will quickly tell you if the database server is able to perform basic read and write operations in a timely manner and without failures.

- Use perl scripts with ePN or shell script queries to read performance data from database system tables and alert when performance is out of acceptable limits as defined by the database staff and Nagios administration staff.

- Most databases include SNMP agents or monitoring programs that will send SNMP traps when the database fails or performance degrades; some also include SNMP sub-agents or SNMP master agents that will allow you to poll the database for performance metrics. Make use of this functionality if the database you are monitoring supports it.

Specialized Hardware

Fast load balancers, efficient SSL termination appliances and proxies, UPSs. The variety of hardware devices that can be found on larger projects is dizzying. Even more confusing is keeping track of all those devices. Some provide SNMP agents (if you are lucky and can use SNMP), others have HTTP interfaces, and even others have no interface to monitor beyond log output. Regardless of the interface, Nagios' simple and easy-to-use plug-in framework will let you monitor your device and free up your memory for more important things like remembering to go to lunch or the name and face of your significant other. In this section, we discuss a number of hardware appliances larger organizations use and help you monitor the right metrics on the devices, the metrics that will enable you to quickly know when things are going wrong.

Bluecoat Application Proxy and Anti-Virus Devices

SNMP-based Checks

The Bluecoat proxy devices (SG410, 510, and 810) and anti-virus (A/V) devices expose a number of very useful SNMP MIBs that allow a network manager to retrieve very useful metrics from them. These MIBs include HTTP status distribution, CPU, memory, and disk utilization, proxy activity, and Web server utilization. One very nice feature of Bluecoat is that all thresholds that are set by a Bluecoat administrator on a Bluecoat device are exposed in the SNMP MIB, so scripts that check service thresholds on the Bluecoats for CPU, memory, and network utilization need no threshold input from the Nagios administrator. These devices also send out a large number of useful traps that can be received by Nagios using SNMPTT (discussed in Chapter 5).

All MIBs used in this section can be downloaded from the Bluecoat Web site at www.bluecoat.com.

Proxy Devices (SG510, SG800)

Bluecoat proxy devices use the concept of *pressure* to describe the amount of work a manageable element of the device is using, be that CPU, network, or memory. From the Bluecoat management console an administrator can configure the warning and critical threshold levels and the alert threshold intervals for each of these checks. A metric is only considered at or above a threshold if it exceeds the threshold for at least the internal configured for the threshold. For example, the CPU utilization threshold might be configured on the Bluecoat device as "95% pressure for 120 seconds," so the device would only consider CPU utilization breached if it stayed above 95% utilization for two minutes or more.

The Bluecoat MIB defines seven different states for manageable elements: ok, low-warning, warning, high-warning, low-critical, critical, and high-critical. We map these states to Nagios alert states as follows:

OK:

- ok

WARN:

- low-warning
- warning
- high-warning

CRITICAL:

- low-critical
- critical
- high-critical

In our opinion, having seven different states does not provide additional value. When an element enters a non-ok state we feel that the alert should be acted on. Having low and high sublevels within each threshold definition means a device manager has to decide to 1) ignore the substates, 2) let the substates trigger an alarm but do nothing about them, or 3) act regardless of the substate. We feel that acting regardless of the substate is the best course of action and simplifies setting the thresholds on the device.

Bluecoat administrators can also configure the Bluecoat to send SNMP traps when thresholds are breached; these traps can be integrated into Nagios using SNMPTT (as discussed in Chapter 5). Bluecoat also allows an administrator to configure the Bluecoat to send email alerts and log events to the Bluecoat's internal logs when alerts occur.

CPU Utilization

MIB needed

BLUECOAT-SG-PROXY-MIB.my

system–resources.my

OIDs used

BLUECOAT-SG-PROXY-MIB.my

- sgProxyCpuBusyPerCent: 1.3.6.1.4.1.3417.2.11.2.1.7.0
- sgProxyCpuIdlePerCent: 1.3.6.1.4.1.3417.2.11.2.1.8.0

system–resources.my

- cpuUtilizationValue: 1.3.6.1.4.1.3417.2.8.1.3.0
- cpuCurrentState: 1.3.6.1.4.1.3417.2.8.1.9.0
- cpuWarningThreshold: 1.3.6.1.4.1.3417.2.8.1.4.0
- cpuCriticalThreshold: 1.3.6.1.4.1.3417.2.8.1.6.0

This check measures CPU pressure on a Bluecoat device. According to the documentation, on SGOS 4.*x*, this check will only return utilization for CPU 0 on a Bluecoat device even if that device has multiple CPUs. On Bluecoats running SGOS 5.*x* we can also retrieve busy and idle CPU utilization for graphing and trending purposes using perfdata.

```perl
#!/usr/local/bin/perl
# nagios: +epn
=pod
=head1 NAME
check_bluecoat_cpu.pl - Check CPU pressure on a Bluecoat device.
=head1 DESCRIPTION
The SNMP agent on Bluecoat devices allows us to query it to see what
thresholds have been set by the Bluecoat administrator. For this reason
we do not need to have the user specify warning nor critical thresholds.

The script will return perfdata for CPU utilization for all Bluecoat
devices; for SGOS 5.x and later this script will also return idle and
busy % CPU utilization.
=cut
sub check_bluecoat_cpu {
    use strict;
    use FindBin;
    use lib "$FindBin::Bin/lib";

    use Net::SNMP;
    use Nagios::Plugin::SNMP;

    my $LABEL = 'BLUECOAT-CPU';

    my $plugin = Nagios::Plugin::SNMP->new(
        'shortname' => $LABEL,
        'usage' => 'USAGE: %s'
    );

    $plugin->getopts;

    my $DEBUG = $plugin->opts->get('snmp-debug');

    # Return from current state will be one of these, each has
    # a value that matches the index position in the array below.
    my @states = qw(ok low-warning warning high-warning
                    low-critical critical high-critical);

    my %oids = qw(
        sgProxyCpuBusyPerCent.0 .1.3.6.1.4.1.3417.2.11.2.1.7.0
        sgProxyCpuIdlePerCent.0 .1.3.6.1.4.1.3417.2.11.2.1.8.0
        cpuUtilizationValue.0   .1.3.6.1.4.1.3417.2.8.1.3.0
        cpuCurrentState.0       .1.3.6.1.4.1.3417.2.8.1.9.0
        cpuWarningThreshold.0   .1.3.6.1.4.1.3417.2.8.1.4.0
        cpuCriticalThreshold.0  .1.3.6.1.4.1.3417.2.8.1.6.0
    );

    my $result = $plugin->get(values %oids);

    # Close and destroy session
    $plugin->close();

    my @perf_data;

    my %cpu;
```

```
    $cpu{'busy'}  = $result->{$oids{'sgProxyCpuBusyPerCent.0'}};
    $cpu{'idle'}  = $result->{$oids{'sgProxyCpuIdlePerCent.0'}};
    $cpu{'util'}  = $result->{$oids{'cpuUtilizationValue.0'}};
    $cpu{'state'} = $result->{$oids{'cpuCurrentState.0'}};
    $cpu{'warn'}  = $result->{$oids{'cpuWarningThreshold.0'}};
    $cpu{'crit'}  = $result->{$oids{'cpuCriticalThreshold.0'}};
    # Not supported on SGOS < 5.x
    $cpu{'busy'} = 0 if $cpu{'busy'} eq 'noSuchObject';
    $cpu{'idle'} = 0 if $cpu{'idle'} eq 'noSuchObject';

    my $level = OK;

    my $output = "$LABEL ";

    if ($cpu{'state'} == 0) {
        $output .= "OK - Utilization $cpu{'util'}%";
    } elsif (($cpu{'state'} > 0) && ($cpu{'state'} < 6)) {
        $output .= "WARNING - Utilization $cpu{'util'}% >= $cpu{'warn'}%";
        $level = WARNING;
    } else {
        $output .= "CRITICAL - Utilization $cpu{'util'}% >= $cpu{'crit'}%";
        $level = CRITICAL;
    }

    print "$output, state $states[$cpu{'state'}] ",
        "| 'busy'=$cpu{'busy'}%;;;0;100 ",
        "'idle'=$cpu{'idle'}%;;;0;100 ",
        "'util'=$cpu{'util'}%;$cpu{'warn'};$cpu{'crit'};0;100 ",
        "'state'=$cpu{'state'};1;6;0;6\n";

    return $level;

    sub debug {

        return unless $DEBUG == 1;

        my $msg = shift;

        print STDERR scalar(localtime()) . ": $msg\n";

    }

}
exit check_bluecoat_cpu();
```

Memory Utilization

MIB needed

BLUECOAT-SG-PROXY-MIB.my

system–resources.my

OIDs used

BLUECOAT-SG-PROXY-MIB.my

- sgProxyMemAvailable: 1.3.6.1.4.1.3417.2.11.2.3.1.0

- sgProxyMemCacheUsage: 1.3.6.1.4.1.3417.2.11.2.3.2.0

- sgProxyMemSysUsage: 1.3.6.1.4.1.3417.2.11.2.3.3.0

system-resources.my

- memPressureValue: 1.3.6.1.4.1.3417.2.8.2.3.0

- memCurrentState: 1.3.6.1.4.1.3417.2.8.2.9.0

- memWarningThreshold: 1.3.6.1.4.1.3417.2.8.2.4.0

- memCriticalThreshold: 1.3.6.1.4.1.3417.2.8.2.7.0

This check measures percentage memory utilization on a Bluecoat device. On devices running SGOS 5.*x* or later we can also retrieve memory available, cached, and system utilization metrics. As with CPU utilization, the warning and critical thresholds are set on the device itself so we do not have to ask the user to provide them as arguments to the script.

```
#!/usr/local/bin/perl
# nagios: +epn
=pod
=head1 NAME
check_bluecoat_mem.pl - Check Bluecoat memory pressure
=head1 DESCRIPTION
This script will check memory pressure on a Bluecoat device. The Bluecoat
SNMP agent also exposes the thresholds the Bluecoat administrator has set
on the device, which means we do not need to have the user provide
warning or critical thresholds.

The script will return memory pressure % as perfdata; for Bluecoats running
SGOS version 5.x or higher, the script will also return cached, sys, and
avail memory as perfdata for trending purposes.
=cut
sub check_bluecoat_mem {
    use strict;
    use FindBin;
    use lib "$FindBin::Bin/lib";
    use Nagios::Plugin::SNMP;
```

```perl
my $LABEL = 'BLUECOAT MEM';

my $plugin = Nagios::Plugin::SNMP->new(
    'shortname' => $LABEL,
    'usage' => 'USAGE: %s'
);

$plugin->getopts;

my $DEBUG = $plugin->opts->get('snmp-debug');

# Return from current state will be one of these:
my @states = qw(ok low-warning warning high-warning
                low-critical critical high-critical);

my %oids = qw(
    sgProxyMemAvailable.0   .1.3.6.1.4.1.3417.2.11.2.3.1.0
    sgProxyMemCacheUsage.0  .1.3.6.1.4.1.3417.2.11.2.3.2.0
    sgProxyMemSysUsage.0    .1.3.6.1.4.1.3417.2.11.2.3.3.0
    memPressureValue.0      .1.3.6.1.4.1.3417.2.8.2.3.0
    memCurrentState. 0      .1.3.6.1.4.1.3417.2.8.2.9.0
    memWarningThreshold.0   .1.3.6.1.4.1.3417.2.8.2.4.0
    memCriticalThreshold.0  .1.3.6.1.4.1.3417.2.8.2.7.0
);

# Get the mem values
my $result = $plugin->get(values %oids);
# Close and destroy session
$plugin->close();

my @perf_data;

my %mem;

$mem{'avail'} = $result->{$oids{'sgProxyMemAvailable.0'}};
$mem{'cache'} = $result->{$oids{'sgProxyMemCacheUsage.0'}};
$mem{'sys'} = $result->{$oids{'sgProxyMemSysUsage.0'}};
$mem{'pressure'} = $result->{$oids{'memPressureValue.0'}};

$mem{'state'} = $result->{$oids{'memCurrentState.0'}};
$mem{'warn'} = $result->{$oids{'memWarningThreshold.0'}};
$mem{'crit'} = $result->{$oids{'memCriticalThreshold.0'}};

$mem{'avail'} = 0 if $mem{'avail'} eq 'noSuchObject';
$mem{'cache'} = 0 if $mem{'cache'} eq 'noSuchObject';
$mem{'sys'} = 0 if $mem{'sys'} eq 'noSuchObject';
$mem{'pressure'} = '' if $mem{'pressure'} eq 'noSuchObject';

my $level = OK;
my $output = "$LABEL ";

if ($mem{'state'} == 0) {
    $output .= "OK - Utilization $mem{'pressure'}%";
} elsif (($mem{'state'} > 0) && ($mem{'state'} < 6)) {
    $output .= "WARNING - Utilization $mem{'pressure'}% >= $mem{'warn'}%";
    $level = WARNING;
} else {
    $output .= "CRITICAL - Utilization $mem{'pressure'}% >= $mem{'crit'}%";
    $level = CRITICAL;
}
```

```perl
      print "$output, state $states[$mem{'state'}] ",
          "| 'avail'=$mem{'avail'}b;;;; ",
          "'cache'=$mem{'cache'}b;;;; ",
          "'sys'=$mem{'sys'}b;;;; ",
          "'pressure'=$mem{'pressure'}%;$mem{'warn'};$mem{'crit'};0;100 ",
          "'state'=$mem{'state'};1;6;0;6\n";
      return $level;
      sub debug {
          return unless $DEBUG == 1;
          my $msg = shift;
          print STDERR scalar(localtime()) . ": $msg\n";
      }
  }
exit check_bluecoat_mem();
```

Network Interface Utilization

MIB needed

system-resources.my

OIDs used

netName: 1.3.6.1.4.1.3417.2.8.3.1.1.2
netUtilizationValue: 1.3.6.1.4.1.3417.2.8.3.1.1.3
netWarningThreshold: 1.3.6.1.4.1.3417.2.8.3.1.1.4
netCriticalThreshold: 1.3.6.1.4.1.3417.2.8.3.1.1.6
netCurrentState: 1.3.6.1.4.1.3417.2.8.3.1.1.9

The Bluecoat exposes network utilization values on a per-interface basis; if the Bluecoat has four interfaces, the SNMP agent on the Bluecoat will return individual states, values, and thresholds for each interface. The script will output perfdata for each interface for graphing and trending purposes.

```perl
#!/usr/local/bin/perl
# nagios: +epn
=pod
=head1 NAME
check_bluecoat_net.pl - Check Bluecoat network pressure
=head1 DESCRIPTION
This script checks network pressure on a Bluecoat Proxy device. It will
return memory pressure % utilization as perfdata for each interface on
the Bluecoat proxy being checked. Network pressure thresholds are set on
the device by the Bluecoat proxy administrator so we do not need to ask
the user to provide warning nor critical thresholds to the script.
=cut
```

```perl
sub check_bluecoat_net {
    use strict;
    use FindBin;
    use lib "$FindBin::Bin/lib";
    use Nagios::Plugin::SNMP;

    my $LABEL = 'BLUECOAT-NET';
    my $plugin = Nagios::Plugin::SNMP->new(
        'shortname' => $LABEL,
        'usage' => 'USAGE: %s'
    );

    $plugin->getopts;

    my $DEBUG = $plugin->opts->get('snmp-debug');

    # Return from current state will be one of these:
    my @states = qw(ok low-warning warning high-warning
                    low-critical critical high-critical);

    # These are all tables, one entry in each per interface
    my %oids = qw(
        .1.3.6.1.4.1.3417.2.8.3.1.1.2 netName
        .1.3.6.1.4.1.3417.2.8.3.1.1.3 netUtilizationValue
        .1.3.6.1.4.1.3417.2.8.3.1.1.4 netWarningThreshold
        .1.3.6.1.4.1.3417.2.8.3.1.1.6 netCriticalThreshold
        .1.3.6.1.4.1.3417.2.8.3.1.1.9 netCurrentState
    );

    my %net;

    for my $oid (keys %oids) {
        debug("Walking table $oid");

        my $results = $plugin->walk($oid);

        for my $result (keys %$results) {
            my $table = $results->{$result};

            for my $item (keys %$table) {
                my ($base, $idx) = ($item =~ m/^(.+)\.(\d+)$/);
                my $key = $oids{$base};

                debug("$idx: $key = $table->{$item}");

                $net{$idx} = {} if ! exists $net{$idx};
                $net{$idx}->{$key} = $table->{$item};
            }
        }
    }

    # Close and destroy session
    $plugin->close();

    my @perf_data;

    my @ok;
    my @warn;
    my @crit;

    my $level = OK;
```

```perl
        for my $idx (sort keys %net) {
            my %net = %{$net{$idx}};
            my $name = $net{'netName'};
            if ($net{'netCurrentState'} == 0) {
                push(@ok, "$name $net{'netUtilizationValue'}%");
            } elsif (($net{'netCurrentState'} > 0) &&
                    ($net{'netCurrentState'} < 6)) {
                push(@warn, "$name $net{'netUtilizationValue'}% " .
                        ">= $net{'netWarningThreshold'}");
                $level = WARNING unless $level == CRITICAL;
            } else {
                push(@crit, "$name $net{'netUtilizationValue'}% " .
                        ">= $net{'netCriticalThreshold'}");
                $level = CRITICAL;
            }
            $name =~ s/ utilization//gi;
            $name =~ s/ /_/g;
            $name =~ s/:/-/g;
            push(@perf_data, "'${name}'=$net{'netUtilizationValue'};" .
                        "$net{'netWarningThreshold'};" .
                        "$net{'netCriticalThreshold'};" .
                        "0;0");
        }
        my $output = "$LABEL ";
        if (scalar(@crit) > 0) {
            $output .= 'CRITICAL ' . join(', ', @crit) . ' ';
        }
        if (scalar(@warn) > 0) {
            $output .= 'WARNING ' . join(', ', @warn) . ' ';
        }
        if (scalar(@ok) > 0) {
            $output .= 'OK ' . join(', ', @ok);
        }
        print "$output | " . join(' ', @perf_data) . "\n";
        return $level;
        sub debug {
            return unless $DEBUG == 1;
            my $msg = shift;
            print STDERR scalar(localtime()) . ": $msg\n";
        }
}
exit check_bluecoat_net();
```

Anti-Virus Devices
A/V Health Check
MIB needed

BLUECOAT-AV-MIB

OIDs needed

avFilesScanned: 1.3.6.1.4.1.3417.2.10.1.1.0
avVirusesDetected: 1.3.6.1.4.1.3417.2.10.1.2.0
avLicenseDaysRemaining: 1.3.6.1.4.1.3417.2.10.1.7.0
avSlowICAPConnections: 1.3.6.1.4.1.3417.2.10.1.10.0

Bluecoat anti-virus devices are used in conjunction with proxy devices to provide fast anti-virus scanning of content passing through the Bluecoat device. Proxies communicate with anti-virus devices using a protocol called ICAP that allows for efficient communication between the two. Bluecoat anti-virus devices do not have the rich SNMP MIB support proxy devices do; however, the SNMP agent on them does provide useful, queryable variables. This AV check script will:

- Alert when the Antivirus scanning license is nearing expiration (user provides days left for warning and critical thresholds)

- Return perfdata that includes the following fields

  - Number of file scanned.

  - Viruses detected.

  - Number of slow ICAP connections—if sustained numbers are seen, check the connections between the proxy and anti-virus devices for problems and check the two devices to see if either is becoming overloaded.

```
#!/usr/local/bin/perl
# nagios: +epn
=pod
=head1 NAME
check_bluecoat_av.pl - Check basic status of a Bluecoat A/V device.
=head1 DESCRIPTION
```

This script will perform several basic checks on a Bluecoat A/V device; the script accepts warning and critical arguments that indicate low water marks for days left on the A/V device Antivirus license on the device. The device will return perfdata for the number of files scanned, the number of virii detected by the device, and the number of slow ICAP connections to the device from compatible Bluecoat proxy devices.

```perl
=cut
sub check_bluecoat_av {
    use strict;
    use FindBin;
    use lib "$FindBin::Bin/lib";
    use Nagios::Plugin::SNMP;

    my $LABEL = 'BLUECOAT-AV';

    my $USAGE = <<EOF;
USAGE %s [--warning days_left_on_license] [--critical days_left_on_license]
EOF

    my $plugin = Nagios::Plugin::SNMP->new(
        'shortname' => $LABEL,
        'usage' => $USAGE
    );

    $plugin->getopts;

    my $DEBUG = $plugin->opts->get('snmp-debug');

    my $WARNING = $plugin->opts->get('warning');
    $plugin->nagios_die('warning threshold is required!')
        if ! defined $WARNING;

    my $CRITICAL = $plugin->opts->get('critical');
    $plugin->nagios_die('critical threshold is required!')
        if ! defined $CRITICAL;

    my %oids = qw(
        avFilesScanned.0 .1.3.6.1.4.1.3417.2.10.1.1.0
        avVirusesDetected.0 .1.3.6.1.4.1.3417.2.10.1.2.0
        avLicenseDaysRemaining.0 .1.3.6.1.4.1.3417.2.10.1.7.0
        avSlowICAPConnections.0 .1.3.6.1.4.1.3417.2.10.1.10.0
    );

    my $results = $plugin->get(values %oids);

    my $files_scanned = $results->{$oids{'avFilesScanned.0'}};
    my $virii_found = $results->{$oids{'avVirusesDetected.0'}};
    my $days_left = $results->{$oids{'avLicenseDaysRemaining.0'}};
    my $slow_icap = $results->{$oids{'avSlowICAPConnections.0'}};

    # Close and destroy session
    $plugin->close();

    my $level = OK;

    my $output = "$LABEL ";
```

```
    if ($days_left <= $CRITICAL) {
        $output .= "CRITICAL - license expiring expire soon! " .
                   "($days_left days <= $CRITICAL days) ";
        $level = CRITICAL;
    } elsif ($days_left <= $WARNING) {
        $output .= "WARNING - license approaching expiration " .
                   "($days_left days <= $CRITICAL days) ";
        $level = WARNING;
    } else {
        $output = "OK - $days_left days left on A/V license ";
    }
    print "$output | 'days'=$days_left;$WARNING;$CRITICAL " .
                   "'scanned'=$files_scanned;0;0 " .
                   "'virii'=$virii_found;0;0 " .
                   "'slow_icap'=$slow_icap;0;0\n";
    return $level;
    sub debug {
        return unless $DEBUG == 1;
        my $msg = shift;
        print STDERR scalar(localtime()) . ": $msg\n";
    }
}
exit check_bluecoat_av();
```

Environmental Probes

Network Technologies Incorporated (NTI) produces a number of environmental monitoring systems. All systems come with SNMP agents and can be easily monitored with Nagios. NTI was kind enough to lend us their Enviromux-Mini for the purposes of this book. This device can monitor temperature, humidity, presence of water using a liquid detection sensor, and has four contacts for dry contact sensors. It additionally comes with an Ethernet port for remote administration and polling using SNMP. The device can also send out alerts via SNMP, syslog, or email using SMTP and can be managed using X-modem as well. While we experienced some minor annoyances during setup (included screwdriver was insufficient to complete the hardware installation, setup CD did not come with a Java installer and the discovery program included requires java, discovery of the device requires a DHCP server, some parts were not labeled correctly), we found the documentation on the device easy to read and comprehend and the Enviromux MIB easy to use as well.

Complete Sensor Check and Alert Script

MIB needed

ENVIROMUX-MINI (NETWORK-TECHNOLOGIES-GLOBAL-REG)

OIDs used

temperatureSensor1CurrentValue: 1.3.6.1.4.1.3699.1.1.3.1.1.1
temperatureSensor1Alert: 1.3.6.1.4.1.3699.1.1.3.1.1.2
temperatureSensor2CurrentValue: 1.3.6.1.4.1.3699.1.1.3.1.2.1
temperatureSensor2Alert: 1.3.6.1.4.1.3699.1.1.3.1.2.2
humiditySensor1CurrentValue: 1.3.6.1.4.1.3699.1.1.3.1.3.1
humiditySensor1Alert: 1.3.6.1.4.1.3699.1.1.3.1.3.2
humiditySensor2CurrentValue: 1.3.6.1.4.1.3699.1.1.3.1.4.1
humiditySensor2Alert: 1.3.6.1.4.1.3699.1.1.3.1.4.2
dryContact1Status: 1.3.6.1.4.1.3699.1.1.3.1.5.1
dryContact1Alert: 1.3.6.1.4.1.3699.1.1.3.1.5.2
dryContact2Status: 1.3.6.1.4.1.3699.1.1.3.1.6.1
dryContact2Alert: 1.3.6.1.4.1.3699.1.1.3.1.6.2
dryContact3Status: 1.3.6.1.4.1.3699.1.1.3.1.7.1
dryContact3Alert: 1.3.6.1.4.1.3699.1.1.3.1.7.2
dryContact4Status: 1.3.6.1.4.1.3699.1.1.3.1.8.1
dryContact4Alert: 1.3.6.1.4.1.3699.1.1.3.1.8.2
waterStatus: 1.3.6.1.4.1.3699.1.1.3.1.9.1
waterAlert: 1.3.6.1.4.1.3699.1.1.3.1.9.2
temperatureSensor1Name: 1.3.6.1.4.1.3699.1.1.3.2.2.1
temperatureSensor1Unit: 1.3.6.1.4.1.3699.1.1.3.2.2.2
temperatureSensor1LowThreshold: 1.3.6.1.4.1.3699.1.1.3.2.2.3
temperatureSensor1HighThreshold: 1.3.6.1.4.1.3699.1.1.3.2.2.4
temperatureSensor2Name: 1.3.6.1.4.1.3699.1.1.3.2.3.1
temperatureSensor2Unit: 1.3.6.1.4.1.3699.1.1.3.2.3.2
temperatureSensor2LowThreshold: 1.3.6.1.4.1.3699.1.1.3.2.3.3
temperatureSensor2HighThreshold: 1.3.6.1.4.1.3699.1.1.3.2.3.4

humiditySensor1Name: 1.3.6.1.4.1.3699.1.1.3.2.4.1

humiditySensor1LowThreshold: 1.3.6.1.4.1.3699.1.1.3.2.4.2

humiditySensor1HighThreshold: 1.3.6.1.4.1.3699.1.1.3.2.4.3

humiditySensor2Name: 1.3.6.1.4.1.3699.1.1.3.2.5.1

humiditySensor2LowThreshold: 1.3.6.1.4.1.3699.1.1.3.2.5.2

humiditySensor2HighThreshold: 1.3.6.1.4.1.3699.1.1.3.2.5.3

dryContact1Name: 1.3.6.1.4.1.3699.1.1.3.2.6.1

dryContact1AlertStatus: 1.3.6.1.4.1.3699.1.1.3.2.6.2

dryContact2Name: 1.3.6.1.4.1.3699.1.1.3.2.7.1

dryContact2AlertStatus: 1.3.6.1.4.1.3699.1.1.3.2.7.2

dryContact3Name: 1.3.6.1.4.1.3699.1.1.3.2.8.1

dryContact3AlertStatus: 1.3.6.1.4.1.3699.1.1.3.2.8.2

dryContact4Name: 1.3.6.1.4.1.3699.1.1.3.2.9.1

dryContact4AlertStatus: 1.3.6.1.4.1.3699.1.1.3.2.9.2

waterName: 1.3.6.1.4.1.3699.1.1.3.2.10.1

waterAlertStatus: 1.3.6.1.4.1.3699.1.1.3.2.10.2

This check script will check the status of all sensors on the device. The Environmux Mini SNMP agent supports only SNMP version 1 (or at least the Net-SNMP agent code we use for our scripts was only able to poll it using SNMP version 1). For each sensor present, the script will output a friendly name for the sensor, the current reading for the sensor, and the low and high thresholds of the sensor if it is in alert status.

Example call to the script

```
check_enviromux_mini.pl --hostname 192.168.3.133 --snmp-version 1
--rocommunity mycommunity
ENVIROMUX-MINI CRITICAL - Dry Contact #2: closed, Dry Contact #3: closed,
Humidity #1: 29.00% (<= 40.0%) OK - Dry Contact #1: open (alert when closed),
Dry Contact #4: open (alert when closed), Temperature #2: 75.70F, Water #1: open
(alert when closed) | 'contact_dry_contact1'=0;0;1;0;1
'contact_dry_contact2'=1;0;1;0;1 'contact_dry_contact3'=1;0;1;0;1
'contact_dry_contact4'=0;0;1;0;1
'humidity_humidity_sensor1'=29.00%;0;40.0:80.0;0;100
'temperature_temperature_sensor2'=75.70F;0;41.0:100.4 'water'=0;0;1;0;1
```

And the code for the script:

```
#!/usr/bin/perl

=pod

=head1 NAME
```

```
check_enviromux_mini.pl - Check status of all sensors on the Enviromux Mini
=head1 SYNOPSIS
```

This script will check the status of all sensors on an Enviromux Mini
Server Environment Monitoring System device. This script will check the
following sensors on the device:

```
=over 4
=item *
Temperature Sensor 1-2
=item *
Humidity Sensor 1-2
=item *
Dry Contact 1-4
=item *
Water Status
=back
```

All thresholds are set from the device administrative interface, so no
threshold specifications need to be passed in by the user.

The script will output Nagios perfdata for all sensors for
trending purposes. If a sensor is not active, it will not be output in
perfdata.

```
=back
=cut
sub check_enviromux_mini {
    use strict;
    use FindBin;
    use lib "$FindBin::Bin/lib";
    use Nagios::Plugin::SNMP;
    use Nenm::Utils;
    my $LABEL = 'ENVIROMUX-MINI';
    my $USAGE = <<EOF;
Usage: %s
EOF
    my $PLUGIN = Nagios::Plugin::SNMP->new(
        'shortname' => $LABEL,
        'usage' => $USAGE
    );
    $PLUGIN->getopts;
    $Nenm::Utils::DEBUG = $PLUGIN->opts->get('snmp-debug');
    my $BASE_OID = '1.3.6.1.4.1.3699.1.1.3';
    my %sensors = (
        'temperatureSensor1' => {qw(
            1.1.1.0 temperatureSensor1CurrentValue
            1.1.2.0 temperatureSensor1Alert
```

```
            2.2.1.0 temperatureSensor1Name
            2.2.2.0 temperatureSensor1Unit
            2.2.3.0 temperatureSensor1LowThreshold
            2.2.4.0 temperatureSensor1HighThreshold
)},
'temperatureSensor2' => {qw(
            1.2.1.0 temperatureSensor2CurrentValue
            1.2.2.0 temperatureSensor2Alert
            2.3.1.0 temperatureSensor2Name
            2.3.2.0 temperatureSensor2Unit
            2.3.3.0 temperatureSensor2LowThreshold
            2.3.4.0 temperatureSensor2HighThreshold
)},
'humiditySensor1' => {qw(
            1.3.1.0 humiditySensor1CurrentValue
            1.3.2.0 humiditySensor1Alert
            2.4.1.0 humiditySensor1Name
            2.4.2.0 humiditySensor1LowThreshold
            2.4.3.0 humiditySensor1HighThreshold
)},
'humiditySensor2' => {qw(
            1.4.1.0 humiditySensor2CurrentValue
            1.4.2.0 humiditySensor2Alert
            2.5.1.0 humiditySensor2Name
            2.5.2.0 humiditySensor2LowThreshold
            2.5.3.0 humiditySensor2HighThreshold
)},
'dryContact1' => {qw(
            1.5.1.0 dryContact1Status
            1.5.2.0 dryContact1Alert
            2.6.1.0 dryContact1Name
            2.6.2.0 dryContact1AlertStatus
)},
'dryContact2' => {qw(
            1.6.1.0 dryContact2Status
            1.6.2.0 dryContact2Alert
            2.7.1.0 dryContact2Name
            2.7.2.0 dryContact2AlertStatus
)},
'dryContact3' => {qw(
            1.7.1.0 dryContact3Status
            1.7.2.0 dryContact3Alert
            2.8.1.0 dryContact3Name
            2.8.2.0 dryContact3AlertStatus
)},
    'dryContact4' => {qw(
            1.8.1.0 dryContact4Status
            1.8.2.0 dryContact4Alert
            2.9.1.0 dryContact4Name
            2.9.2.0 dryContact4AlertStatus
)},
```

```perl
        'water' => {qw(
            1.9.1.0 waterStatus
            1.9.2.0 waterAlert
            2.10.1.0 waterName
            2.10.2.0 waterAlertStatus
        )}
    );
    my @critical;
    my @ok;

    my $perfdata = "";

    for my $sensor (sort keys %sensors) {
        if ($sensor =~ m/temperature/) {
            $perfdata .=
                check_temp($sensor, $sensors{$sensor}, \@ok, \@critical);
        } elsif ($sensor =~ m/umidity/) {
            $perfdata .=
                check_humidity($sensor, $sensors{$sensor}, \@ok, \@critical);
        } elsif ($sensor =~ m/ontact/) {
            $perfdata .=
                check_contact($sensor, $sensors{$sensor}, \@ok, \@critical);
        } elsif ($sensor =~ m/water/) {
            $perfdata .=
                check_water($sensor, $sensors{$sensor}, \@ok, \@critical);
        }
    }
    my $output = "$LABEL ";
    my $level = OK;
    if (scalar(@critical) > 0) {
        $output .= 'CRITICAL - ' . join(', ', @critical) . ' ';
        $level = CRITICAL;
    }
    if (scalar(@ok) > 0) {
        $output .= ' OK - ' . join(', ', @ok);
    }
    print "$output | $perfdata \n";

    return $level;
    sub check_temp {
        my $name = shift;
        my $data = shift;
        my $ok = shift;
        my $critical = shift;
        Nenm::Utils::debug("Checking temperature sensor $name");
        my $rs = snmp_get($data);
        if ($rs->{"${name}CurrentValue"} eq "655350") {
            Nenm::Utils::debug("$name not active: skipping");
            return '';
        }
```

```perl
    my $value = sprintf("%.2f", $rs->{"${name}CurrentValue"} / 10);
    my $unit = $rs->{"${name}Unit"};

    my $low = $rs->{"${name}LowThreshold"};
    my $high = $rs->{"${name}HighThreshold"};

    my $s_unit = ($unit =~ m/^(.)/)[0];
    my $output = $rs->{"${name}Name"} . ": $value$s_unit";

    if ($rs->{"${name}Alert"} == 1) {

        $output .= " - ALERT ";

        if ($value >= $high) {
            $output .= "(>= $high$s_unit)";
        }

        if ($value <= $low) {
            $output .= "(<= $low$s_unit)";
        }

        push(@$critical, $output);

    } else {
    push(@$ok, $output);
    }

    my $perf_label = $name;
    $perf_label =~ s/([a-z])([A-Z])/$1_\L$2/g;

    return "'temperature_${perf_label}'=$value$s_unit;0;$low:$high ";

}
sub check_humidity {

    my $name = shift;
    my $data = shift;
    my $ok = shift;
    my $critical = shift;

    Nenm::Utils::debug("Checking humidity sensor $name");

    my $rs = snmp_get($data);

    if ($rs->{"${name}CurrentValue"} eq "655350") {
        Nenm::Utils::debug("$name not active: skipping");
        return '';
    }

    my $value = sprintf("%.2f", $rs->{"${name}CurrentValue"} / 10);

    my $low = $rs->{"${name}LowThreshold"};
    my $high = $rs->{"${name}HighThreshold"};

    my $output = $rs->{"${name}Name"} . ": $value\%";

    if ($rs->{"${name}Alert"} == 1) {

        if ($value >= $high) {
            $output .= " (>= $high\%)";
        }

        if ($value <= $low) {
            $output .= " (<= $low\%)";
        }
```

```perl
            push(@$critical, $output);
        } else {
            push(@$ok, $output);
        }

    my $perf_label = $name;
    $perf_label =~ s/([a-z])([A-Z])/$1_\L$2/g;
    return "'humidity_${perf_label}'=$value\%;0;$low:$high;0;100 ";
}
sub check_contact {
    my $name = shift;
    my $data = shift;
    my $ok = shift;
    my $critical = shift;
    my %alert_on_states = qw(
        0 open
        1 closed
    );
    my %states = qw(
        0 open
        1 closed
    );
    Nenm::Utils::debug("Checking contact sensor $name");
    my $rs = snmp_get($data);
    my $state = $states{$rs->{"${name}Status"}};
    my $alert_on = $alert_on_states{$rs->{"${name}AlertStatus"}};
    my $output = $rs->{"${name}Name"} . ": $state";
    if ($rs->{"${name}Alert"} == 1) {
        push(@$critical, $output);
    } else {
        $output .= " (alert when $alert_on)";
        push(@$ok, $output);
    }

    my $perf_label = $name;
    $perf_label =~ s/([a-z])([A-Z])/$1_\L$2/g;
    return
        "'contact_${perf_label}'=" . $rs->{"${name}Status"} . ';;' .
        $rs->{"${name}AlertStatus"} . ';0;1 ';
}
sub check_water {
    my $name = shift;
    my $data = shift;
    my $ok = shift;
    my $critical = shift;
```

```perl
    my %alert_on_states = qw(
        0 open
        1 closed
    );

    my %states = qw(
        0 open
        1 closed
    );

    Nenm::Utils::debug("Checking water sensor $name");

    my $rs = snmp_get($data);

    my $state = $states{$rs->{"${name}Status"}};
    my $alert_on = $alert_on_states{$rs->{"${name}AlertStatus"}};

    my $output = $rs->{"${name}Name"} . ": $state";

    if ($rs->{"${name}Alert"} == 1) {
        push(@$critical, $output);
    } else {
        $output .= " (alert when $alert_on)";
        push(@$ok, $output);
    }

    my $perf_label = $name;
    $perf_label =~ s/([a-z])([A-Z])/$1_\L$2/g;
    return
        "'${perf_label}'=" . $rs->{"${name}Status"} . ';0;' .
        $rs->{"${name}AlertStatus"} . ';0;1 ';

}

sub snmp_get {
    my $data = shift;

    local($_);

    my @oids = map { "${BASE_OID}.$_"; } keys %$data;
    Nenm::Utils::debug("SNMP get " . join(', ', @oids));

    my $get_results = $PLUGIN->get(@oids);

    my $results;

    for my $oid (keys %$get_results) {
        my $value = $get_results->{$oid};
        $oid =~ s/$BASE_OID\.//;
        $results->{$data->{$oid}} = $value;
        Nenm::Utils::debug("Set $data->{$oid} to $value");
    }

    return $results;

    }
}
exit check_enviromux_mini();
```

244 Chapter 4 • Plug-ins, Plug-ins, and More Plug-ins

Summary

In this chapter, we presented a number of example checks we hope you will find useful and inspire you to develop your own checks. While Nagios traditionally has been used as a network and systems monitoring framework, it can be used to monitor the health of any device, application, or system you can get metrics from. All the checks presented in this chapter are also available online from the book site.

## Chapter 5

Add-ons and Enhancements

Solutions in this chapter:

- **Checking Private Services when SNMP Is Not Allowed**

- **Visualization**

- **PNP—PNP Not PerfParse**

- **Cacinda**

- **NLG—Nagios Looking Glass**

- **SNMP Trap Handling**

- **SNMPTT**

- **NagTrap**

- **Text-to-Speech for Nagios Alerts**

- ☑ **Summary**

Introduction

Thanks to a very enthusiastic user/developer base, there is a large and continually growing set of add-ons and enhancements available for Nagios. These projects manipulate, massage, ingest, and display data in ways that extend far beyond the capabilities of the core Nagios system. In this chapter we discuss a number of enhancements and add-ons we feel are very useful in a larger environment.

Checking Private Services when SNMP Is Not Allowed

NRPE

Download it from: http://www.nagios.org/download/addons/

    Windows version: http://www.miwi-dv.com/nrpent/

    Monitoring and security requirements often clash when the monitoring server sits in one security zone and the managed server sits in a different security zone. For example, web servers are often hosted in DMZ zones. With most DMZs, SNMP traffic is not allowed, yet IT staff is still expected to monitor systems in the DMZ and identify issues early. Outages to servers in a high-visibility security zone like a DMZ means trouble for most companies as quite often corporate web servers are located in a DMZ.

DMZs and Network Security

NRPE allows Nagios to monitor systems that sit in security zones where traffic is only allowed to flow either from the client to the Nagios server or from the Nagios server to the managed client. Security policies generally dictate that systems in high-visibility security zones (like a DMZ) may not initiate communications with systems sitting in more trusted zones; however, often a monitoring system in the more trusted security zone will be allowed to communicate with clients in the DMZ for monitoring purposes. These same policies also often prohibit the use of SNMP v1 or SNMP v2c as the two are not encrypted and depend on UDP as their layer 4 transport. NRPE uses TCP and can encrypt traffic between the server and client using SSL (Figure 5.1).

Figure 5.1 NRPE Information Flow across a Security Zone

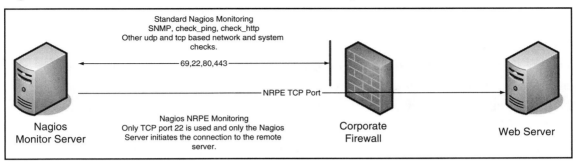

In order to use NRPE in your network, you should make the following changes to the firewall that sits between the Nagios server and the DMZ host being monitored:

1. Create a firewall ACL that allows the Nagios host to communicate with the DMZ host over TCP port 5666, which is the default port the NRPE client uses to listen for incoming connections requests.

2. Connections initiated from the DMZ Web server to the internal network are not permitted.

3. All traffic between the Nagios server and Web server is encrypted using TLS (SSL) encryption.

4. On the DMZ Web server, tcp_wrappers should be configured to only accept NRPE connections from the internal Nagios server or firewall IP address (if NAT is in use) on TCP port 5666.

Security Caveats

If NRPE is run with the configuration parameter *dont_blame_nrpe* set to 1, it will allow remote clients to send arbitrary command arguments to the NRPE daemon. If NRPE is allowed to run in this mode it essentially acts as a remote shell for any server that can connect to the NRPE client. We highly recommend that you do not enable this mode of NRPE.

NRPE Details

NRPE allows the Nagios server to run Nagios plug-ins on a managed client. To install NRPE, you will need both the Nagios plug-ins and OpenSSL installed on the Nagios server. Install the OpenSSL libraries on the Nagios server to allow the *check_nrpe* plugin to communicate with remote NRPE clients using TLS / SSL. The NRPE documentation is quite good and from this point on we assume that you have an NRPE daemon running on a remote server and we assume that check_nrpe has been compiled and installed on your Nagios server using the default settings.

NRPE in the Enterprise

By default, NRPE is configured to monitor basic system metrics. We see many configurations where basic measures of system health are checked: disk usage, memory utilization and whether or not critical network-based system services are running (SSH, Apache)—but often administrators do not take the time to fully exploit NRPE to check higher-level application functionlity.

Scenario 1: The Internet Web Server

You have a small business Web server. You are running NRPE on the host and checking basic services based on your web_server template. This includes disk space utilization, memory utilization, number of active Apache processes, and number of active tomcat Java processes. With these settings in place you know you will be alerted when there is a critical service failure. Do not stop here; there are other types of failures that can mean big problems for your web server and NRPE can help you spot them.

This is where we use NRPE as the eyes of our environment. For example, we can use *check_http* to check for a variety of problems with our web server. We can use the command *check_http -e -N <server-name>* to verify that the layer 7 firewall we use stops invalid HTTP requests from reaching our web server. We can use the –s option of check_http to verify that critical parts of our web site return the content we expect them to contain. HTTP content returned from the web server. The value of this type of checking is that we verify that our application is functioning as expected from the perspective of a customer.

When using NRPE on a DMZ Web server, it is best to identify standard text in the Web page near the bottom of the document (not in a header or footer) that you can check with check_http's –r or –s options. By checking for content on a web page, you can identify when problems occur in the application that impact your users.

NSCA

Download it from: http://www.nagios.org/download/addons/

NSCA (Nagios Service Check Acceptor) allows you to configure devices and applications to send asynchronous events to Nagios. The event information can be encrypted in a variety of ways, and a password can be required in order for the server-side of NSCA to accept the incoming event. This framework is a terrific alternative or supplement to having devices send out SNMP traps and then ingesting them into Nagios using a framework like SNMPTT.

NSCA can be downloaded from the main Nagios site (www.nagios.org). The installation instructions are easy to follow and installation is simple. Once installed, the NSCA server can be run on the Nagios server as a daemon (the package comes with a SysV-style init script that can be placed in /etc/init.d/ to start and stop the NSCA daemon). The daemon will listen for incoming NSCA requests sent by the client-side send_nsca utility. When received, requests are authenticated using one of over a dozen encryption algorithms along with an optional administrator-configured password. The password chosen must be entered in the NSCA server configuration file and every NSCA client configuration file. If you are not using NSCA in a trusted environment, we highly recommend creating a complex password and using a strong encryption algorithm. We also recommend that in untrusted environments you use firewall rules to limit which client servers can communicate with your NSCA daemon. Once an NSCA client and server are configured, you can use the send_nsca utility to send events from the client for anything you can script—from hard disk errors, to application-level events, to security events (Figure 5.2).

Figure 5.2 NSCA Information Flow

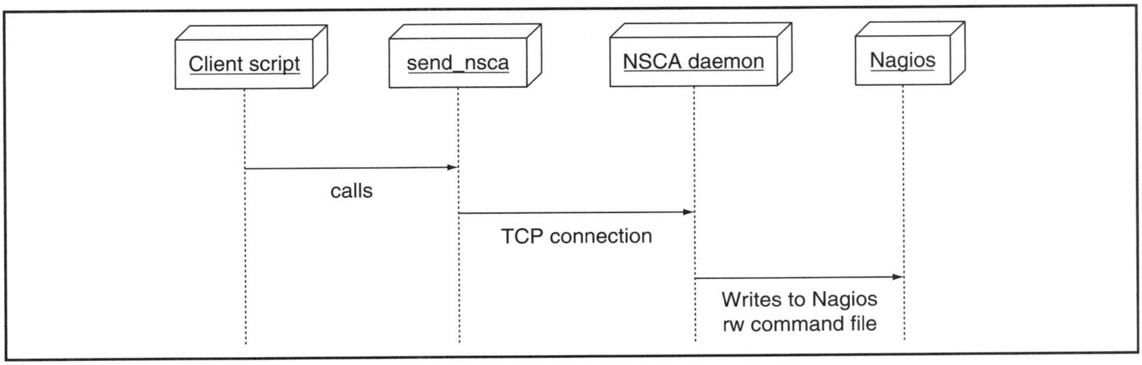

Visualization

While Nagios has a very easy to read and well-designed network map front end, there are times when a logical view by device is not what your users want. For example, developers and application-specific support personnel might prefer a view that shows status organized logically and by service as that is the focus of their work—ensure the application they are responsible for is running and responding in a reasonable amount of time.

NagVis

Download it from: http://www.nagvis.org/

In larger, heterogeneous organizations, the number of system and host problems that occur in any given day can easily clutter up a screen, even a big one. There will also be staff members in your organization who do not want to see network maps or tables of problems, be that because they find the data intimidating or because they only care about application health as opposed to system and network health. Enter NagVis, another very useful add-on that lets you visualize data from Nagios in a variety of useful and creative ways. NagVis uses a PHP-based front and can either read host and service data directly from the Nagios CGIs (not recommended) or from a MySQL database that has been populated with Nagios status information using the NDO Utils package. In this section, we give you tips on installing and configuring this add-on, and show examples of how to make best use of NagVis.

We recommend (the NagVis team does, too) that you use the database back end for service and host data. For large groups, this greatly reduces the overhead of NagVis on a system and provides much better performance than the CGI-based back end does. Configuring NagVis to use a database involves the following steps:

1. Enable the event broker in Nagios.
2. Download and install NDO Utils.
3. Download, install, and configure NagVis.
4. We cover each of these steps in this section.

Enable the Event Broker in Nagios

If you did not enable the event broker functionality in Nagios 3 when you installed it, you can re-run *configure* in the Nagios 3 distribution directory and pass it the switch *--enable-event-broker*. After running *configure*, re-run *make* and then *make install-base* and *make install-commandmode* to re-install just the Nagios daemon with the event broker capability enabled. You then must tell Nagios to broker everything through the event broker by setting the following parameter in your nagios.cfg file:

```
event_broker_options=-1
```

Finally, you must restart Nagios so your new event-broker enabled Nagios daemon is running.

Install the NDO Utils Package

Download it from: http://www.nagios.org/download/addons/

The NDO Utils package captures service and host configuration information and host and service events from Nagios and populates a database with the information. It is available for download from the main Nagios site under the Downloads section. While the module developers warn in the README that it is experimental/beta quality, we have not experienced any problems with this module in a production environment. NDO consists of two parts: the NDOMOD event broker module that receives events from Nagios and then makes the events available to remote clients over a TCP/IP socket or appends data to a file on the Nagios server, and a data ingestion program that processes the data. NDO comes with two programs that read events produced by the NDOMOD module; FILE2SOCK reads the NDOMOD data from the file output of NDOMOD and sends it over the network to a remote instance of NDO2DB, and NDODB, which can receive data from FILE2SOCK or NDOMOD directly and populate a database with the information. If you have the good fortune of having a separate machine to use just for visualization, make use of FILE2SOCK and offload the data ingestion and visualization functions onto the second machine. We will assume for the rest of this section that you are running Nagios and NagVis on the same host, as that is likely to be the most common situation Nagios integrators will encounter (Figure 5.3).

Figure 5.3 How Nagios, NDOMOD, and NDO2DB Interact to Populate a Database with Nagios Events

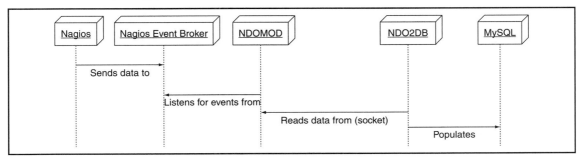

Follow the instructions in the README that comes with NDO Utils carefully and you will have NDOMOD and NDO2DB installed and running in no time. If you have multiple versions of MySQL installed on your host or have MySQL installed in a nonstandard location, use the command *mysql_config --libs* to determine which directory your MySQL libraries are installed in and then pass that directory to the configure script as *--with-mysql-lib=/path/to/mysql/lib*. also keep in mind that if you do not have Nagios installed in the default location (*/usr/local/nagios*), you need to pass the base path of your installation to the NDODB configure script using the *--prefix* option of configure. Finally, if you are not using the user and group *nagios* for your Nagios daemon, pass the names of the group and user to configure using the *--with-ndo2db-user* and *--with-ndo2db-group* switches.

After you make NDO, install the NDOMOD and NDO2DB files according to the instructions in the README. The README does not currently include an init script, so here is one you can use on Redhat-like Linux systems to control the NDO2DB daemon:

```
#!/bin/bash

# chkconfig: - 50 50

# description: NDO2DB - Nagios NDO to database daemon
#
# processname: ndo2db
# pidfile: /var/run/ndo2db.pid

NBASE=/home/nagios
ndo2db=$NBASE/bin/ndo2db

# source function library
. /etc/init.d/functions
case "$1" in
  start)
     echo -n $"Starting ndo2db: "
     daemon $ndo2db -c $NBASE/etc/ndo2db.cfg
     RETVAL=$?
     Echo
  ;;
stop)
   echo -n $"Stopping ndo2db: "
   killproc $ndo2db
   RETVAL=$?
   echo
;;

restart)
   echo -n $"Restarting ndo2db: "
```

```
   $0 stop
   sleep 30
   $0 start
;;
status)
   status ndo2db
   RETVAL=$?
;;
*)
   echo $"Usage: $0 {start|stop|status|restart}"
   RETVAL=1

Esac

exit $RETVAL
```

After installing NDO2DB and NODMOD by following the README file, restart Nagios to activate the NDOMOD module, and then start NDO2DB to activate the NDO database daemon:

```
/etc/init.d/ndo2db start
```

If everything is installed and configured properly, you will see a line like the following in your /var/log/messages file:

```
Jan 6 17:44:31 hostname nagios: ndomod: Successfully flushed 117 queued
items to data sink.
```

Download and Install NagVis, Configure It to Use the Database Back End You Set up with NDO

Now we will install and configure NagVis. Download the latest stable distribution from http://www.nagvis.org and follow the instructions in the INSTALL file to install NagVis. Note that when the instructions mention "Move the nagvis directory tree," they mean the distribution directory, not the nagvis directory you see under the distribution directory. Following the instructions, configure NagVis to use the database you set up when installing and configuring NDO utils on your system. Finally, integrate links to the project into the Nagios GUI to make it easy for users to find by adding code like the following to <path-to-nagios>/share/side.html:

```
   <br/>
   <br/>
```

```
<table width="150">
 <tr>
  <td>
   <table width="100%" class="NavBarTitle" cellspacing="0">
    <tr>
    <td class="NavBarTitle">Add-Ons</td>
   </tr>
   </table>
  </td>
 </tr>
</table>


<br/>


<table width="150" border="0" cellpadding=0 cellspacing=0>
    <tr>
    <td width=13><img src="images/greendot.gif" width="13" height="14"
        name="config-dot"></td>
    <td nowrap width=134><a href="/nagios/nagvis/" target="main"
        onMouseOver="switchdot('nagvis-dot',1)"
        onMouseOut="switchdot('nagvis-dot',0)"
        class="NavBarItem">NagVis Maps</a></td>
    </tr>
</table>
```

Now that you are done with installation, the sky is the limit. The NagVis home page has many examples of the kinds of visualization you can do with NagVis. Many people use NagVis to show network and system paths in a manner that is more visually appealing than the default Nagios status map; however, we have found it works very well for showing high-level application and service status as well.

Example one: You work in a software development shop and find yourself monitoring multiple development and integration environments. In these environments, it is typical for services to go up and down regularly and for a number of people to want to know the status of services in each environment at-a-glance. Your users are most likely not going to appreciate receiving large numbers of emails about service and host outages, as they are expecting services and hosts to be relatively instable. This is the type of situation in which NagVis shines; at a glance, developers, system administrators, and system integrators can easily see the status of multiple environments from one place. As with any enhancement to Nagios, talk to your users and customers when you install this add-on; educate them on what it can do and solicit their feedback on how it can be used to best meet their needs.

Example two: Network Operations Center (NOC). In many NOCs, staffing is 24×7 and staff are hired and quit on a regular basis. Educating and training staff about applications on a network or set of networks quickly is very important. Using NagVis, you can create maps that show the status of applications and make it visually very easy for staff to learn about the relationships between the pieces of the applications without having to spend hours reading system and network documentation (most NOC staff do not ever get the time to do that). Additionally, this has the benefit of making it easy for NOC staff to communicate to application- or network-specific personnel what has gone wrong and where that piece sits within an application.

PNP—PNP Not PerfParse

Download it from: http://www.pnp4nagios.org/pnp/

PNP is a gem of an add-on; it allows a Nagios administrator to easily add RRD-style graphs and efficient long-term trending (four years per metric by default) capabilities to Nagios. Like the rest of the Nagios configuration framework and much like Cacti (at least one piece of PNP is borrowed from Cacti), this graphing framework makes extensive use of templates and is easy to customize. It consists of a PHP-based front end that lives under the Nagios web document directory and a Perl/C based back end that processes performance data produced by Nagios using RRDtool (www.rrdtool.org). RRDtool manipulates RRD files efficiently, and includes a powerful graphing language. The RRD files PNP produces are space efficient; a single metric takes up approximately 400k of space for four years' worth of trending. If you are familiar with Cacti, once you have PNP installed and integrated with Nagios you will find it very easy to use and very useful. We highly recommend you choose the *Batch Mode + NPCD* of operation (explained later).

In this section, we provide recommendations on the installation and configuration of PNP. We then describe how to add performance data to your scripts in a format Nagios and PNP can read. We finish with an example of a custom PNP template to make an easy-to-read, useful graph from the output of a custom Nagios check (CPU utilization in this case). Examples in this section all assume PNP is using the batch mode and NPCD daemon mode of operation.

There are three ways to configure Nagios and PNP to get data from Nagios into PNP:

- **Default mode** Configure Nagios to directly call the PNP RRD (round-robin database) file creation script (process_perfdata.pl) with performance data from Nagios every N seconds.

- **Batch mode** Configure Nagios to create host and service performance data files, and add process_perfdata.pl commands to the service and host file processing command directives of Nagios. process_perfdata.pl will then be called by Nagios to read and process the service and host performance files and update the RRD and XML files the PNP Web interface reads.

- **Batch mode + NPCD** Configure Nagios to create host and service performance data files, and to move those configuration files to a spool directory every N seconds. Then, compile and run npcd, a C-based daemon included with the PNP package. The daemon reads the performance files from the spool directory, and then spawns N instances of the graphing script at a time to ingest the files into RRD databases.

Option three provides the best scalability for large organizations and will allow your Nagios server to process the most performance data at a time without impacting the operation of Nagios, as in this mode, all Nagios does is create performance data files and periodically move them to a spool directory (Figure 5.4).

Figure 5.4 How PNP Processes Nagios Performance Data

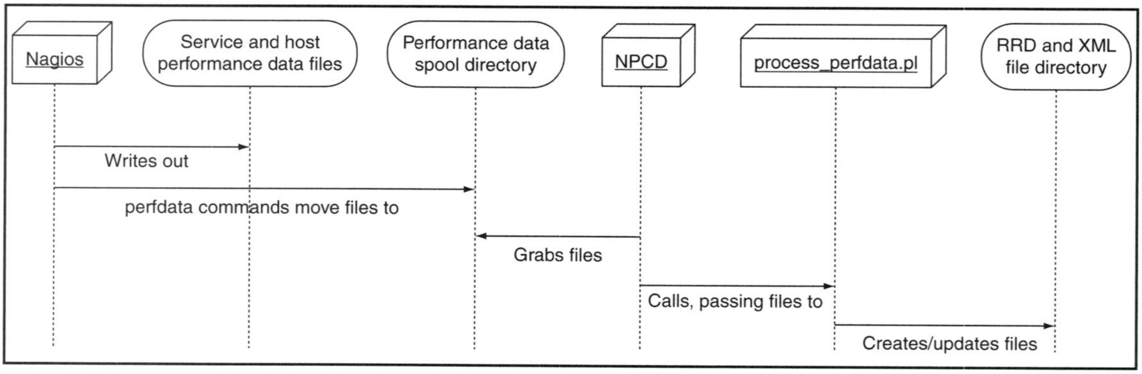

For best RRD creation and update performance, make sure you have the RRDs Perl module (comes with the source distribution of RRDtool) installed. You can check to see if you have this module by running the command:

```
perl -MRRDs -e 1
```

If you see no output from Perl when you run this command, the RRDs module is installed. If you see an error message, you might need to download and compile RRDtool from source yourself; the options *--with-perl* and *--with-perl-site-install* will enable the RRDs module and place it in your site-wide Perl library directory.

Configuring Nagios to create the performance data files the PNP npcd daemon reads and setting up base PNP configuration files is fairly easy. The documentation on the PNP site is very well done, so we will not repeat basic installation instructions here. We do recommend you follow the documentation carefully, as the process will fail if you miss any steps. Especially critical are the host and service performance data templates; make sure you enter those into your configuration file correctly.

Once you have PNP installed and configured correctly, you need to understand how to modify your scripts to produce performance data output in a manner Nagios understands. Nagios 3 parses any data in the output of a service check that follows a pipe "|" symbol as performance data. Performance data can include multiple metrics, and each metric can contain discreet warning, critical, minimum, and maximum values. From the Nagios perfdata documentation (http://nagiosplug.sourceforge.net/developer-guidelines.html#AEN203):

```
| 'label1'=value;[warn];[crit];[min];[max] … 'labelN'=value;[warn];[crit];[min];[max]
```

Sample output from a service check that uses this format:

```
ROBOTIC_TEST OK: 340 results in 3.034 seconds |'Retrieve home page'=1s;3,5;;;
'Perform search'=15s;20;30;;
```

From the output of this check, we know:

- The test performed acceptably and involved a Web search that returned 340 results.
- Home page retrieval took 1 second, has a warning threshold of 3 seconds, a critical threshold of 5 seconds, and no min or max output values.
- Logout took 2 seconds, has a warning threshold of 5 seconds, a critical threshold of 15 seconds, and no min or max output values.

NOTE

Your performance data can include data that goes well beyond the single status your check returns, yielding a very nice separation of fault management data vs. service performance trending data.

Now that we have our performance data in a format Nagios and PNP will recognize, we need to configure the service so Nagios processes performance data from it by setting the service parameter *process_perf_data* to 1 and restarting Nagios. We then create a PNP graph template so we can see all the performance data from our Nagios check in one place. PNP templates are PHP files that generate a custom command line that will be passed to rrdtool along with a string containing the RRD tool language necessary to create your graph. For more information on the RRD tool and RRD language, see www.rrdtool.org/.

PNP first looks for templates under <nagios-share>/pnp/templates.dist, and then under <nagios-share>/pnp/templates for a PHP template file to use to display a custom graph for a service. Custom template files should be named for the service with which they are associated. If no custom template file is found, the default template default.php will be used.

We will place our custom check graph template in the directory <nagios-share>/pnp/templates. An easy way to get started on a custom template is to find an existing template under the templates.dist directory, copy it to the templates directory, and then modify it to meet your needs. For this check, we copied the check_load.php template, as it shows multiple RRD sources on a single graph. Here is the template we created based on the Net-SNMP CPU check shown in Chapter 4 in this book:

```php
<?php
$opt[1] = "--vertical-label '% Utilization' " .
    "--title '$hostname: $NAGIOS_SERVICEDESC' -X 0 -M";

$colors = array(
   'idle' => '00FF00',
   'user' => '0000FF',
   'system' => 'FF0000',
   'kernel' => '999999',
   'interrupt' => '999900',
   'wait' => 'FF9900',
   'nice' => '00FF00'
);

$graph = "";

$i = 1;

foreach ($DS as $d) {
   if ($NAME[$d] == 'idle') {
      continue;
   }

   $type = 'STACK';
```

```
   if ($i == 1) {
      $type = 'AREA';

   }
   $i++;

   $label = sprintf("%-9s", ucfirst($NAME[$d]));
   $graph .= <<<EOF
DEF:var$d=$rrdfile:$DS[$d]:AVERAGE
$type:var$d#{$colors[$NAME[$d]]}:"$label"
GPRINT:var$d:LAST:" Cur %6.2lf "
GPRINT:var$d:MAX:"Max %6.2lf \\n"

EOF;
   if ($i == 1) {
      $type = 'AREA';
   }
   $i++;

   $label = sprintf("%-9s", ucfirst($NAME[$d]));

   $graph .= <<<EOF
DEF:var$d=$rrdfile:$DS[$d]:AVERAGE
$type:var$d#{$colors[$NAME[$d]]}:"$label"
GPRINT:var$d:LAST:" Cur %6.2lf "
GPRINT:var$d:MAX:"Max %6.2lf \\n"

EOF;

}

$def[1] = preg_replace('/[\r\n]/', ' ', $graph);

?>
```

Now we browse to http://example.org/pnp?host=myhost to see our new graph. Figure 5.5 is a screenshot of what the output looks like.

Figure 5.5 PNP-based Net-SNMP CPU Utilization Graph

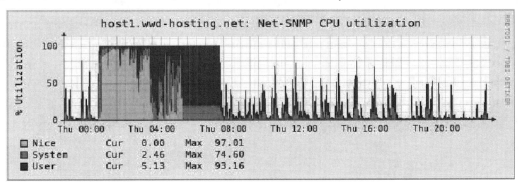

The power of this framework is that this graph will be generated for any new hosts you add to Nagios that are associated with this Nagios check.

Finally, integrate PNP into the Nagios HTML GUI by adding some custom HTML code to <path-to-nagios>/share/side.html. This example adds HTML that will take you to the custom pages section of PNP when the "PNP Graphs" link is clicked (just remove the word *page* from the link to go to the default PNP index page). Add the code to the bottom of the file, before the ending </body> tag:

```
<br/>
<table width="150" border="0" cellpadding=0 cellspacing=0>
  <tr>
      <td width=13><img src="images/greendot.gif" width="13" height="14"
      name="config-dot"></td>
  <td nowrap width=134><a href="/nagios/pnp/index.php?page" target="main"
      onMouseOver="switchdot('pnp-dot',1)"
      onMouseOut="switchdot('pnp-dot',0)"
      class="NavBarItem">PNP Graphs</a></td>
  </tr>
</table>
```

Cacinda

Download it from: http://cacinda.sf.net/

If your shop is more Cacti-oriented and you use Nagios purely for service and status checks or you have a very large Cacti install and are just starting to use Nagios, Cacinda can help you create HTML-based dashboards that integrate the information from Cacti and Nagios along with live SNMP data from your devices. Warning: Cacinda is an alpha release; when it is stable, it will be released as a Cacti plug-in. Despite its new status, getting it set up and running is straightforward. Like most Nagios and Cacti add-ons, Cacinda uses templates to allow you to handle multiple device types easily and create customized HTML views for metrics from a variety of SNMP devices.

Installation of Cacinda is straightforward; just download the source code from http://cacinda.sf.net, untar it into a directory under your Web server's document root, and configure it by editing the config.pnp file that comes with the distribution. The first section of the Cacinda configuration file is used to configure Cacinda so it can select data from your Cacti database. The second section is to tell Cacinda the base URL for Nagios, and configure a username and password to use to log in to Nagios if Nagios requires authentication. Finally, you may configure a search and replace string pair that will help you match Cacti host names to Nagios names. For example, if you use fully qualified host names in Cacti, but short names in Nagios, you can use this to strip the domain portion of each Cacti host name so the names will work with Nagios.

Cacti uses templates for each device type you wish to display a dashboard for; the current release supports Cisco devices, Microsoft SNMP agents, and Net-SNMP agents. Cacti checks the SNMP sysDescr.0 and sysObjectId.0 SNMP OIDs to try to match devices with templates; if a suitable template cannot be found, a descriptive error page will appear. A template can include graphs from Cacti, output from Nagios, and live SNMP data. Cacinda uses the PHP package Image_Graph for creating live graphs.

Once you have Cacinda properly configured, you can create useful and aesthetically pleasing dashboards for your users and administrators to use to view host status. Dashboard pages will refresh every five minutes to display data updates. Eventually, the author of this project plans to make Cacinda a Cacti plug-in to make it easier to install and configure (Figures 5.6 and 5.7).

Figure 5.6 How Cacinda Retrieves Data from Nagios and Cacti

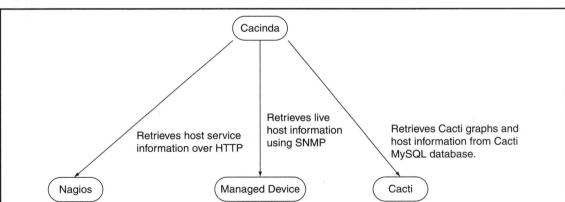

Figure 5.7 Cacinda Screenshot

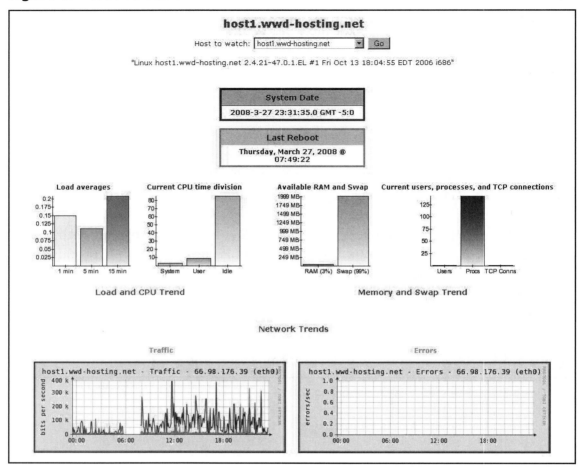

NLG—Nagios Looking Glass

Download it from: http://www.nagioslookingglass.co.uk

Nagios Looking Glass (NLG) is a PHP-based project that allows you to set up a read-only status site that sits outside your Nagios security zone (DMZ for example). The software consists of two pieces: a client that resides on the system end users will access to view Nagios host and service status; and a server piece that sits on the Nagios server (under the *share* directory) that communicates with the client to retrieve Nagios status files. We tried version 1.10 b1 for the purposes of this book, as it supports Nagios 3.

The software requirements for the system are fairly standard; it does require PHP 5.1 or newer for both the client and server sides (we used php 5.2.5). The project allows the administrator to customize the look, feel, and output of the NLG site. Even the thresholds for the front-end screen network and metric health bars can be customized. Most users will find the default look and feel aesthetically pleasing. NLG provides views that non-technical staff and managers will find especially pleasing, although technical staff will find much of the same detailed information available in the NLG Web GUI the core Nagios GUI produces (Figures 5.8 and 5.9).

Figure 5.8 Nagios Looking Glass Data Flow

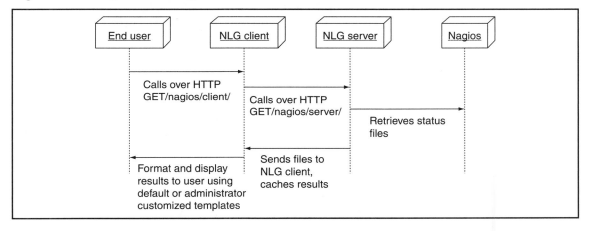

Figure 5.9 Nagios Looking Glass in Action

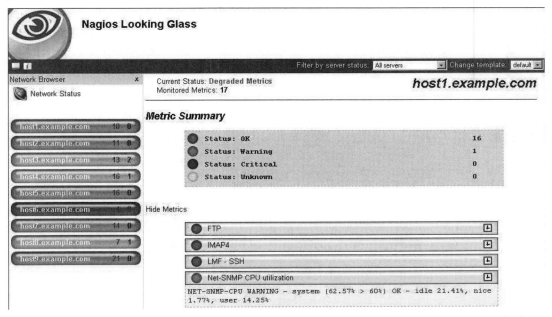

SNMP Trap Handling

Many open source monitoring packages lack the capability to ingest and process SNMP traps. While Nagios does not come "out of the box" with this capability, enabling it is fairly easy due to the open nature of Nagios. While configuring SNMP agents to send traps is sometimes a bit complex, the benefits of being able to receive traps are that events are received much closer to when they occur compared to waiting for polling to happen and those events take fewer system resources to process than do polled events. In this section, we give an overview of SNMPTT, a trap-handling program that hooks into Net-SNMP's snmptrapd. We then discuss how to make use of NagTrap, an open source trap viewer for Nagios.

Net-SNMP and snmptrapd

Download it from: http://net-snmp.sourceforge.net/

If you use SNMP with Nagios and are not familiar with Net-SNMP, you either are not managing Unix and Unix-like systems or you are fortunate enough to have a budget that allows you to use a commercial agent. Net-SNMP is an open source, extensible SNMP agent and suite of SNMP utilities. The only commercial agent we have used that exceeds its functionality is the CA (formerly Empire Technologies) SysEdge agent, which retails for over $3k per instance. Net-SNMP runs on a wide variety of Unix and Unix-like platforms and Windows. snmptrapd is a trap listener included with the Net-SNMP distribution; it will receive traps and then has a very flexible configuration that allows you to specify hooks to handle traps based on source IP, authentication, and/or OID. SNMPTT relies on snmptrapd, so make sure you download and install snmptrapd before installing SNMPTT.

SNMPTT

Download it from: http://www.snmptt.org/

SNMPTT (SNMP Trap Translator) is a Perl-based program developed by the Net-SNMP group. It translates traps from SNMP to more human-readable formats (or other computer-parsable formats). It can also populate databases or files with the traps. NagTrap reads SNMPTT translated traps from a MySQL database. Download and install SNMPTT and follow the directions to enable it to store traps in MySQL before installing NagTrap.

Configuring SNMPTT for Maintainability and Configuration File Growth

SNMPTT allows an administrator to specify multiple configuration files for event definitions; take advantage of this feature to divide your configuration into files by device type or event type. For example, if we have events coming in from Oracle Enterprise Manager (OEM), Digi devices, and Bluecoat proxies, we might use the directory /usr/local/snmp/etc/snmptt/ to place configuration snippets for each device type in. We tell SNMPTT to look at multiple files by adding them to the snmptt_conf_files variable in the SNMPTT main configuration file; since SNMPTT is written in Perl, it uses an INI parser that understands Perl HERE document syntax. For example:

```
snmptt_conf_files = <<EOF
/usr/local/snmp/etc/snmptt/oem.conf
/usr/local/snmp/etc/snmptt/digi.conf
/usr/local/snmp/etc/snmptt/bluecoat.conf
EOF
```

NagTrap

Download it from: http://www.nagtrap.org/

NagTrap is an open-source Nagios add-on that reads SNMP traps from a database created by SNMPTT (SNMP Trap Translator). It allows you to view, query, and filter traps by host name, severity, and category from a PHP-based Web interface. It also allows you to archive traps through the GUI. Finally, it includes a script to help you get traps from SNMPTT into Nagios (Figure 5.10).

Figure 5.10 NagTrap Data Flow

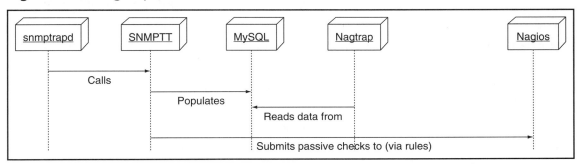

Download NagTrap from http://www.nagtrap.org. Installation is straightforward and well documented. Two changes we recommend making are:

1. Change the format line field in the snmptt database from type varchar(255) to text(2000) as a number of traps will exceed the varchar(255) limit.

2. Add indexes to the SNMPTT table; we recommend adding indexes to the category and severity fields at a minimum.

While SNMPTT comes with a script that can be run as a check from Nagios that polls the SNMPTT database for new traps, we believe you will get better performance by adding script triggers to your SNMPTT configuration files that submit passive checks to Nagios as this keeps Nagios from having to poll yet another data source. We discuss how to do this and show an example script that will allow you to do this in the next section of this chapter. Ingesting Traps into Nagios.

SNMPTT allows you to specify a custom script to be called when a match for an OID is found in a configuration file you create. This hook makes it easy for us to then submit alerts to Nagios as passive checks. Since most devices we deal with will likely send dozens if not more events to your SNMPTT instance, we find it easiest to create a passive check per device type and then define the severity of the event in the SNMPTT configuration line. For example, if we have a Raritan configured to send Nagios SNMPT traps we might create a "Raritan Event" passive check that can be used to accept any of the 30 or so SNMP traps the Raritan can send.

The hardest part of ingesting traps from SNMPTT into Nagios is mapping the device names and IPs to your Nagios names and IPs. Since some devices are multihomed, you might receive a trap from a device with a source IP address in the trap that does not match the IP you have configured for the device in Nagios. There are several ways to work around this situation. First, you can change your Nagios configuration for the device in question so the IP used for traps matches the IP you use for polling. Second, you can make sure every device you receive events from has a DNS PTR (reverse IP to name) record in DNS, and turn on DNS in SNMPTT. Third, and most flexible, you can just add a local database table or flat file where you can map these additional outside IPs to your inside IPs and write your script so it looks up the IP in this local cache before it tries to match the IP address in your Nagios to IP address data store.

There are two ways to query Nagios to get the official hostname for a device for which you have an IP address. The first is to write a wrapper script that will let you query your Nagios configurations, or a script that parses your Nagios host configurations and writes the IP to host name mappings to either a flat file or a database. This method places custom development effort on you but then means you have no extra components to add to Nagios to retrieve hostname or IP address information. The second way is to install NDO (mentioned earlier in this chapter) and then just query the Nagios event database using your favorite scripting language's database abstraction API.

For this SNMPTT to Nagios script, we chose to use NDO because we had it installed already for NagVis (mentioned earlier in this chapter). This made the SNMPTT to Nagios script very short and easy to write.

Here is an example of what an event configuration in SNMPTT looks like, including calls to our custom script:

```
EVENT kvmLoginSuccess .1.3.6.1.4.1.0.1.1 "KVM" warning
EXEC /path/to/script $ar $s "KVMi Event" "$Fz"
FORMAT Successful login: $1

EVENT kvmiLoginFailed .1.3.6.1.4.1.0.1.2 "KVM" critical
EXEC /path/to/script $ar $s "KVM Event" "$Fz"
FORMAT Failed login: $1

EVENT kvmGeneric 1.3.6.1.4.1.0.1.* "KVM" ok
EXEC /path/to/script $ar $s "KVM Event" "$Fz"
FORMAT $+*
```

Here is what a passive check configuration in Nagios that receives events from this script looks like; note that we set up a "reset" freshness check that will be called to reset the state of the event to OK if a new event is not received within a period of time.

First, we define a base service template for the passive service:

```
define service {
  use                     generic-service
  name                    passive-base
  check_period            24×7
  flap_detection_enabled  0
  max_check_attempts      1
  active_checks_enabled   0
  passive_checks_enabled  1
  normal_check_interval   1
  retry_check_interval    1
  check_freshness         1
  freshness_threshold     3600
  process_perf_data       1
  contact_groups          admins
  notifications_enabled   0
  register                0

}
```

Then, we define a template for the Digi event service:

```
define service {
  use                     passive-base
  check_command           check_digi_freshness
  hostgroup_name          digi-hosts
  service_description      Digi Event
  contact_groups          admins
}
```

Finally, the command definition for the command that will reset the service to OK after one hour (3600 seconds) without a new event arriving:

```
define command {
  command_name check_digi_freshness
  command_line $USER1$/check_dummy 0
}
```

You can write the script to submit traps to Nagios from SNMPTT in whichever language you prefer. SNMPTT calls the script using the arguments you pass to the EXEC directive of SNMPTT. The script then should take the IP address of the device passed to it ($ar argument) and look that IP address up in the NDO nagios_hosts table by checking the value against the *address* field of the table. If the host name is not found, the script should exit with an error. If the host name is found, the script should then submit the check to Nagios by writing it in passive check format to the Nagios command file (/var/nagios/rw/nagios.cmd by default). Nagios will periodically read from this named pipe and associate any passive alerts with the devices they refer to. Here is an example diagram showing how this workflow all fits together:

Figure 5.11 SNMPTT to Nagios workflow

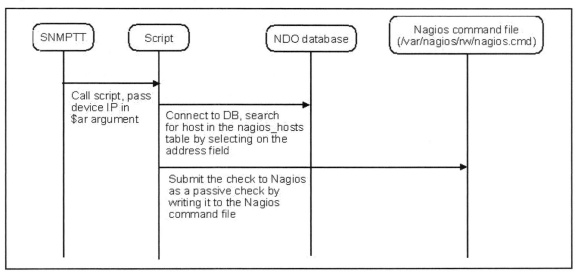

Translating SNMP trap MIBS to SNMPTT format is an easy process, and receiving events from all of our specialized devices and monitoring programs (like Oracle's OEM) has proven very useful.

Text-to-Speech for Nagios Alerts

Often, data center or technical managers or NOC staff think that having the alerting system speak alerts will make their lives much easier. Before long, however, you will see them shrink down in their seat as alerts are spoken or just quietly turn the volume down on the speakers of the alerting station. Spoken alerts must be implemented judiciously. Only have the text-to-speech system "say" the most critical alerts.

Something else to keep in mind when implementing text-to-speech is that even the better text-to-speech libraries will not pronounce words the way we might expect them to. Therefore, it will most likely be necessary to include in any text-to-speech scripts the capability to add custom word and phrase transformations that change words that trip up voice libraries into phonetic spellings that make them sound truer to their original spellings. For an example text-to-speech daemon that polls Nagios and "speaks" alerts, see Chapter 2.

Summary

As you can see, a wide variety of add-ons and enhancements let Nagios do much more than just monitor networks and systems by running plug-ins. A major strength of Nagios (and a feature that can be intimidating to new users) is its flexibility and openness. We have covered just a small portion of the add-ons available for Nagios in this chapter; we hope that the add-ons we discussed will get you excited about the Nagios community and the power that Nagios brings to administrators and users.

## Chapter 6

Enterprise Integration

Solutions in this chapter:

- Nagios as a Monitor of Monitors (MOM)
- LDAP Authentication
- Integration with Splunk
- Integrating with Third-Party Trend and Analysis Tools
- Multiple Administrators/Configuration Writers
- Integration with Puppet
- Integration with Trouble Ticketing Systems
- Nagios in the NOC

☑ Summary

Introduction

In an ideal world, an organization would choose one tool that would enable them to monitor and perform performance trending on every device and application in the organization, regardless of operating system. In reality, most organizations end up choosing a mix of best-of-breed tools. All these pieces need to be tied together to ensure your customer and your teammates do not spend all of their time remembering what tool to use. This chapter focuses on how to integrate Nagios with the types of tools, frameworks, and operational models commonly used in larger organizations.

Nagios as a Monitor of Monitors

A monitor of monitors (MOM) is a centralized console that receives events from remote applications, displays alerts, and can poll locally managed devices for status. It is important when designing a monitoring system to empower the staff who manage applications and systems within an organization with as much control over their monitoring systems as possible (Figure 6.1). It is also very important to let specialists in an organization use the tools they know work best for the type of monitoring they wish to do. For example, a network security team might prefer to manage its own instances of Snort, Tripwire and Nessus. Even these specialized systems will produce some alarms and events that your tier-1 and tier-2 staff need to know about due to their potential impact. Instead of forcing them to have to learn and use multiple tools to see these alerts, simplify their lives by letting the application experts decide which alarms need to be seen, and have the specialists configure their tools to forward these alerts to the central management server. SNMP traps or the Nagios NSCA frameworks can both be used for this purpose.

Figure 6.1 Monitor of Monitors in an Organization

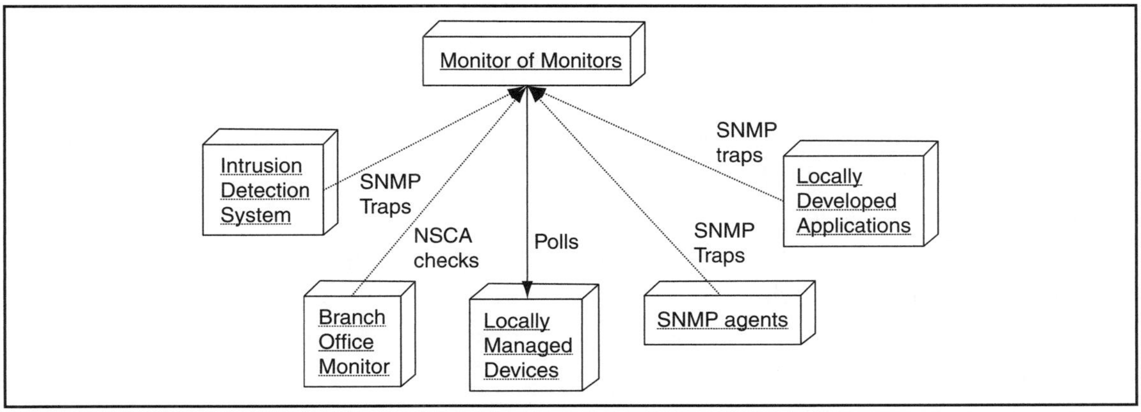

Nagios can fill this manager of managers role quite well. It can receive and display SNMP traps using SNMPTT and some simple integration code, it can receive passive events using the NSCA framework, and it can poll systems and applications in an organization for status. With its extensive visualization add-ons (NagVis, PHP, Nagios Looking Glass, to name a few), Nagios can provide end users with a multitude of customized views of data stored in Nagios. When planning a new Nagios installation or integrating Nagios into an existing organization, think about how Nagios might work in this role. Using Nagios as a Monitor of Monitors can make your life easier as an integrator. It also may make it much easier to convince an organization to adopt Nagios; not much thrills IT managers (especially service desk managers) more than hearing that they can simplify life for their staff while providing them with greater insight into IT operations.

LDAP Authentication

In this section, we discuss how to use LDAP as an authentication source for Nagios. We first discuss using LDAP for simple authentication based on mapping Nagios contacts to LDAP users. Then, we discuss how to make LDAP work for group authentication with Nagios.

One LDAP User, One Nagios User

Basic Nagios integration with LDAP is straight-forward. For most distributions of Linux and flavors of BSD, use the package administration tools that come with the operating system to install an Apache LDAP authentication module like mod_authnz_ ldap. For some flavors of Unix you might have to custom-compile the module. Set up a <Location> section in an .htaccess file or in one of the Apache server configuration files with mod_authnz_ldap directives so the configuration points to an LDAP server that contains the user accounts needing access to Nagios. Create the contact objects in Nagios so that the user IDs from LDAP map to the Nagios usernames. Finally, establish a base set of privileges for all users and hard-code the names of the Nagios administrators in the Nagios CGI configuration file. Keep in mind that with this method of authentication, the Nagios administrator will have to manually assign users to hosts or host groups for those users to view hosts within Nagios unless the special token * is used in the configuration file with the *authorized_for_all** configuration directives (authorized_for_all_hosts, authorized_for_all_services, authorized_for_all_ service_commands, authorized_for_all_host_commands) to grant access to view all hosts and services to everyone (Figure 6.2).

Figure 6.2 Basic LDAP User Authentication Data Flow

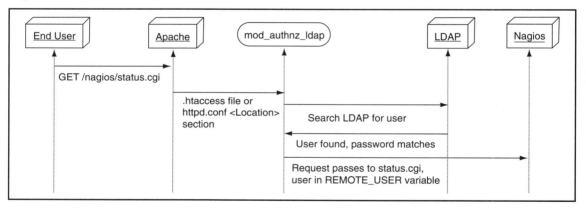

One LDAP Group, One Nagios User

In this scenario we use shared group accounts for LDAP authentication instead of individual user accounts. This makes maintaining contact configurations easier but provides less fine-grained auditing on who is doing what in Nagios. It also may simplify how a Nagios administrator thinks about authentication as the contact groups can map to corporate email groups. Only use this method of authentication in a trusted environment and do not give all authenticated users permissions to modify the state of Nagios as it runs from the web interface unless everyone can be trusted. As with the first LDAP authentication scenario in this section, we hard code the names of groups that receive elevated permissions in the Nagios CGI configuration file.

Integration with Splunk

Nagios has been integrated with graphing tools like Cacti and other performance data tools for years now, using a variety of different methodologies. In the 3.*x* release of Nagios, Ethan has started to integrate Nagios with Splunk, a commercial product that acts as like "Google for your logs." Nagios allows us to monitor just about anything, Splunk allows us to ingest and search just about any file format or textual output we feel is important, be that system logs, output from programs, or text ingested using custom connectors. Splunk indexes this data and gives us flexible, full-text searching capabilities.

This functionality is a perfect companion for Nagios. When something is broken, the next question is "Why did it break?" For that we often turn to system and application log files. Currently, Nagios to Splunk integration is very basic. There are a few configuration options to change in the Nagios CGI configuration file, cgi.cfg. These options are shown below:

```
# SPLUNK INTEGRATION OPTIONS
# These options allow you to enable integration with Splunk
# in the web interface. If enabled, you'll be presented with
# "Splunk It" links in various places in the CGIs (log file,
# alert history, host/service detail, etc). Useful if you're
# trying to research why a particular problem occurred.
# For more information on Splunk, visit http://www.splunk.com/

# This option determines whether the Splunk integration is enabled
# Values: 0 = disable Splunk integration
#         1 = enable Splunk integration

enable_splunk_integration=1

# This option should be the URL used to access your instance of Splunk
splunk_url=http://splunk.localhost.net:8000/
```

Figure 6.3 Nagios Status Screen Showing Link to Splunk

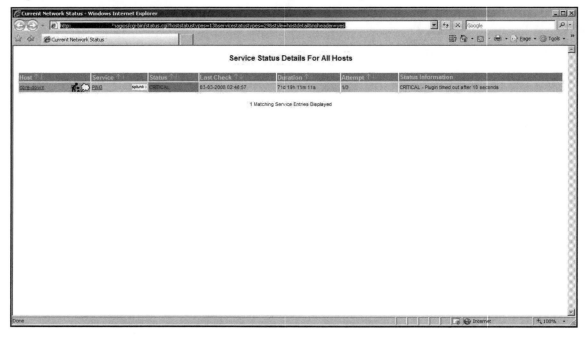

The Splunk icon then appears as a link that will take the end user to your Splunk Web site and execute a query for the host or service having an issue. Currently, this is the extent of Splunk integration with Nagios; it is by no means where we believe the integration will end. The open architecture and vast number of uses Splunk has means that we expect to see increased integration between Nagios and Splunk in future versions of Nagios.

Integrating with Third-Party Trend and Analysis Tools
Cacti

Cacti (www.cacti.net) is an open-source trending tool that uses the round-robin database tool (RRD tool) to create long-term trending graphs of device and application performance. When integrated with Nagios, MySQL, and SNMPTT, Cacti can be used to create network monitoring trend reports and graphs. Cacti has a very flexible plug-in framework and can be enhanced to perform additional functions Examples include: watching for configuration changes on network devices, alerting when trended metrics exceed configured thresholds, and displaying bandwidth utilization maps. While Cacti is very good at trending, its fault management capabilities do not match those of Nagios. When used with Nagios, we recommend you use Cacti for long term trending and Nagios for fault management.

One of the difficulties of integrating Cacti and Nagios is authentication. Cacti directly supports LDAP authentication. Nagios can be made to use LDAP by using the mod_authnz_ldap module for Apache. Unfortunately, even with LDAP authentication on for both programs it will still be necessary to create user accounts for each application to limit access within each program. If your user base is trusted you can give read-only permissions for all devices to the "guest" user account in Cacti.

Another way to integrate the two programs is to use the Cacinda add-on (http://cacinda.sf.net/). Cacinda is a PHP-based set of scripts that allows you to set up dashboards for devices on your network by device type and then display information from those devices in Nagios. It accesses the Cacti database directly for graphs, SNMP authentication information, and device information so there is no need to create individual user accounts in both Cacti and Nagios. Cacinda pages can be linked to from Nagios by using the extra notes or action URL configuration directives for devices. See the section on Cacinda in Chapter 5 for more information on how Cacinda works.

Finally, you might conclude that it is best to not fully integrate them. Many users will set up Cacti to focus on network devices as it has several very useful network-centric plug-ins and use Nagios solely for monitoring systems and applications. Here is a very small sampling of the plug-ins available for Cacti:

- Network Weathermap for Cacti (http://www.network-weathermap.com/)

- MAC address and port status tracking (http://docs.cacti.net/plugins/mactrack/info)

- Netflow graphing (http://docs.cacti.net/plugins/Flowviewer)

Your level of integration may be just placing a link from the Nagios main GUI that will let users view Cacti pages while staying within the Nagios HTML frame set. This is the beauty of Nagios, many ways to do what needs to be done to meet the goals of your organization—just pick the method that works best for you and your customers.

eHealth

eHealth is a commercial trending and trap management suite of programs sold by Computer Associates (CA). eHealth does an excellent job of reporting and is designed to let you store and then query metrics across large numbers of devices. It comes with a number of well thought-out reports and a flexible report creation tool that allows you to create reports tailored to your organization. eHealth is designed to be a monitor of monitors and additionally comes with a very flexible trap handling and filtering program, Trap Exploder.

eHealth does performance predication based on past performance. By default it watches element performance over a six-week period; as future performance deviates from this rolling six-week baseline, eHealth will generate alerts that tell the percent deviation in performance an element is showing and whether the element performance is degrading or improving. For example, one of these alerts might read "CPU utilization is 100% higher than normal." These traps can be kept in eHealth or forwarded to Nagios.

eHealth also comes with a limited set of visualization tools; it does not, however, come with network path visualization tools or application-level or service-level customizable visualization tools. We suggest that when using eHealth and Nagios together, eHealth is used as the data repository of all system and network metrics, while Nagios is used for nonstandard application, system, and network checks. We also suggest making use of eHealth's trap viewer but use Nagios as the Monitor of Monitors and forward traps that need to be acted on to Nagios for alerting and notification. Finally, for DMZ hosts where SNMP may not be allowed, Nagios' NSCA add-on can be used to send application-level events from DMZ devices to Nagios.

The ideal role for Nagios if integrated with eHealth would be as the master fault manager. We recommend you use Nagios for visualizing services and applications on your network and make use of eHealth for long-term trending and analysis of system and network devices. In this role, eHealth should be configured to forward all traps to Nagios for display and notification where applicable. eHealth comes with an easy-to-use Web interface and uses Apache authentication for application login; to ease integration of users between the two applications you should either use the .htpasswd file eHealth creates for users to authenticate users under Nagios or set up a cron job that will copy this file from your eHealth host to your Nagios host using scp using PKI.

Figure 6.4 Nagios and eHealth Together

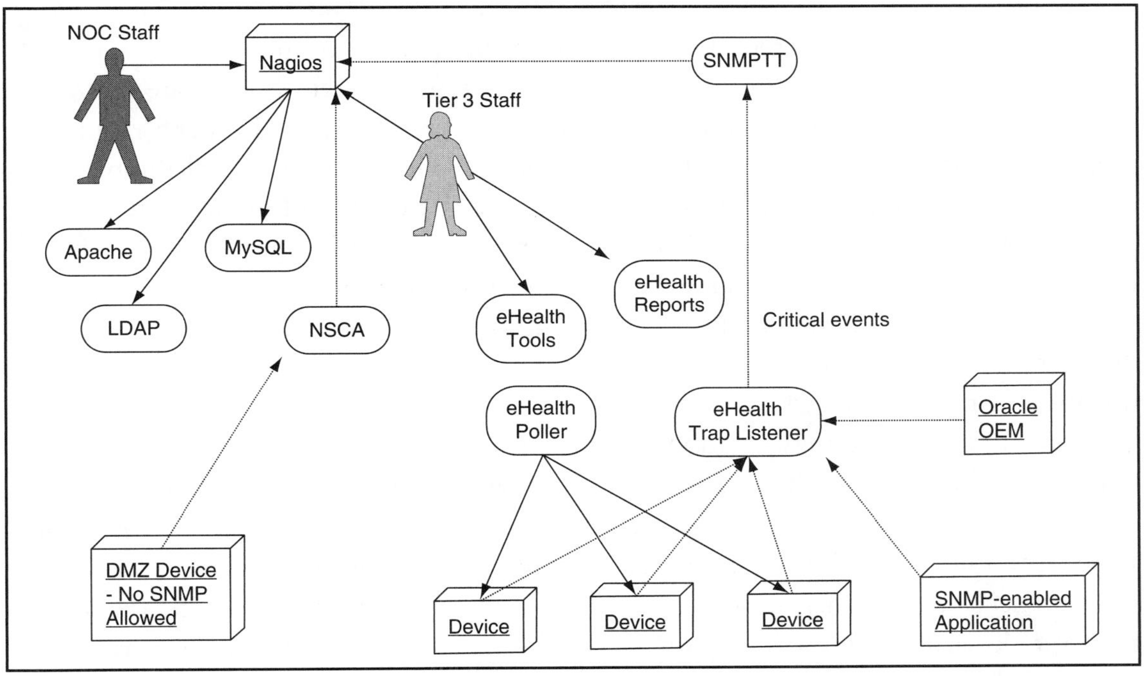

Multiple Administrators/ Configuration Writers

In larger organizations there will often be more than one person involved in writing and maintaining Nagios configuration files. There are several administration GUIs available for Nagios; while the current set of GUIs available does not provide the full flexibility of configuration that hand-creation of configuration allows, they all do allow for creation of user accounts and user roles. If your staff is technically proficient, you might opt instead to design your Nagios configuration so it can be checked into a source code control system like CVS or SVN; access to various parts of the configuration tree can then be controlled by server-side ACLs. Finally, you might even choose an LDAP-based configuration where Nagios objects are stored in LDAP and a custom script pulls the configuration from LDAP periodically and applies it to your system, restarting Nagios if changes have been made.

Integration with Puppet

Puppet (http://www.reductivelabs.com/projects/puppet) is an open source systems administration automation and management framework. System polices are configured using a declarative configuration language very similar to Ruby. Each managed server runs a Puppet agent that retrieves its configuration from a central Puppet server (called the Puppet master). Once an agent has a valid configuration, it will periodically apply the policies and rules it receives from the Puppet Master to the managed system and can also send the results of each run to a Puppet reporting server. Policies and rules range from watching for changes in critical files and directories to ensuring no changes are made to specific files, to installing and updating software packages on managed hosts.

Puppet and Nagios make a good team. Puppet provides an "inside-out" view of a network of systems and helps automate many types of system administration tasks. Nagios, on the other hand, is very good at providing "outside-in" views of applications, systems, and networks. A typical arrangement would entail Nagios reporting status for service checks on a managed host, while Puppet actually performs the systems administration tasks that would normally be done if human intervention were required. Together, the two provide a very complete tool set for monitoring and managing an organization's IT infrastructure (Figure 6.5).

Figure 6.5 Nagios and Puppet Together

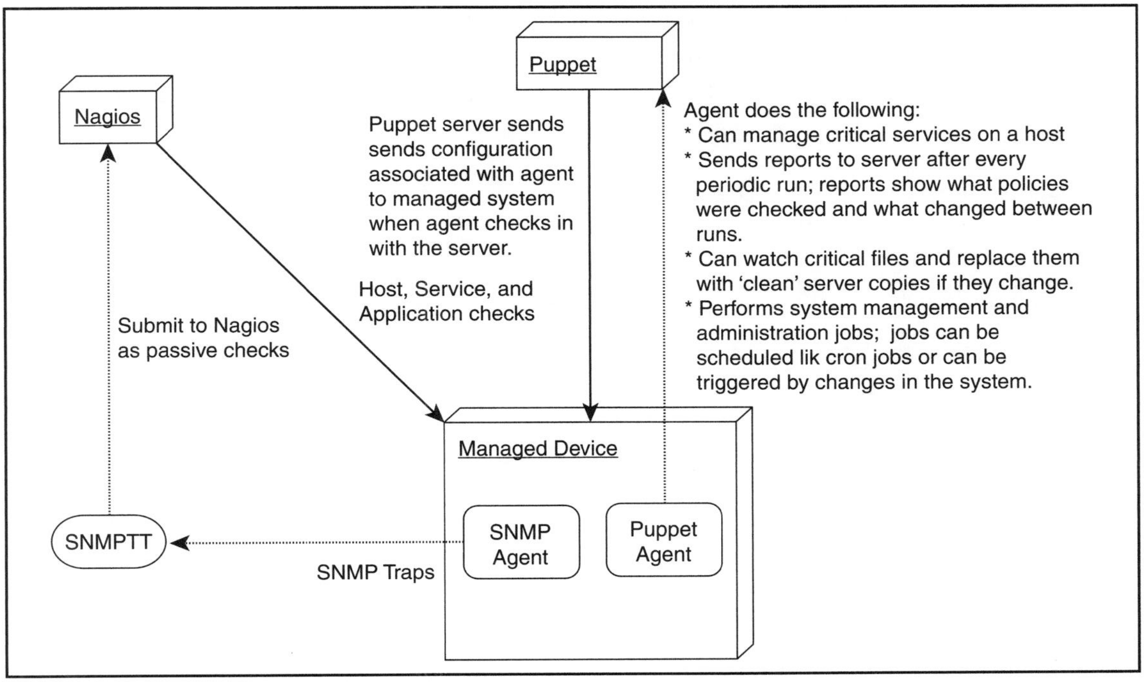

Puppet

Nagios

Puppet server sends
sends configuration
associated with agent
to managed system
when agent checks in
with the server.

Host, Service, and
Application checks

Agent does the following:
* Can manage critical services on a host
* Sends reports to server after every
  periodic run; reports show what policies
  were checked and what changed between
  runs.
* Can watch critical files and replace them
  with 'clean' server copies if they change.
* Performs system management and
  administration jobs; jobs can be
  scheduled lik cron jobs or can be
  triggered by changes in the system.

Submit to Nagios
as passive checks

Managed Device

SNMPTT

SNMP Traps

SNMP
Agent

Puppet
Agent

Integration with Trouble Ticketing Systems

We recommend that you only allow your fault management software to create trouble tickets if the alerts triggering the tickets are so application specific and free from false positives (like a passive check) that you can ensure the event requires attention by a real person. On the other hand, we highly recommend you take advantage of help desk systems that allow you to associate fault manager event IDs and information with your trouble tickets. For example, it would make sense to have your help desk software have the capability to acknowledge an open alert in Nagios, or to have the help desk software clear an alert as soon as the issue is resolved by the help desk person working on the event in question.

Core Nagios exposes a large number of macros that enable scripts to use the information Nagios gathers from hosts, services, and other sources. Macros can be employed by event handlers that execute scripts to email, send text messages, or call external programs. Trouble ticketing systems often provide programs that can be used to inject tickets into the service desk system from the command line; many allow end users to open new tickets by sending email to a specific email address, for example support@example.com. Nagios' event handlers can call these external programs or send email to a trouble ticketing system to open new tickets, providing URLs in the ticket body that link the ticket back to the originating Nagios event. Again, be sure any events set up to automatically open new trouble tickets only do so for events that require immediate human attention (Figure 6.6).

Figure 6.6 Nagios Opens a Trouble Ticket

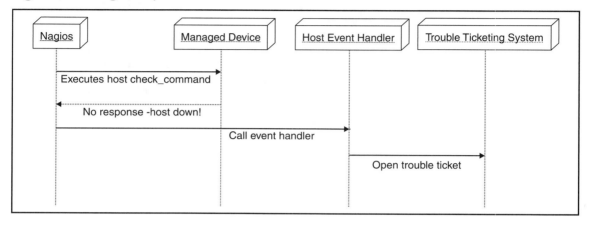

Nagios in the NOC

There are usually three types of NOCs. We will discuss the Enterprise NOC first and then explore two smaller types of NOCs as well.

The Enterprise NOC usually is divided into three tiers. The tier one group takes phone calls, opens tickets, and acts as the front line of problem resolution. This group is typically the one that should be seeing a problem-only view of Nagios. They should see hosts and services that report warnings and start to work those issues while starting a problem ticket. Tier two will usually have more specific skills or specialties and will have problems escalated to them based on that expertise. Tier two should take on any issues that have been open for longer than your established escalation threshold or that the tier one group is unable to complete. Tier three is usually made of non-NOC staff who are application or system specific experts who are called in to look at issues after second or third escalation timers have expired. Some NOCs will include a separate group that sits organizationally between the first and second or second and third tiers based on the systems in use within the organization. Another variation is that once past tier one problems are branched off to other second-level teams that specialize in application, hardware, or network issues.

In all of these cases it is important to define escalation timers and notification rules. Improper notifications and unrealistic escalation times lead to "cry wolf" conditions that will cause your staff to become complacent about alerts and issues. Preventing false positives before they send out notification is the number-one priority of your Nagios administrator. We will now discuss some important issues to consider should you decide to integration Nagios into your organizations' NOC.

The Nagios Administrator

This can be a full-time job. Nagios is not an install and forget application, and like the rest of your systems and applications, it requires maintenance. Depending on the number of systems you may need more than one person to administer and maintain Nagios; this is especially true in larger organizations. For any Enterprise Nagios installation you need at least one dedicated Nagios administrator. This person can then work with individual system administrators and their teams to maintain Nagios host and service definitions. The Nagios administrator should be someone who works with the applications in your organization daily. This person should be experienced with all aspects of Nagios and with the large number of add-ons and customizations that are available for Nagios. The lead Nagios administrator should have strong organization skills, an ability to interact with multiple teams at your organization, and be able to listen well and determine what is important to monitor and what is not as new applications are added to an organization's network. Additionally, the Nagios administrator needs to be able to communicate effectively and train and educate other staff members on network and systems management concepts and benefits.

The Nagios Software

For Nagios to be effective, its monitoring plug-ins and software need to be installed before a system goes live. You need to test the failure scenarios for that system and validate that your thresholds are set correctly. You also need to validate that performance data is being collected properly by plugins and establish a performance baseline. By planning your deployment early as described in Chapter 2, you will have base configurations and templates that only need to be slightly modified for new systems and applications. You also only need to define all of your system and application dependencies to keep your status screens clean; ensure that network paths are properly defined so that when a network device fails all hosts that depend on it are shown as unreachable by Nagios (as opposed to all of them being shown as down). In addition, new versions of Nagios and the plug-ins are released several times throughout the year. Planning for upgrades and deploying updates to both software and custom plug-ins and the Nagios configuration can be a task for your Nagios administration team, or it can be delegated to desk staff if upgrade and installation processes are properly documented.

Integration

When preparing a system for roll out into a production environment, your Nagios administrator and System adminsitrators should work together to deploy the system and configure Nagios to starting monitoring it. For any enterprise deployment you should have a develop and test Nagios system where you can test plug-ins and configurations. This allows a team to identify failure scenarios, configure alerts, and test notification policies before the system is in use. For a large enterprise installation you should have a second Nagios server that just handles integration and test environment systems so you can validate configuration changes and file configurations before moving the changes to your production Nagios server.

Deployment

Deployments should be done in phases. We recommend you deploy applications and systems in groups; this allows operations staff to learn the systems, validate the systems function properly, and test that health checks for the systems are implemented as agreed upon by operational and development staff. Your main goal is to remove as many false positives as possible and ensure that alerts sent by the system are meaningful to operational staff.

When deploying new Nagios servers, make sure notifications are off by setting the parameter *notifications_enabled* to 0 in the nagios.cfg configuration file. If possible, have notifications go to a separate testing mailbox so you can validate the notification process and details. Many people do not appreciate the value a monitoring system can bring to an organization; the especially dislike systems that fill up their mail boxes with notifications. Using templates you can quickly change the notification destinations for an entire set or host group of systems, allowing you to quickly transition the monitoring to the local system admins once your deployment testing is done.

While it may not be the most glamorous of tasks, as you add new system and application checks to Nagios, be sure to monitor your Nagios server for resource and performance problems. Make sure you are running checks on your base monitoring system. Watch for changes in execution times. If you are using the performance data gathering features of Nagios, carefully watch processing times and performance.

While Nagios operates well in large environments, performance data processing can easily become a bottleneck for a Nagios system. If you are planning to roll Nagios out on a large deployment with performance data processing in place, we recommend you look at distributed Nagios monitoring.

Maintenance

Even after Nagios is configured to monitor a new system, you will need to maintain the configuration—watch for repetitive failures and be sure to update configuration rules to match changes in the system or application. If your configuration and monitoring environment are large, you should schedule periodic reviews of the systems and devices being monitored to check for changes or new services. You also need to plan for the scheduled maintenance cycle of the system to make sure you have scheduled maintenance planned in your Nagios configuration. Sending alerts out at 2 A.M. for planned work makes everyone unhappy. In many cases, you will also need to plan alert outages around network backup and other regularly scheduled system and network maintenance activities that can cause false positive alerts.

Depending on your environment, you may already have software deployment or patch management software in place. If not, keep Nagios in mind when planning your deployment and maintenance. For the most part we have seen Nagios plug-ins work for years without needing replacement. However, when a new plug-in comes out that you just have to have, having a way to easily deploy the changes to many systems at once can make your life as a Nagios administrator much easier.

If you don't have patch management, we highly recommend you look at your Nagios user account. In many environments you may be able to allow SSH access to your systems using SSH keys instead of passwords. With SSH keys in place, you can implement a script on your Nagios server that parses Nagios and other system configuration files, determines which systems require updates, and then deploys updates to those systems. Regardless of the method you decide to use to manage your updates, the update process needs to be considered and accounted for on the list of required resources and required time per server when planning a deployment.

The Process

Nagios can add a lot of value to an organization provided you monitor changes to your systems and eliminate false positives. Define a change process that includes notifying Nagios administration staff when something changes in the environment. System administrators need to come to you early in the integration process so you can have complete application and system monitoring in place for a system or application when it does finally go live. Ensure a process is in place that makes it easy for operational staff to report problems that Nagios did not catch to Nagios administrators so that the problem situation can be monitored by Nagios in the future. Your Nagios administrator should have the ability to review support tickets to see which issues were not identified before a phone call was received or users noticed that a problem was occurring. When a problem is found, you should consider the basic questions—what caused the issue, what resolved the issue, how can we detect it in the future, and how can we prevent it or automatically recover from it? Your biggest return on investment overall from monitoring is to end "known issues" or repetitive maintenance work; this type of continual re-fixing is part of what leads to lower morale and more common mistakes from your NOC staff.

In conclusion, remember that Nagios does not replace people; you normally cannot reduce your admin or network staff once a monitoring system is in place. A proper deployment of any monitoring tool will help make your staff more effective and your outages less expensive and damaging. When Nagios alerts your staff, it should be pointing them to the exact problem that needs to be resolved. Too often we depend on phone calls or emails from users that present symptoms of the issues but not the actual problem. Through intelligent setup and proper configuration of Nagios, you present your staff with a tool that tells them exactly where issues are occurring so they can quickly resolve host and application problems.

The Operations Centers

The Enterprise NOC

The enterprise NOC is the primary customer of your Nagios installation. Nagios provides NOC staff with early insight into problems. If host and service checks are properly defined, warnings are seen by the NOC before end users are impacted. Your Nagios configuration should be simple and geared toward users' needs. Just as you gather requirements before adding new hosts, you need to document how your NOC works today and what needs improvement. In most environments there will be some kind of monitoring tool in place well before you suggest Nagios. Work with NOC staff to identify what they like and do not like about the current set of tools they use. Many times, the problem is not that the tool currently in place is not useful but rather that it is not integrated into the build, test, and deploy processes an organization uses for new and existing systems. Looking at a typical service desk workflow we can see how Nagios can integrate into an existing service desk process. (Figure 6.7).

Figure 6.7 Typical Workflow

Existing Helpdesk Flow

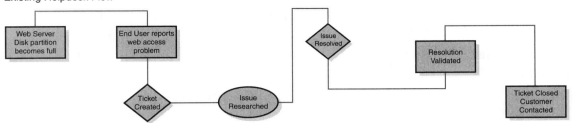

Issues with Non Monitored Fault Management:
* Helpdesk is dependent on end users to report problems after they have impacted the customer base.
* End users reports usually describe symptoms and not true root cause of issues or specific system with fault.
* Faults are only found when they impact systems.
* Helpdesk is continuously in a reactionary mode "fighting fires" instead of pro-actively maintaining systems.

Nagios Helpdesk Flow

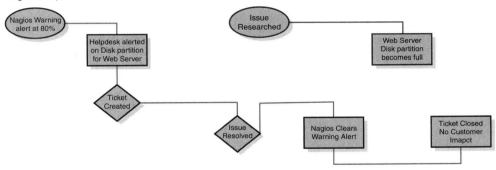

Advantage of Fault Monitoring:
* Helpdesk is able to identify Root Cause issues at "Warning" State before issue is "Critical"
* Root Cause Research time and false symptoms are greatly reduced.
* Helpdesk is able to methodically work issue without rushing.
* Issue is resolved before any user impact and without additional resource usage of end user reporting.

Existing Flow:
1. User calls helpdesk -> Helpdesk opens ticket and attempts to identify root issue. Depending on the service outage there can be a high volume of calls for one issue.
2. Helpdesk is able to either work issue and resolve or escalates to second level.
3. Second level works to identify root cause and resolve issue. If unable to resolve issue, they may need to contact third-level support.
4. Once issue is resolved, helpdesk works to close ticket and notify users of service recovery.

Nagios Flow:
1. Nagios display shows service in Warning status -> Helpdesk opens a ticket knowing a base root issue as Nagios has a failing or failed service and pre-defined service check. Since the issue being reported is from a pre-defined service check there is less work involved in identifying the root cause of the failure. You are also able to then have the helpdesk check against previous tickets or documentation for this type of check failure. Helpdesk also acks the alert on Nagios. With this ack, any other administrator knows that the issue is now being worked on.
2. Helpdesk is able to resolve issue or escalates to second level.
Nagios continues to monitor, and if pre-defined time limit has passed or service fails it will then automatically notify second-level staff.
3. Second-level staff is able to begin troubleshooting and either resolve issue or involve third-level support.
Once the issue is resolved, Nagios is able to automatically show service recovery, which acts as a redundant confirmation to staff that issue has been completely resolved.

Many issues are not isolated. With an automated testing tool like Nagios you can see when multiple problems occur at the same time and you can usually easily see what top level system or application caused the two or more related problems; this keeps operational staff from getting stuck 'in the weeds' when an application or system problem occurs. When a user calls, he or she may report a problem accessing a web server. If the real issue is that a network device between the web server and the end user has failed, Nagios can display this graphically and keep your operational staff from spending time on trouble shooting application-level issues when in fact the problem is network-related.

Nagios saves your operational staff time. If your helpdesk receives a notice Nagios that a service or host is in a warning state, they may be able to fix the impending problem before any customers notice. Many help desk personnel spend more time answering calls to repeat the same outage information to a group of users than they do working on and resolving problems. In addition, when new issues are reported by users, your first-level helpdesk will become tied up in telephone and user task work and they may not be able to work any issues to resolution. As a result, tier two staff may become stressed and overworked on tasks that can and should be done by tier one staff. Finding issues before users do can save your organization both time and money.

The scenario we have just described is typical of a NOC with a more traditional, tiered approach to support. In this environment, operations staff sit in a shared work area and communication between staff members is as easy as standing up and shouting at a neighbor. In cases where NOC personnel are not in a common area, more work has to be done to keep people informed. Investing in a large, easy to read status screen for each common area used by your NOC staff on any level drastically increases their awareness of system status. Status screens should never be limited to one location and should never be left out of the data center. When placing a status screen, keep in mind what we discussed earlier on scaling the GUI. Sit at the desks of your staff and look at the status screen; if you cannot read all text on the screen neither can they. The data shown should be easy to read, simple, and always current. A good analogy for this is driving: when you look out your windshield you look at everything around you; if you see a sign that warns you of danger ahead, you process that information and act accordingly. If that sign is too far away or in such small type that you cannot see it you will ignore it or worse, lose focus on the road as you attempt to read it, and now that sign has hurt your driving experience rather than help it.

NOTE

In the data centers we have visited we rarely see status monitors on the data center floor. Yet a high percentage of time, outages are caused by work being done in the data center. We feel that more administrators need to consider the benefit of putting system status screens in the data center. When an operational staff member is done replacing a cable, or installing a new server, the data center monitor will provide near-instant configuration that the work done did not break other systems in the data center.

The Incident

For discussion purposes, lets pretend that a hard disk on a web server is 98% full. With no monitoring at all, we will not know there is an issue until the drive is full and the application stops operating correctly. In this case, the first report of an issue is when a customer contacts the helpdesk and reports that the Web site is broken. Administrative staff begin researching why the Web server has failed. By this time the drive is 100% full and the SSH server on the system fails as a result, making trouble-shooting even more difficult. At this point, many users are impacted and the issue has become a critical problem for end users and the help desk staff!

Nagios allows us to configure both WARNING and CRITICAL thresholds for alerts. The warning threshold should cause the alert to be triggered at least 30 mintues before an issue becomes critical. Once an issue is critical, it will most likely impact end users. In the preceding case, we could have been are alerted to the issue before the disk was full. The helpdesk would have been able to log in to the system, identify the cause of the issue, and resolve it. With the issue resolved, no application or systems would have been affected and no customers would have called to report a problem.

Fires rarely occur in a well managed and organized help desk. All administrative staff from level 1 to 3 should have a general of system and network performance at all times. Management should be able to tell what issues exist and how well they are being managed. Many helpdesks today base their staffing levels on metrics, usually based on the ratio of tickets open/closed, system uptime/downtime, and overall application availability. Proactive monitoring with a fault management system allows you to lower your system downtime and improve your time gap for ticket open/close interval.

Ongoing Maintenance

There will be times when a system breaks in such a way that Nagios is not aware of. You need to have the option in your ticket system to flag those issues so that Nagios staff can easily see them. Once the problem and resolution are known the Nagios system can be updated to monitor for that failure condition. With this type of continual quality management, you can simealtaneously grow your monitoring configuration and, at the same time, reduce the number of system and host outages that occur. System and software upgrades, integration of new systems, and addition of new checks to catch system and host problems before they become critical will keep a NOC staff very busy. We feel that in the long run the happiness customers and end users experience and the reduced stress placed on a NOC staff justify the additional time and effort required to integrate Nagios into the processes in use in a NOC.

Smaller NOCs

In the beginning of this section, we mentioned that there are two other types of NOCs that typically use Nagios. Enterprise NOCs in some ways are easier than smaller NOCs. They have a larger staff with more well-defined roles and responsibilities. Smaller NOCs have fewer resources to allocate to problems; in some cases the "NOC" may just be a single person sitting behind a PC. First, we will look at the NOC that has a small helpdesk staff where one group of personnel perform the duties of both tier one and tier two staff. When this type of helpdesk is unable to resolve an issue they escalate the issue directly to a developer or a direct vendor for additional support. In these situations you will find that helpdesk staff is committed to each issue for a longer amount of time as they follow each issue to completion regardless of their experience level with the problem at hand. This can become a problem if too many issues occur at once. By identifying issues before they are critical problems, Nagios it helps prioritize problems. Moreover, the ability to acknowledge issues and add notes directly to Nagios means additional staff can easily see the status of issues and handle those with the higher impact first.

The other type of NOC typically seen has staff members at multiple locations who may support systems locally and then act as secondary support or even primary support for remote locations. When working with remote staff support or de-centralized NOCs, it is important that staff in each location can communicate easily and quickly with each other. Allow staff members to use email or instant messenger to communicate with each other as they work on current issues (do not allow end users to communicate with NOC staff using instant messenger as this circumvents your help desk processes!). We recommend you not use email as a trouble ticketing system as it does not provide any one person with ownership or accountability of issues. Effective tools for group chat include private IRC, IM Group channels, even VOIP or Skype conference channels can be used for this purpose.

The biggest bottleneck in de-centralized NOCs is that the ability for staff members to quickly communicate with each other is reduced dramatically when compared to a NOC where the support staff can see and interact with each other directly. It is imperative that when possible as much of your support staff should work in a location that promotes direct interaction. Your goal is to allow and support unstructured conversations. Quite often several issues that occur at or around the same time will be related. If NOC staff cannot easily talk with each other about outstanding issues the link between related issues can easily be lost. This results in longer outages and repeated effort by your staff. Small or de-centralized NOCs have an uphill battle in fighting this communication barrier. Individual status screens separate from desktops in every office area can help greatly in keeping people aware of network status and health. Organizations that use Nagios should consider implementing direct methods of communications like paging, instant messenger, and text messages as these methods of communication are quite effective at conveying the importance of an alert.

Summary

In this chapter, we described how to best integrate Nagios into your NOC. Far too often today, we see NOCs that are run using outdated methodologies that do not stress proactive monitoring and direct communication best practices. Times and systems have changed. With software and hardware load balancing we can now monitor systems and resolve issues well before any end users are affected. When looking at Nagios or any other monitor of monitors (MOM) software, we must consider our current environment and what processes are in use by our help desk management and staff. When we review our help desk practices and procedures, our first task is to pose as an end user, place a ticket, and see how things operate from the point of view of a customer. Everyone in IT has had to interact with vendor help desk systems; we all know how frustrating it can be to struggle through a traditional, tiered help desk system, especially one that is de-centralized. Take a hard look at your help desk systems and processes and find ways to improve it so users will not need to call; if they do have to call, ensure that they are helped quickly, directly, and politely. The less time the user is put on hold or transferred, the better. The sooner users can be given a real answer, the happier they are with your level of service. Your happiest customer is one who never has to call; the customer who will recommend you to someone else is the one who does call and is provided real assistance.

Be willing to change. Talk to and listen to the different tiers of your helpdesk. They will tell you what issues they fix daily and where the process can be improved. There should be a zero tolerance policy on daily repetitive issues. If you had to change your car tire every day you went to work, you would not keep that car. Applications should not experience the same problems and band-aid solutions over and over nor should your NOC have to waste time on a regular basis on issues that should be escalated and resolved so they do not occur again. We also recommend that you visit other NOCs. See how similar helpdesks in your field work. Finally, look at how helpdesks in other fields work; many times you can find processes and applications in other fields that apply very well to your field. We need to re-examine how we manage the systems we operate and how we help the users who use the systems and applications we monitor for them.

## Chapter 7

Intrusion Detection and Security Analysis

Solutions in this chapter:

- **Know Your Network**
- **Watching for Session Hijacking Attacks**
- **Nagios and Compliance**
- **Securing Nagios**

☑ **Summary**

Know Your Network

One of the axioms of computer security is "know your network." Unfortunately, many network security professionals tend to think this means purchasing more security software, running more scans, or hiring an external firm to run a penetration test. However, the real core of good network security is not the tools you run or the firms you hire to document that you are "secure," but how well you understand your systems and your network architecture.

There are a great number of different tools available to a security professional. None of them is as valuable as the ones that provide true visibility into the systems and services of a network. This is where the true power of Nagios comes in. It is not an IDS; it is not a vulnerability assessment scanner; it will not tell you that you have been hacked; it won't even stop an attacker. However, it still can be one of the most powerful tools in your security arsenal. Nagios forces you to understand and monitor the normal and approved operating parameters of your systems. This is a key point because when something "abnormal" happens, you will have a good baseline and understanding of what changed and why it is important to you. After all, how can you know what abnormal is if you don't know what normal is first?

Security Tools under Attack

We are seeing many of the core security technologies we have come to depend on beginning to be attacked and bypassed. The research of Mike Poor and Ed Skoudis has shown how simple modifications like fragmentation and different versions of Metasploit attack code causes it to not be identified or stopped by many intrusion prevention systems (ISPs). We are seeing the re-emergence of master boot record (MBR) viruses, malware that attacks anti-virus products directly, and robust command and control mechanisms for botnets. These are only the beginning of a new trend in hacking that is going to force us to better understand our systems rather than rely on various tools to tell us we are secure or hacked.

It is becoming more and more important for security professionals to understand what is happening on their networks. It is also important to know what is leaving your network (extrusion detection) and to understand that some attacks, like smb_relay, do not involve exploits in the traditional sense and may be difficult to detect with traditional security technologies like IDS and IPS.

To read more about MBR viruses returning, see the article at www.f-secure.com/weblog/archives/00001393.html.

To read about the work of Ed Skoudis and Mike Poor, see the article at www.toplayer.com/pdf/IS_110105.pdf.

To learn more about extrusion detection, check out the site from Richard Bejtlich at www.taosecurity.com.

Enter Nagios

So, how can Nagios help a security professional know what is normal? Configuring Nagios starts from a different perspective than most security tools. Many security tools are built around the concept of blacklisting. This is where the developer(s) focus on identifying malicious traffic and either alert you or block the traffic (hopefully alerting you in the process). This paradigm in computer security is failing. The excellent article "Six Dumbest Ideas in Computer Security" by Marcus Ranum articulates this point very well by stating that the amount of malicious traffic is growing faster than the security community can develop new signatures and methods to detect it.

The whole paradigm shifts with a tool like Nagios. Rather than having a tool tell you that something bad is happening, Nagios has to be configured to periodically check what is normal and presumably good. Configuring a tool to automatically audit normal process states sounds like a fair amount of work to many people who have been trained to purchase the security product that has the best marketing and/or sales force. However, identifying normal states is a far more efficient way to secure your network, because it will reduce the amount of time it takes for your security team to identify that an incident has occurred and restore operations (Figure 7.1).

Figure 7.1 Service Status Details for Hosts

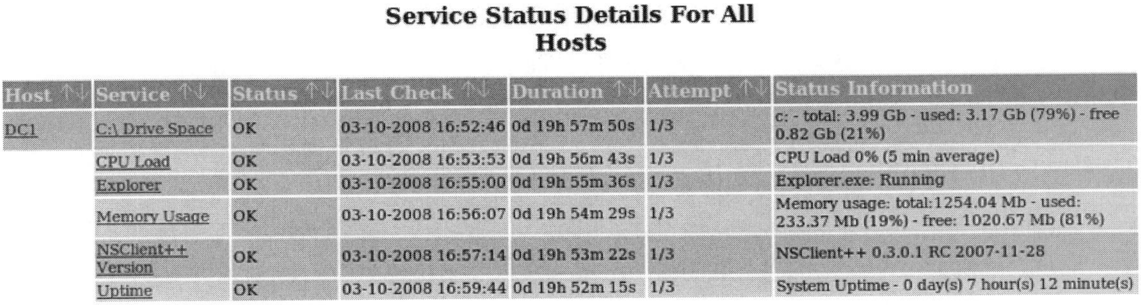

Service Status Details For All Hosts

Host	Service	Status	Last Check	Duration	Attempt	Status Information
DC1	C:\ Drive Space	OK	03-10-2008 16:52:46	0d 19h 57m 50s	1/3	c: - total: 3.99 Gb - used: 3.17 Gb (79%) - free 0.82 Gb (21%)
	CPU Load	OK	03-10-2008 16:53:53	0d 19h 56m 43s	1/3	CPU Load 0% (5 min average)
	Explorer	OK	03-10-2008 16:55:00	0d 19h 55m 36s	1/3	Explorer.exe: Running
	Memory Usage	OK	03-10-2008 16:56:07	0d 19h 54m 29s	1/3	Memory usage: total:1254.04 Mb - used: 233.37 Mb (19%) - free: 1020.67 Mb (81%)
	NSClient++ Version	OK	03-10-2008 16:57:14	0d 19h 53m 22s	1/3	NSClient++ 0.3.0.1 RC 2007-11-28
	Uptime	OK	03-10-2008 16:59:44	0d 19h 52m 15s	1/3	System Uptime - 0 day(s) 7 hour(s) 12 minute(s)

In this section of this book, we are not going to try to portray Nagios as a centralized security-monitoring platform. There are a great number of tools available to you, and you should learn how to work with as many of them as possible.

Snort, Squil, and OSSEC are all great products that complement Nagios in any size environment; here are the links to learn more about these products:

- www.snort.org/

- sguil.sourceforge.net/

- www.ossec.net/

Attackers Make Mistakes

Unfortunately, many administrators have been desensitized to their systems or critical services crashing. In the days of Windows 2000 or NT, a system or service crashing was considered more "normal" than a service or system staying up for long periods of time. Unfortunately, this thought process has carried over to today. Systems like modern flavors of Linux and the Windows server family are far more stable than the 2000 and NT versions of Windows. Because of this, when a system or service crashes, it should be investigated immediately. In Figure 7.2, we can see that the Explorer process has crashed on a Windows 2003 server due to an unsuccessful attempt by an attacker to install the AFX rootkit.

Figure 7.2 Explorer Process Has Crashed

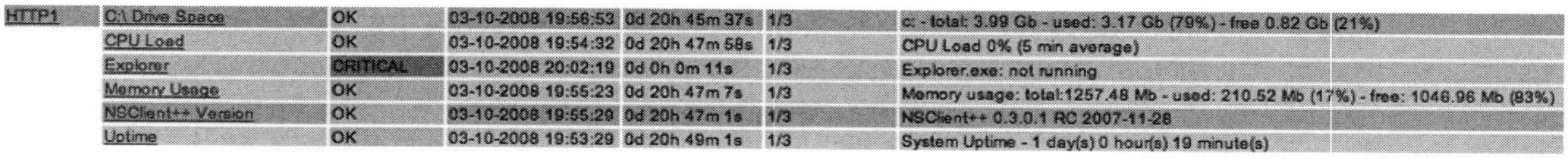

HTTP1	C:\ Drive Space	OK	03-10-2008 19:56:53	0d 20h 45m 37s	1/3	c: - total: 3.99 Gb - used: 3.17 Gb (79%) - free 0.82 Gb (21%)
	CPU Load	OK	03-10-2008 19:54:32	0d 20h 47m 58s	1/3	CPU Load 0% (5 min average)
	Explorer	CRITICAL	03-10-2008 20:02:19	0d 0h 0m 11s	1/3	Explorer.exe: not running
	Memory Usage	OK	03-10-2008 19:55:23	0d 20h 47m 7s	1/3	Memory usage: total:1257.48 Mb - used: 210.52 Mb (17%) - free: 1046.96 Mb (83%)
	NSClient++ Version	OK	03-10-2008 19:55:29	0d 20h 47m 1s	1/3	NSClient++ 0.3.0.1 RC 2007-11-28
	Uptime	OK	03-10-2008 19:53:29	0d 20h 49m 1s	1/3	System Uptime - 1 day(s) 0 hour(s) 19 minute(s)

Attackers make mistakes. Their tools don't always compile and run correctly. Sometimes, they crash a service or a system. Sometimes, they crash systems or services intentionally for new malicious configurations to take effect. These abnormalities need to be investigated by the systems administrators and the security team. It is not acceptable to simply reboot a system or restart the service. Root cause analysis must be preformed to identify why a service or system crashed.

In the next few sections, we address some Nagios plug-ins that may assist in detecting an attacker on a system for Windows, Linux, and service-based checks like DNS.

NSClient++ Checks for Windows

We are going to start by going through the standard NSClient++ Windows plug-in checks that can be performed by having the NSClient++ installed on a remote Windows system. The directions to install NSClient++ and configure the Nagios server to monitor a Windows system can be found at http://nagios.sourceforge.net/docs/3_0/monitoring-windows.html.

We will address some the functions of the NSClient++ plug-in and how it can be used to identify potentially malicious activity on remote Windows systems.

The first NSClient++ check we will review is the ability to monitor the memory usage of a remote system. By defining the following configuration parameter on the Nagios server, we can monitor the memory utilization on a remote Windows system:

```
define service{
  use                   generic-service
  host_name             <Your Server Name Here>
  service_description   Memory Usage
  check_command         check_nt!MEMUSE!-w 80 -c 90
}
```

The check_command portion of the configuration tells Nagios to check the memory usage and generate a warning when memory usage is 80% and a critical alert when it is 90% (Figure 7.3).

Figure 7.3 Critical Alert

FP2	C:\ Drive Space	OK	03-10-2008 18:13:34	0d 19h 6m 24s	1/3	c: - total: 3.99 Gb - used: 1.51 Gb (38%) - free 2.48 Gb (62%)
	CPU Load	OK	03-10-2008 18:13:41	0d 0h 6m 17s	1/3	CPU Load 7% (5 min average)
	Explorer	OK	03-10-2008 18:15:46	0d 0h 34m 12s	1/3	Explorer.exe: Running
	Memory Usage	CRITICAL	03-10-2008 18:19:43	0d 0h 0m 15s	1/3	Memory usage: total:161.43 Mb - used: 160.14 Mb (99%) - free: 1.29 Mb (1%)
	NSClient++ Version	OK	03-10-2008 18:13:49	0d 0h 6m 9s	1/3	NSClient++ 0.3.0.1 RC 2007-11-28
	Uptime	OK	03-10-2008 18:15:28	0d 0h 34m 30s	1/3	System Uptime - 0 day(s) 0 hour(s) 4 minute(s)

There could be a variety of reasons why a potentially compromised Windows host would have its memory resources exhausted. Many attackers use large numbers of systems under their control to attack other networks via denial-of-service attacks, spam, or possibly utilizing multiple systems to perform distributed password cracking.

The second NSClient++ check we are going to look at is the drive space check:

```
define service{
  use                   generic-service
  host_name             <Your Server Name Here>
  service_description   C:\ Drive Space
  check_command         check_nt!USEDDISKSPACE!-l c -w 80 -c 90
}
```

The preceding check watches how much space is being used by the system being monitored. If the utilization is greater than 80%, a warning will be issued. If the utilization is greater than 90%, a critical alert will be issued (Figure 7.4).

Figure 7.4 Critical Alert

| FP2 | C:\ Drive Space | CRITICAL | 03-10-2008 18:57:23 | 0d 0h 4m 29s | 3/3 | c: - total: 3.99 Gb - used: 3.60 Gb (90%) - free 0.39 Gb (10%) |

Many attackers prefer to store incriminating evidence on other people's systems. This way, when the FBI breaks down a door to seize evidence, it won't be their door. It should be noted that some of the more advanced rootkits like Hacker Defender have the capability to mask the true amount of hard drive space that is being used.

The final NSClient++ check we are going to look at is the explorer.exe check. This check monitors the status of explorer.exe:

```
define service{
  use                   generic-service
  host_name             <Your Server Name Here>
  service__description  Explorer
  check_command         check_nt!PROCSTATE!-d SHOWALL -l Explorer.exe
}
```

This process is associated with the Windows GUI. If this service is not running, it makes it very difficult to interact with the computer that is being monitored. Many of the different tools attackers often use try to inject their malicious code into explorer.exe. Tools like Metasploit have the capability to migrate to this process, and rootkits like AFX use the explorer.exe process as a place to inject and hide their malicious code. However, often explorer.exe will become unstable during the process. If the service crashes, you should investigate the root cause of the crash.

To learn more about dll injection, we recommend Jim Shewmaker's excellent presentation on the topic: bluenotch.com/files/Shewmaker-DLL-Injection.pdf.

Securing Communications with NSClient++

It is strongly recommended that you set two parameters in the NSC.ini file on the Windows clients you are monitoring. You should set a password to access the NSClient++ plug-in and restrict access to only the Nagios server's IP address.

The two parameters to set on the remote systems being monitored are:

```
password=<Your password here>
```

and

```
allowed_hosts=<Nagios Server IP address>
```

Do not use the same password as the Administrator account of the system being monitored, or of any other system on your network for that matter. Use a password that is unique to the NSClient++ function.

Another great check with NSClient++ is CheckEventLog. The following brute force password attack check was provided by Mick Douglas:

```
$ARG1$ = "security"
$ARG2$ = max before warn
$ARG3$ = max before crit
$ARG4$ = "529"

./check_nrpe -H $HOSTNAME$ -c CheckEventLog -a filter=new file="$ARG1$"
MaxWarn=$ARG2$ MaxCrit=$ARG3$ filter-generated=\<2h filter-eventID==$ARG4$
filter-eventType==error filter=in filter=all
```

Security Checks with NRPE for Linux

check_load

This check checks the total processing load on a remote system. As with the NSClient++ checks in Windows, this check is useful for identifying potentially malicious programs that are using your system's CPU cycles either to launch attacks or processing such as password cracking.

```
define service{
    use                 generic-service
    host_name           <Your Server name here>
    service_description CPU Load
    check_command       check_nrpe!check_load
}
```

check_users

This check monitors the total number of users currently logged in to a system. If there are servers that should rarely be interacted with by administrators except in controlled change management functions, you may want to have this check alert you when a system is logged on to:

```
define service{
  use                 generic-service
  host_name           <Your Server name here>
```

```
    service_description     Current Users
    check_command           check_nrpe!check_users
}
```

check_total_procs

This check gets to the core of knowing your network. You should have a solid understanding of what services are running on your systems. With this check, you can tell if a system has a service shutdown or if an additional service has been started. Often, attackers may start additional services like ftp or IRC chat relays once they have compromised a system.

check_by_ssh

One of the favorite checks in Nagios is the check_by_ssh plug-in. With this plug-in it is possible to run any script on a remote machine via ssh. It is not recommended to use this check for checks that need to reoccur on a regular and short time basis because of the bandwidth involved. However, it is a great plug-in to use when there is something the default NRPE plug-ins will not do. For example, it is possible to run a bash script that runs various rootkit detection checks and then emails the results to you every morning. It is nice to have some security checks initiated remotely rather than via a local cron job. Once attackers compromise a system, they often check the local cron jobs to see what the maintenance operations are. By initiating some of these checks remotely, you may catch an attacker off-guard.

Watching for Session Hijacking Attacks

Many attackers attempt to hijack the sessions of servers, services, and users on your network. There are two main points where attackers will attempt to proxy or intercept user, server, and/or service sessions. The first is by controlling DNS queries and responses, and the second is by launching a targeted arp-cache poising attack. We will cover both of these attack scenarios and show how Nagios can assist in identifying these attacks.

DNS Attacks

There are a couple of different ways an attacker can manipulate DNS queries. The first is by directly changing the records stored on a DNS server through a remote cache poisoning attack, or an attacker can take over the DNS server and then change the records. In either case, Nagios can assist a security team in identifying these attacks. By running the check_dns plug-in from Nagios, an administrator can specify and monitor which DNS entries should be stored on your DNS server. For example, there may be an internal Sugar CRM server in an environment. This would be a great target for an attacker to compromise. By manipulating the DNS records, an attacker can force internal users to go to the attacker's system instead of the legitimate Sugar server. At this point, an attacker can either proxy the connection to the real Sugar server or mimic the logon screen of the legitimate Sugar server, collect user IDs and passwords, and return an error page. In both scenarios, the DNS entries will appear modified to a Nagios server check. By configuring the check_dns plug-in, you can monitor what the DNS records should be and receive a notification when they have changed.

For example, you could run the following check:

```
check_dns -H www.localsugar.com -s 192.168.1.1 -a 192.168.1.100
```

which states that the DNS server at 192.168.1.1 is going to look up www.localsugar.com. The expected address is 192.168.1.100. However, check_dns returns the following:

```
DNS CRITICAL - expected '192.168.1.100' but got '17.250.248.34'
```

Arp Cache Poisoning Attacks

Another vector used by many malicious attackers is an arp-cache poisoning attack. This attack is similar to the DNS attack insofar as they redirect traffic to a system they control. However, they are achieving redirection by manipulating the arp entries on the victim hosts on a local network segment or LAN.

The problem with arp is that any unsolicited arp responses will be stored for future reference by the machines that receive them. Because of this "feature" of the arp protocol, an attacker can pretend to be any system on the local segment he wants to be. For example, he could be an internal company Web server, or pretend to be the default gateway for the network. By becoming the default gateway, all traffic sent beyond the current network segment or out to the Internet would be sent to a machine the attacker owns, where it can be captured, sniffed, hijacked, and routed to the legitimate destination.

If an attacker spoofs an internal IP address on a local network segment in this way, the normal Nagios checks that would be run against the spoofed system may fail. This is because the Nagios checks sent to the legitimate host will be run against the IP address of the attacker's system. It should be noted that attackers can mimic Nagios client responses to the centralized server requests.

It is also possible for an attacker to spoof the IP address of the default gateway for a LAN segment. Nagios has the capability to run a number of SNMP checks against SNMP enabled devices. Again, if an attacker is spoofing the address of the SNMP enabled gateway, these Nagios queries will not be answered correctly and will generate alerts for the network and security administrators to respond to. As a special note, whenever possible use SNMP v3, as it has multiple security improvements over previous versions.

Let's look at an arp spoofing attack and its effect on Nagios monitoring. First, let's look at the arp table of our monitoring system.

```
monitor# arp -a

Router1.localhost.net (10.98.63.97) at 00:12:01:a9:75:00 on fxp0 [ethernet]
monitor.localhost.net (10.98.63.111) at 00:06:5b:04:d3:39 on fxp0 permanent
[ethernet]
Router2.localhost.net (10.98.63.115) at 00:01:80:10:50:25 on fxp0 [ethernet]

We then initiate an ARP Spoof from another host on the same switched network.

./arpspoof -i fxp0 10.98.63.115
00:06:5b:04:d3:39 ff:ff:ff:ff:ff:ff 0806 42: arp reply 10.98.63.115 is-at
00:02:b3:d0:28:4c
00:06:5b:04:d3:39 ff:ff:ff:ff:ff:ff 0806 42: arp reply 10.98.63.115 is-at
00:02:b3:d0:28:4c
00:06:5b:04:d3:39 ff:ff:ff:ff:ff:ff 0806 42: arp reply 10.98.63.115 is-at
00:02:b3:d0:28:4c
00:06:5b:04:d3:39 ff:ff:ff:ff:ff:ff 0806 42: arp reply 10.98.63.115 is-at
00:02:b3:d0:28:4c
00:06:5b:04:d3:39 ff:ff:ff:ff:ff:ff 0806 42: arp reply 10.98.63.115 is-at
00:02:b3:d0:28:4c
00:06:5b:04:d3:39 ff:ff:ff:ff:ff:ff 0806 42: arp reply 10.98.63.115 is-at
00:02:b3:d0:28:4c
00:06:5b:04:d3:39 ff:ff:ff:ff:ff:ff 0806 42: arp reply 10.98.63.115 is-at
00:02:b3:d0:28:4c
00:01:80:10:50:25 ff:ff:ff:ff:ff:ff 0806 42: arp reply 10.98.63.115 is-at
00:02:b3:d0:28:4c
00:01:80:10:50:25 ff:ff:ff:ff:ff:ff 0806 42: arp reply 10.98.63.115 is-at
00:02:b3:d0:28:4c
00:01:80:10:50:25 ff:ff:ff:ff:ff:ff 0806 42: arp reply 10.98.63.115 is-at
00:02:b3:d0:28:4c
```

We also see that we lose our connectivity to the original device:

```
monitor# ping 10.98.63.115
PING 10.98.63.115 (10.98.63.115): 56 data bytes ^C

--- 10.98.63.115 ping statistics ---160 packets transmitted, 0 packets received,
100% packet loss
```

and that the new device is listed in our arp table now.

```
monitor# arp -a
Router1.localhost.net (10.98.63.97) at 00:12:01:a9:75:00 on fxp0 [ethernet]
monitor.localhost.net (10.98.63.111) at 00:06:5b:04:d3:39 on fxp0 permanent
[ethernet]
Router2.localhost.net (10.98.63.115) at 00:02:b3:d0:28:4c on fxp0 [ethernet]
```

Finally, we see the effect of this attack from our Nagios Web page (Figure 7.5).

Figure 7.5 Nagios Displays Attack Effect

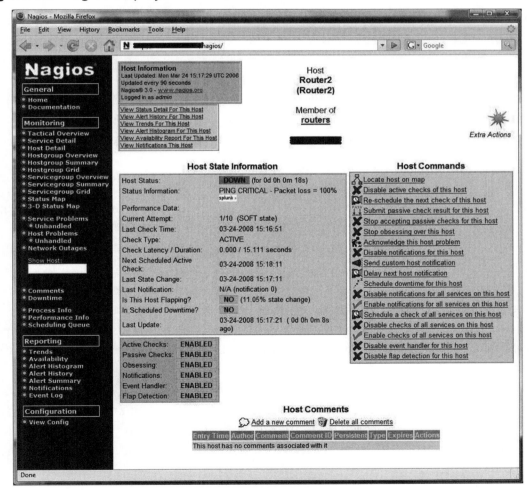

As you can see, as far as Nagios is concerned the device it is supposed to be monitoring is down.

Nagios and Compliance

Unfortunately, many network and security administrators fear external and internal audits more than they fear an attack. Further, many security teams spend far more time documenting and "proving" that they are secure than actually securing their networks or trying to identify possible intrusions. This may be one of the reasons why many security professionals put so much trust in their security appliances and software. They just do not have enough time to do anything else.

In this section, we identify ways in which Nagios can assist network and security administrators to provide "proof" that they are compliant.

One of the key points any security manager needs to understand is that compliance rules change over time. What qualifies as due diligence this year may not be the same next year. Many security managers spend a tremendous amount of time trying to "meet the minimum" when it comes to their security architecture and expenditures. While a good risk assessment and a solid cost benefit analysis is always a good way to plan architecture modifications, utilizing tools like Nagios to monitor the status of systems and services will be an applicable addition in most compliance-driven security environments.

Sarbanes-Oxley

Passed in 2002, the Sarbanes-Oxley (SOX) or Public Company Accounting Reform and Investors Protection Act is focused on protecting shareholders. It is the direct result of a wave of corporate scandals and outright fraud. For your company to fall under the SOX Act it has to be a publicly traded company.

The majority of SOX relates to the accounting practices of a company and how it is to undergo financial reporting. Section 404 of SOX requires that a company must safeguard its data and provide controls to protect its integrity. Failure to comply with SOX can have a dire impact on a company in the form of penalties and possible jail time for the CEO and CFO.

SOX 404 requires the use of an internal control framework. Under COBIT and COSO (which are commonly used for SOX compliance), there are requirements for the monitoring of internal systems and services. Nagios can help your organization in areas ranging from monitoring systems and services to assisting in verifying they are in a trusted state.

SOX and COBIT

COBIT's main goal is to align the business drivers of an organization with the management of their information technology. It also includes the ability to incorporate metrics or measurable objectives to the management of information technology, which includes large portions of a company's security architecture.

All IT management plans, processes, and procedures need to meet the following two criteria from the COBIT 4.1 executive overview:

- Business objectives are achieved.

- Undesired events are prevented or detected and corrected.

These two objectives tie in very closely with using network-monitoring software like Nagios. While an organization may not be looking for specific signs of a compromise, detecting and preventing "Undesirable events" definitely falls under the Availability aspect of the Confidentially, Integrity, and Availability (CIA) triad.

Under COBIT, four core domains cover the life cycle of an information system. While Nagios can be helpful in most core domains, the two where it provides the greatest value to an organization is *Delivery and Support* and *Monitor and Evaluate*. Under *Delivery and Support*, the control objective most applicable to Nagios is *DS13: Manage Operations*. However, your organization may also want to check DS7, which is *Educate and Train Users*. One of the main problems facing many organizations is how to retain talent, and the institutional knowledge of their IT teams. It would be a good idea for your team to have a cross-training plan on how to monitor and effectively manage your Nagios installation.

Under *Monitor and Evaluate*, Nagios can directly support all the control objectives (ME1-4) listed here:

- ME1 Monitor and Evaluate IT Processes

- ME2 Monitor and Evaluate Internal Control

- ME3 Ensure Regulatory Compliance

- ME4 Provide IT Governance

SOX and COSO

Under the Committee of Sponsoring Organizations of the Treadway Commission (COSO), five components of the internal control framework for Nagios can be directly applied to the fifth component, *Monitoring*. While the majority of the COSO framework applies to financial processes, the *Monitoring* component can apply to IT and financial monitoring.

It should be noted that under SOX it is not enough to run a tool like Nagios. Your team needs to document how it is using Nagios and how it supports the core objectives of your SOX-compliant environment. As with any compliance framework, if you don't document how you do something and prove it is being done, it will not matter in an audit.

Payment Card Industry

The Payment Card Industry (PCI) Data Security Standard (DSS) was created in late 2004 when all the major credit card companies stopped their respective security standards and merged them into a unified standard.

Under the PCI DSS are six groups of security principals that break down further into 12 requirements. The group most applicable to utilizing Nagios on your network is *Regularly Monitor and Test Networks*. Under this principal, the two requirements are:

- **Requirement 10** Track and monitor all access to network resources and cardholder data.
- **Requirement 11** Regularly test security systems and processes.

While it may seem that Requirement 10 is not applicable to Nagios, remember that you need to monitor the systems and processes that are performing transactions involving cardholder data. For Requirement 11, using Nagios to regularly poll security systems and processes can support this requirement.

DCID 6/3

The Director of Central Intelligence Directive (DCID) 6/3 puts forth seven goals for protecting Sensitive Compartmentalized Information (SCI) and information relating to Special Access Programs (SAPs):

- Provide policy and procedures for the security and protection of systems that create, process, store, and transmit intelligence information.
- Provide administrative and system security requirements, including those for interconnected systems.

- Define and mandate the use of a risk management process.

- Define and mandate the use of a certification and accreditation process.

- Promote the use of efficient procedures and cost-effective, computer-based security features and assurances.

- Describe the roles and responsibilities of the individuals who constitute the decision-making segment of the IS security community and its system users.

- Require a life-cycle management approach to implementing system security requirements.

- Introduce the concepts Levels-of-Concern and Protection Level of information.

The Director of Central Intelligence Directive 6/3 specifically relates to the protection of information systems that process sensitive compartmented information. The two main sections of DCID 6/3 that can be addressed by Nagios are:

[SysAssur1] System Assurance shall include...

1. *features and procedures to validate the integrity and the expected operation of the security-relevant software, hardware, and firmware; and*
2. *features or procedures for protection of the operating system from improper changes.*

and

[SysAssur2] System Assurance shall include...

1. *control of access to the Security Support Structure (i.e., the hardware, software, and firmware that perform operating systems or security functions); and*
2. *assurance of the integrity of the Security Support Structure.*

It should be noted that during audits performed by the Designated Accrediting Authority (DAA) Representative, the concept of what is part of the Security Support Structure and what is not tends to become elastic, meaning that almost every component of an architecture can qualify as being part of the Security Support Structure. With this in mind, it is helpful to have a tool like Nagios regularly check the systems and services on your network to validate that they are operating in an expected and approved manner.

Finally, there are additional classified sections of the DCID 6/3. Please, verify with your DAA whether these sections apply to you.

DIACAP

The DoD Information Assurance Certification and Accreditation Process (DIACAP) is the replacement for the Department of Defense Information Technology Security Certification and Accreditation Process (DITSCAP). The main difference is that the DIACAP treats risk and the assessment of a system's risk as an ongoing process.

The Department of Defense Information Assurance Certification and Accreditation Process references DoD 8500.2 for the Information Assurance Controls that are to be utilized when reviewing DoD systems for IA compliance. Within the 8500.2 section, DCSS-2 relates specifically to the functions Nagios provides.

DCSS-2 System State Changes

System initializations, shutdowns, and aborts are configured to ensure the system remains in a secure state. Tests are provided and periodically run to ensure the integrity of the system state. It should be noted that definition of a "system" could include the critical processes as well. In this section, we covered a few of the many compliance controls that can be bolstered utilizing Nagios. It should be clear that other compliance standards may not call out specifically for system and service monitoring (e.g., HIPPA), but Nagios can still be very valuable in these environments.

Securing Nagios

We have discussed a variety of different ways to use Nagios to help secure your network and identify when a possible attack has occurred. However, we also need to discuss how Nagios can be hardened against attack. There are few targets as useful to an attacker as the very systems used to identify potentially malicious activities. Nagios has the capability to interact with Windows systems via the NSClient++ plug-in, which runs as the local System account on a Windows system. The System account has virtually unlimited privileges on a local Windows computer. On Linux, Nagios interacts with the NRPE plug-in, which is running with root level permissions. If an attacker compromises your core Nagios server, he will get virtually unlimited access to the systems being monitored.

Hardening Linux and Apache

A full write-up on securing a Linux system with Apache is beyond the scope of this section. However, a number of different tools will assist you in securing the underlying operating system and Web server of your Nagios server.

The first recommendation is Bastille by Jay Beale (www.bastille-linux.org) (Figure 7.6).

Figure 7.6 Bastille

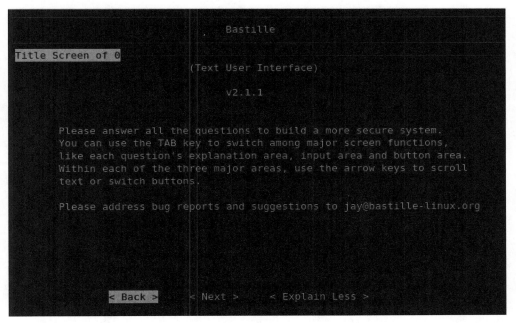

The second recommended tool is the Center for Internet Security's scoring tool for Linux. They also have an excellent guide for securing Apache. Please note that the CIS guide for Apache has a write-up on utilizing SSL on your Apache server. SSL should be used with every Nagios installation (www.cisecurity.org/) (Figure 7.7).

Figure 7.7 SSL

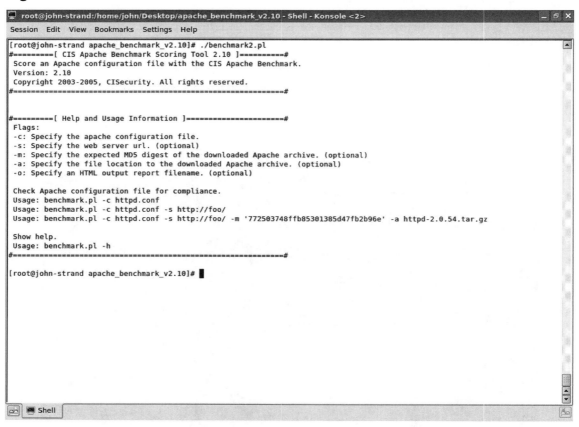

Finally, there are the Defense Information Systems Agency's Security Readiness Review (SRR) scripts for Linux and Apache (http://iase.disa.mil/stigs/SRR/index.html).

Basics

One of the core basics for securing Nagios is to establish different user accounts to log on to the Nagios Web server. Too often, organizations use the same Nagios admin account for all of the networks and systems administrators to monitor Nagios. This makes it extremely difficult to identify who did what, and when. Attackers love shared accounts because they make it easy for them to blend in their attacks and activities along with standard maintenance activity. A good rule to follow is that every user of the Nagios system should have his own uniquely identified accounts, and no one should use the nagiosadmin account unless he has to for a specific and justified purpose.

The next key to securing a Nagios server is to restrict who can even see the server at all. Nagios is installed on a Linux platform, so use iptables to restrict which systems or subnets can access the server. An excellent resource on iptables is www.netfilter.org.

Summary

This section explained some basic ways you can use Nagios to support your security posture. It should be noted that this should serve as a starting place for your organization to expand and tune Nagios to best suit your environment. No two environments are the same. Do not ever use "one size fits all" tools.

Chapter 8

Case Study: Acme Enterprises

315

Case Study Overview

Nagios is a free, powerful, open source software application designed to monitor hosts, services, and networks. Large organizations that invest in information technology—government, commercial, research, or academic—would be hard-pressed to not employ an effective network and systems monitoring solution. The following case study demonstrates how a fictitious large organization, ACME Enterprises, leverages the monitoring and reporting capabilities of Nagios to oversee network and service operations. The focus of this case study consolidates the concepts of the previous chapters, and ties them all together by showing the technologies and Nagios add-ons you might wish to consider when deploying Nagios.

Who Are You?

In this case study, you are part of the systems integration team in the European office with some experience in implementing a network and systems monitoring solution. For the sake of simplicity, systems integrators in this scenario also act as systems administrators, who in turn, work closely with IT support personnel. Keep in mind that there is a separate systems administration group dedicated to servicing end users; your core objective is to deploy Nagios, verify the installation, and hand off the operations and maintenance (O&M) duties of this new Nagios installation to systems administration staff. In addition, your job is to shadow the more experienced systems integrators and assist them as needed. Finally, the more senior systems integrators insist that you follow system design, implementation, and verification best practices to verify that Nagios is effectively monitoring the hosts and services it is configured to monitor.

ACME Enterprises Network: What's under the Hood?

Acme Enterprises is a Fortune 500 company that writes commercial Web-based software in the supply-chain management market. It has offices in Europe, North America, and Japan. Each office implements a multi-layer security model for its' network.

Security zones are:

- **DMZ** Load balancer, Web services, and DNS services sit in the DMZ along with the incoming mail server.

- **Developer network** Developers and system integrators work here, corporate does not want them to have access to any production equipement; access rules are enforced by a hardware firewall.

- **Corporate** HR, accounting, and other overhead groups work on this network segment.

- **IT** Desktop support services, network services, corporate data center.

Each company office is connected to the others by hardware-based VPNs routing over the public Internet. Each company also hosts a regionalized version of the company's Website. Europe is the headquarters for monitoring although each office does have personnel experienced in configuring and troubleshooting servers and network devices. SNMP is allowed only within the developer, corporate, and IT zones. SNMP may be used across the VPN links but is also not allowed to traverse the open Internet.

Acme runs the following applications on its global networks:

- Three-tiered Web application on production Web sites:
- Bluecoat web proxies on the front-end
- Apache/PHP application middle tier
- MySQL database back end
- Oracle database servers may be sprinkled within ACME Enterprises as there is "talk" about supporting both Oracle and MySQL
- Windows-based Active Directory (AD) network for desktop users with two domain controllers at each site.

Network layout:

- All three offices have VPN connections between them
- Each office is scheduled for Nagios deployment, starting with Europe (Figure 8.1)
- USA—Slave
- Japan—Slave
- Europe—Master

Figure 8.1 ACME Enterprises

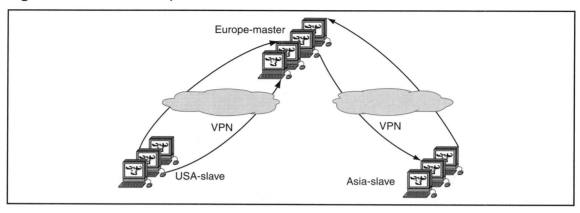

ACME Enterprises Management and Staff: Who's Running the Show?

ACME has the following technical and management groups, show in Table 8.1, who need to be notified when services or hosts are down.

Table 8.1 ACME Management and Staff

ACME Group	Role and Description within ACME Enterprises
IT managers	IT managers represent the system administrators, system integrators, developers, and network staff. This group makes purchasing decisions, drives the software release schedules for developers, and ensures technical personnel have the tools, training, and environment needed to maximize productivity.
System administrators	System administrators report to the IT managers and support all of the servers within ACME Enterprises. This group ensures that all other groups are able to access servers. They provide second-level application support on servers, and work to ensure high availability of servers for all end users employed by ACME Enterprises.

Continued

Table 8.1 Continued. ACME Management and Staff

ACME Group	Role and Description within ACME Enterprises
Developers	Developers report to IT managers; developers design, implement, and test the software packages they create for Acme enterprises. Developers, IT managers, and non-technical staff are the major consumers of network and host services, which are maintained by the system administrators, system integrators, and network staff.
System integrators	System integrators report to IT managers; they maintain the hardware and software services in the developer network. Unlike system administrators, the system integration team provides third-level support for server applications, troubleshoots server environment issues, and works closely with the system administrators and network staff in diagnosing problems that are software, operating system, or network related.
Network staff	The network staff reports to the IT management group and supports all network devices within ACME Enterprises. They also work to ensure that all end users are able to connect to network resources as well as the host servers and software applications maintained by the system administrators and system integrators.

ACME Enterprises and Nagios: Rubber Meets the Road!

Recall that ACME Enterprises has offices throughout the world, and each office location implements a multilayer security network broken into four zones. These security zones are the DMZ zone, the developer zone, the corporate zone, and finally the IT support zone. The systems integrators are enthusiastic, but methodical (yes, "methodical") in their deployment of Nagios to monitor ACME Enterprise networks. The systems integrators are seasoned professionals, and have successfully deployed software-driven systems and hardware-oriented solutions employing network appliances. While every organization is different, the systems integrators are accustomed to their internal customers, which are generally managers, other administrative personnel, and of course engineers, developers, and other IT support staff. As with all successful systems deployments, the systems integrators divide their plan to deploy Nagios into three phases—pre-deployment, deployment, and post-deployment.

Table 8.2 captures most of the activities the systems integrators within ACME Enterprises will be following. The provide a high-level picture of the efforts needed to successfully deploy Nagios. What's more, the system integrators working for ACME Enterprises wear two hats—the non-technical information gathering hat and the technical soup-to-nuts hat.

Entries shown in **BOLD** under the Activities column are discussed below the table. As can be seen, pre-deployment and deployment phases are the main focus of this case study.

Table 8.2 Nagios Deployment Phases

Nagios Deployment Phases	Activities
Pre-deployment	■ **Determine where Nagios will be deployed!**
	■ **Engage the customer early, and determine what goals the customer wishes to achieve through the use of enterprise-wide monitoring with Nagios.**
	■ **Determine what network servers, services, and applications will be monitored. Prioritize them accordingly.**
	■ **Identify the resources, people, and equipment that will actually carry out or assist in the scheduled deployment of Nagios.**
	■ **Survey and evaluate possible strategies that will be used to integrate Nagios within the enterprise network.**
	■ Determine the scope of deployment including the scheduling, level of effort, and trade-offs in applying certain technologies (for integration) over another.
	■ Download Nagios software.
	■ Download Nagios add-ons and other software that will be deployed if integrating Nagios with other software packages deployed within the enterprise.

Continued

Table 8.2 Continued. Nagios Deployment Phases

Nagios Deployment Phases	Activities
Deployment	■ **Nagios configuration strategies**
	■ Software staging of Nagios add-ons, and other software
	■ Verify installation of Nagios software on server
	■ Verify installation of Nagios add-ons
	■ Test Nagios and verify that alerts are being sent by Nagios and SNMP traps and NSCA messages are being collected properly by Nagios
Post-deployment	■ Training of end users
	■ Train the IT support staff that will maintain Nagios in the enterprise
	■ Official hand off to operations and maintenance personnel
	■ Provide technical and consulting support as needed

Nagios Pre-Deployment Activities: What Are We Monitoring?

Determine where Nagios will be deployed! This step is crucial and is the main precursor before deployment. If Nagios will be deployed into your network, it must have a home. Sure, you can slap Nagios onto any Unix box and have it start collecting traps in no time flat, right? Yes, no, maybe?

In all cases, the Nagios server should be installed onto a host that can "see" all of the hosts it will be monitoring. At a minimum, monitored hosts should be able to send traps to the Nagios server. Unless Nagios and the database used to store SNMP traps are installed on the same physical server, we'll need at least two servers—one for Nagios, and one for the back-end database. These two servers form the hardware core of our Nagios deployment. We will elaborate on the layout of Nagios and the minimum components needed to successfully monitor all of the hosts we will be monitoring with Nagios at Acme Enterprises.

Engage the customer early, and determine what meaningful alerts can be captured /collected in a needs assessment. Pre-deployment planning is critical to the success of a Nagios implementation. During this phase we determine what personnel and hardware resources will be needed for our Nagios implementation. We also create a deployment schedule, determine what dependencies exist for each deployment phase, and then add some small additional time to the schedule for unexpected delays and problems that may occur. Management must be involved with this process and must approve of our plan. The end result of pre-planning is a document that clearly explains the deployment process.

Needs assessment starts by soliciting technical requirements from customers and users. Engaging the customer from the very outset of the requirements process establishes expectations systems integrators begin by conducting a needs assessment, identifying their internal customers, and surveying the actual computer network that will be monitored. There will be requirements planning meetings, information gathering, resource gathering (personnel and equipment), schedule planning, risk assessment, verifying connectivity, and of course, management approval.

At this point you have convinced both your customers and management to use Nagios as a monitoring solution. A needs assessment has been conducted, and both the requirements plan and a risk assessment have been approved. The resources, which are the people and equipment needed to deploy Nagios monitoring, that will be supporting the systems integrators have been identified. What's next?

Now is the time to determine which systems are the most critical to monitor, identify any other stakeholders who need to be involved with the implementation process, and schedule deployment and post-deployment activities. We will discuss deployment and post deployment activities in later sections of this chapter. The systems integration team should now schedule meetings with management, technical leads, and the customer to answer the following general questions. The responses to these questions will influence the scope, level of effort, and scheduling of the overall Nagios rollout.

- Who are the stakeholders?
- Who needs to be informed of system outages?
- Which users are directly impacted from deployment?
- Who will be using the monitoring solution?
- What metrics are important to the customer?
- What critical network servers and devices are important to monitor?
- Which alerts will be meaningful to the customer?
- Which alerts will be meaningful to IT management?

- Which alerts will be meaningful to the systems administrators?

- Which alerts will be meaningful to the software developers?

- Which alerts will be meaningful to the network staff?

- Which alerts will be meaningful to us, the systems integrators?

- Who at ACME knows the most about the important devices within ACME Enterprises?

- Who at ACME knows the most about the important applications operating within ACME Enterprises?

After this set of meetings, the systems integration team summarized the general network monitoring requirements (see Table 8.3) and expectations from all technical groups (including themselves).

Table 8.3 ACME Management and Staff Monitoring Requirements

ACME Group / Internal Customer	Monitoring Information Needed / Monitoring Requirements
IT managers	Want to know that service level agreements (SLAs) are being met for production hosts, would like a graphical dashboard to make it very easy for them to see the status of services and devices on each network at the office they work in.
System administrators	Status of all servers on all networks; need to know immediately if any servers are unreachable; second-tier support for applications on the servers.
Developers	Need to know that all hosts and services on hosts in the developer network are available.
System integrators	Maintain hardware and software services in the developer network; need to know if applications are performing poorly, critical software services go offline, or hosts become unavailable.
Network staff	Need to know how network devices are performing, if any network paths become unavailable, or if any connections between the offices or security zones become congested.

Although the information-gathering efforts by the system integrators are general, the monitoring requirements collected are precursors in answering questions specific to the internal customers within ACME Enterprises. In all cases, Nagios has the ability to monitor the health of hardware, services, or applications via plug-ins and event handlers. Nagios can also ingest data from external applications via passive checks and external commands.

Identify the resources, people, and equipment needed to deploy Nagios. Sure, the systems integration team is a bright bunch, and you are part of that elite team (cough cough). Let's not forget that information gathering also includes identifying the personnel who know the most about the important devices and applications within ACME Enterprises. This includes systems administrators, developers, and yes, IT managers.

Determine what network devices, servers, services, and applications will be monitored. Prioritize them accordingly. Ok, so we have ACME management's blessing to keep going. At this point, it's important to take inventory and build a list of the servers and services, devices, and applications that warrant monitoring. As you go through the list of servers in ACME Enterprises, be sure to the purpose of the server, what security zone the server resides in, which users directly log in to the server, and what services and applications are running on each server. We'll create a sample list of servers, the security zones they reside in, and look at some possible approaches in monitoring the server itself, or what's running on those network servers.

Nagios has rich capabilities that allow it to transmit notifications to external applications used by IT support and systems administrators. The systems integrators look under the hood again of ACME Enterprises' network to take an inventory of what will be monitored. While the comprehensive list neither provides the total number of server hosts to be monitored, nor their operating system we continue, knowing that Nagios is flexible enough to monitor every server, device and application at our organization. We can use clustering as well to expand the number of devices and services we monitor if one Nagios server is not able to monitoring everything at ACME by itself (see Chapter 2, "Designing Configurations for Large Organizations," and Chapter 3, "Scaling Nagios").

Table 8.4 ACME Enterprises Comprehensive List of Network Host Servers

ACME Stakeholder Group	Security Zone	Network Host Servers
System administrators System integrators Network staff	DMZ	Load balancers Bluecoat proxy appliances Mail servers DNS servers Web servers
IT management Developers System integrators	Developer Network	Development Web servers Development mail servers Development portal servers Development application servers Development database servers Development LDAP servers Development software build servers Development configuration management (CM) server
All end users, which include technical and nontechnical staff	Corporate Network	Corporate database servers Corporate backup servers Corporate file and document management servers
IT management System administrators System integrators Network staff	IT Support	Enterprise CM server Enterprise backup servers Enterprise FTP servers

Now that the system integration team has put together its comprehensive list of host servers to monitor, they can work with other teams in identifying what services and applications for each server should be monitored based on customer input, and then prioritize accordingly.

Survey and evaluate possible strategies that will be used to integrate Nagios within the enterprise network. This is the meat and potatoes of Nagios integration, and builds on the previous section capturing the list of host servers and services that can be monitored.

Nagios offers a rich set of core monitoring capabilities for both servers and services. Nagios provides self-explanatory status codes, for servers: **UP, DOWN, PENDING,** or **UNREACHABLE.** Host service states (or application services running within the server hosts) are **OK, WARNING, CRITICAL, UNKNOWN,** or **PENDING.**

The system integration team decides that their approach will entail the following:

1. **Determine the minimum "basic host metrics" that will be monitored for all server hosts (Table 8.5).** These metrics will be monitored and collected from all servers. Although it is possible to capture a large number of metrics using the core Nagios "checks" library, the systems integration staff, will start monitoring a few a metrics per server host, and then expand as needed.

Table 8.5 Basic Server Metrics

Metric	Description
CPU	Monitors CPU utilization on a server
Disk utilization	Monitors hard disk space utilization
Load average	Monitors the overall system load on a server
RAM	Monitors RAM utilization on a server
Swap space	Monitors virtual memory utilization on a server

2. **Determine the different types of servers by purpose or role (Table 8.6).** Nagios provides the flexibility to monitor server hosts according to their role. For example, Web servers and database servers each run different services that require different types of checks. An alternative monitoring approach would be to focus on host monitoring and group devices by environment. This approach works well for system administrators and network administrators who are more concerned with the health of the system and network infrastructure within an organization.

Table 8.6 Types of Server Hosts Inside ACME Enterprises

Type of Server Host	Special Host Service Metrics Beyond Basic Host Service Metrics
Load balancers	
Bluecoat proxy appliances	
Mail servers	SSH, SMTP, or POP3
DNS servers	SSH, DNS
Web servers	SSH, HTTP, Apache, and Tomcat
Portal servers	SSH, HTTP, Apache, and Tomcat
Application servers	SSH
Database servers	SSH, Oracle TNS Listener
LDAP servers	SSH, LDAP/TLS, Bluecoat agents
Software build servers	
Configuration management (CM) servers	
Backup servers	
File and document management servers	
FTP servers	SSH, FTP

3. **Determine what core Nagios functionality and add-ons will be integrated with Nagios (Table 8.7).** Core functionality includes basic host checks and a suite of plugins that perform a variety of protocol level checks, from HTTP to SMTP to FTP. Active checks, passive checks, and add-ons will be evaluated by the sytem integration team. While Nagios is excellent out of the box, it is even better when augemented with complimentary software packages and plugins such as eHealth or NagVis. The system integration team has decided to use the core technologies and add-ons listed in Table 8.7.

Table 8.7 Nagios Core Technologies and Add-ons for ACME Enterprises

Core Technology	Brief Description
Host Escalations	Escalates notifications for a particular server host
Service Escalations	Escalates notifications for a particular service within a server host
Nagios Clustering	Distributed monitoring of server hosts and services
Read-only front-end	Provides a Nagios UI for reviewing conditions of server hosts and services
Plug-ins	Custom or third-party code to augment capabilities of Nagios
Nagios Add-ons	
NRPE	Allows monitoring host to execute plug-ins on remote server hosts
NSCA	Allows remote server hosts to send passive check results to monitoring host
NagVis	Visual display alternative for Nagios that displays network and system paths, and high-level application and service status
eHealth	Commercial trending and trap management software as Nagios add-on
Puppet	An agent-based open source system administration and configuration management automation tool that allows remote server hosts running the puppet to apply policies and rules from the Puppet server (Master)
Splunk	Provides full text search capabilities for system and application log files.

4. **Decide on an alerting or notification scheme for each ACME stake-holder group (our internal customers).**

Nagios Deployment Activities: Can You See Me?

Before proceeding in the deployment phase, the systems integration team does a sanity check by reviewing all completed activities. So far we have done the following:

- Meet with internal customers (IT managers, developers, network and system administration staff) to determine what is important to monitor.

- Determine where Nagios, will live on the network.

- Determine which hosts and services will be monitored

- Get an idea of which core Nagios checks and which plugins will be used to implement the monitoring solution

Time to deploy; let's take a quick look at the ACME Enterprises network environment.

We will monitor three offices: one in Japan, one in the United States, and one in Europe.

Each office implements multi-layer network security:

- DMZ—load balancer, Web services, and DNS services sit in the DMZ along with the incoming mail server.

- Developer network

- Corporate network

- IT support network

- SNMP is allowed only within the developer, corporate, and IT zones.

- SNMP may be used across the VPN links, but is not allowed to traverse the open Internet.

ACME Enterprises runs the following applications on its global networks:

- Three-tier Web application on production Web sites

- Bluecoat front end

- Apache/PHP application middle tier

- MySQL database back-end

- Some Oracle database servers may be sprinkled within ACME Enterprises as there is "talk" about supporting database vendors.

- AD network for desktop users with two domain controllers at each site

Since the European ACME office is home for monitoring operations, we'll start by going over the most suitable Nagios core technologies followed by the add-ons.

The system integration team in the European office has decided that it makes sense to start Nagios deployment in their local office first, then roll out to the U.S. and Japan office locations. The remaining portion of the deployment phase section will introduce Nagios core technologies, followed by add-ons, and apply those components relative to ACME Enterprises' monitoring needs. Let's step through the implementation approaches of how Nagios can be deployed in ACME Enterprises by determining where certain technologies may be used in the ACME Enterprises.

Enterprise and Remote Site Monitoring

Since the European office is the network monitoring headquarters for ACME Enterprises, it also hosts the Nagios master monitoring server. The American and Japanese offices host slave Nagios servers that monitor each offices' system and network resources and then report results back to the European office.

In the European office the master Nagios server a combined Nagios configuration. Furthermore, the European monitoring server runs the NSCA daemon, and accepts incoming passive checks from the U.S. and Japan Nagios monitoring servers. This topology allows the master monitoring server to capture an entire view of the network and systems being monitored within ACME Enterprises. The master Nagios server holds the configurations for notifications and host/service escalations, and requires that any host and service definitions at the remote offices are loaded in the master monitoring server's configuration. To make maintaining the configuration easier, the system integration team in the European office created the following directories in the master monitoring server:

```
$NAGIOS_ROOT/etc/usa
$NAGIOS_ROOT/etc/japan
```

The system integration team leverages Nagios' ability to read configurations from multiple directories; combined with a custom shell script running as a cron job we will be able to keep configurations synchronized between the slave servers and master Nagios server. The system integration team decides to schedule the configuration file synchronization cron job every 24 hours.

Nagios clustering is ideal when monitoring multiple offices in geographically distant locations. The advantage of an distributed approach is load sharing, especially if bandwidth between each office location is limited. Clustering allows each remote office to easily view the status of devices and services on their network. The system integration team and NOC team at the central office can easily monitor all networks from one location, making troubleshooting easier and lowering response time to problems that occur at any location. Now that we have our basic fault management architecture in place, how about trending?

eHealth

eHealth, a commercial trending and trap management suite of programs, can act as a monitor of monitors (MOM) in Figure 8.2. In our scenario, eHealth would be installed in the European office location, but not on the same physical server hardware as Nagios eHealth is designed to be a MOM, and comes with Trap Exploder, which provides flexible trap handling and filtering. Within ACME, eHealth serves as the monitor of monitors, leveraging it's strength in trap handling, while Nagios is used as the master fault manager and network visualization console. In this scenario, eHealth will forward all traps to Nagios for display and notification where applicable.

Figure 8.2 eHealth as a Monitor of Monitors (MOM)

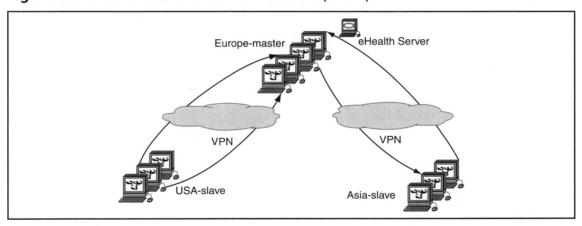

ACME IT staff will implement both active and passive checks within Nagios as both are useful and necessary in a large-scale installation. For example, NRPE is an active checking plug-in Nagios add-on that can be used to monitor servers at remote office locations. NRPE will be covered when we discuss how the system integration team will monitor hosts and services in the DMZ.

A variety of add-ons may be integrated with Nagios. The remainder of this section describes how the different groups within ACME Enterprises might use several of the Nagios add-ons described in this book. Specifically we will discuss NagTrap, NagVis, Puppet, and Splunk.

NagTrap

NagTrap is an open-source Nagios add-on that reads SNMP traps from a database created by SNMPTT (SNMP Trap Translator). Both the system integration and system administration teams would use NagTrap to view, query, and filter traps by host name, severity, and category from a PHP-based Web interface running on one an Apache Web server. The system integration team will make use of the custom script described in the section on SNMPTT to forward traps from SNMPTT to Nagios as passive checks.

NagVis

Remember that ACME Enterprises is a large company. In global enterprises where a large number of system and host problems are captured on the monitoring server's console, the sheer number of alerts may clutter up the screen. The different groups within ACME may not care about network maps, alert tables, or they might care about application health and not care about system and network health. For example, the IT managers and developers within ACME may care tremendously about application health, while systems integration, systems administration, and network staff pay attention to system and network health. Whatever the case, NagVis is a Nagios add-on with a PHP front end that allows Nagios administrators to set up service-oriented views of the host and service check data collected by Nagios. NagVis can read host and service data directly from the Nagios CGIs (not recommended) or from a MySQL database using the NDO Utils add-on. The systems integration team chooses to use NDO Utils and a database backend for performance and scalability reasons.

NagVis enables system administrators, system integrators, and developers to visualize the status of multiple environments from a single interface. In system or network operation centers, NagVis may shorted the learning curve of new NOC staff at ACME. How? We can take the logical network maps created by the network staff and drag and drop icons representing the hosts and services onto the network maps. New network staff now immediately see where a host or service resides on the network when a problem occurs. This allows network operations staff to easily communicate problem status and context with developers, other network staff, or more senior staff members at ACME.

Puppet

Puppet is an agent-based open source system administration and configuration management automation tool; each managed server runs a Puppet agent. The Puppet agent on each server retrieves its configuration from a central Puppet server (Puppet master), and applies the policies and rules it receives from the Puppet master to the managed system. Puppet is a standalone open source project that complements the network and system monitoring capabilities of Nagios. For example, the policies and rules enforced by Puppet clients may range from reporting changes in critical files and directories to ensuring no changes are made to specific files, managing and monitoring services and objects (cron jobs, groups, users, mail aliases), or running periodic jobs when specific system conditions are set. A typical example would entail deleting old core files under /var/core if the /var file system is nearly full. From the perspective of Nagios, the just described example would ensure that the disk usage check (i.e., check_disk) does not send alerts. The output of the results from these rules and policies may be used for troubleshooting or investigating alerts generated by Nagios for managed devices and services.

Splunk

Splunk integration was introduced in Nagios release 3.x. Splunk provides sophisticated "Google-like" search capabilities for text-based log files. The Splunk integration serves to enhance both the monitoring and troubleshooting capabilities of Nagios by allowing users of Nagios to easily "jump" to the Splunk web UI from Nagios using the name of a service or host as the search term within Splunk.

Host and Service Escalations, and Notifications

Host and service escalation types allow an organization to configure Nagios to conform to tiered support systems where group N is initially notified but then after X notifications to group N group P needs to be notified. The systems administration team supporting ACME Enterprises may have a dedicated two-tiered group, and in cases where a particular server host is DOWN or in the UNREACHABLE state after several notifications, a tier-three system administration or system integration group would be notified and begin to investigate the issue. Keep in mind that host escalation intervals are configurable, and can be associated with host groups. This flexibility simplifies trouble ticket assignment to specialized technical groups within an organization.

Service Escalations

Like host problems service problems can also be escalated to different technical support personnel within ACME based on problem duration. For a large organization such as ACME, if services are escalated and associated with host groups rather than hosts or services, it becomes quite easy to apply service escalation rules across large groups of services. For example, ACME Enterprises may have Web and database server host groups for each office location. In this scenario, any new host added to either the Web servers or database servers group immediately inherits the service escalation policies created for that host group.

Notification Schemes

Email is the undisputed king of notification, but there are alternative means to reach network monitoring support personnel. Other methods include one-way pagers, SMS, and instant messenger. There are plenty of situations in which administrators might prefer to send or receive alerts using methods other than email. In all cases, support personnel and management need to discuss and agree on what notification methods will be used to ensure timely delivery of alerts to Acme staff. All companies, including our lovely ACME Enterprises, should regularly review notification methods and survey the staff receiving notifications to ensure that methods chosen are effective and efficient.

Nagios Configuration Strategies

DMZ Monitoring—Active versus Passive Checking

Why Passive Service Checks?

Passive service and host checking is not an end-all be-all solution, but rather an approach. Passive checks minimize the load on the monitoring server and scale well for a distributed set up; they will not provide host UNREACHABLE or DOWN alerts as quickly as active checks do nor will they in general alert us as quickly to service problems as active checks will. For these reasons, Acme chooses to use a combination of passive and active checks.

Why Active Service Checks?

In a typical network, Internet-facing hosts reside in a DMZ with restrictions placed on the traffic allowed to the managed systems from both the Internet and the internal network. While SNMP traffic within DMZs is often not allowed (this is the case for ACME), DMZ systems still must be actively monitored by Nagios. Managed servers within the DMZ represent a company's Internet presence; any outage to DMZ hosted managed servers directly impacts key applications hosted within most organizations. ACME chooses to use NRPE, the Nagios monitoring agent. This agent does not use SNMP and all traffic between Nagios and the agent is encrypted, a perfect fit for exposed servers that may not run SNMP agents. NRPE uses TCP as it's layer 4 transmission protocol, making it also easy to restrict the traffic between the Nagios server and the managed agent via firewall rules.

NRPE and ACME Enterprises

NRPE allows the Nagios monitoring server to run any normal Nagios plug-ins on a managed server and collect the results as if the plugin were run on the Nagios server itself. Any Nagios check plugin installed on the managed Nagios client can be executed from the Nagios server using the *check_nrpe* plugin from the Nagios server. Each NRPE client must have any required Nagios check plugins installed on it and must have SSL installed as well before NRPE can be used on it. After OpenSSL is installed, the *check_nrpe* plugin will be able to communicate with the NRPE client using SSL. The Nagios monitoring server performs active checks by executing commands on remote monitored server hosts via NRPE.

Keep in mind that a single NRPE client should be installed onto the DNS, mail, and Web servers to collect basic server metrics (see Table 8.5), by calling check commands such as *check_load* or *check_disk* on the remote server hosts. Simply put:

Nagios monitoring server (check_nrpe) -> Nagios client (NRPE)-> *check_command* on monitored hosts.

Monitoring for the Load balancers and Bluecoat proxy servers would be approached by employing plug-ins. In this book you will find several examples of Bluecoat plugins that use SNMP to poll Bluecoat devices for a variety of basic metrics, including CPU and memory utilization. These proxy devices (SG410, 510, and 810) provide a set of SNMP MIBs that include HTTP status distribution, CPU, memory, and disk utilization, proxy activity, and Web server utilization.

Developer, Corporate, and IT Support Network Monitoring

NSCA to the Rescue!

NSCA is a Nagios add-on that allows you to send passive check results from managed remote server hosts to the Nagios daemon running on the monitoring server. Passive service and host checking is ideal when restrictions on management traffic type do not exist the way they do in a restricted security zone. In ACME Enterprises, NSCA will be used extensively within corporate, developer and IT networks. NSCA will also be used by the slave hosts in the Nagios cluster; they will submit passive checks to the central Nagios server using NSCA. In general, a passive checking scheme proves useful in distributed and redundant/failover monitoring setups.

NSCA uses a client server approach; a passive check is submitted by the managed client to the NSCA daemon which runs on the Nagios hosts. Each client that wishes to submit NSCA checks to the Nagios server must have the *send_nsca* installed on the client along with a configuration file that specifies the type of encryption the *send_nsca* utility should use to communicate with the client along with an optional password (highly recommended). Of course, managed servers can also be monitoring also monitoring servers in a monitor-of-monitors setup. NSCA allows devices and applications to send asynchronous events to Nagios.

NRPE Revisited

So, in the grand scheme of things, the distributed monitoring approach may call for a monitoring server for each security zone—one for the developer, corporate, and IT support networks reporting to an overall monitoring server at that remote site. In turn, the main monitoring server for each office location may monitor peer monitoring servers for each office location. Thus, the main Nagios monitoring server observes the main monitoring servers in the U.S. and Japan:

Figure 8.3 NSCA and NRPE in Action

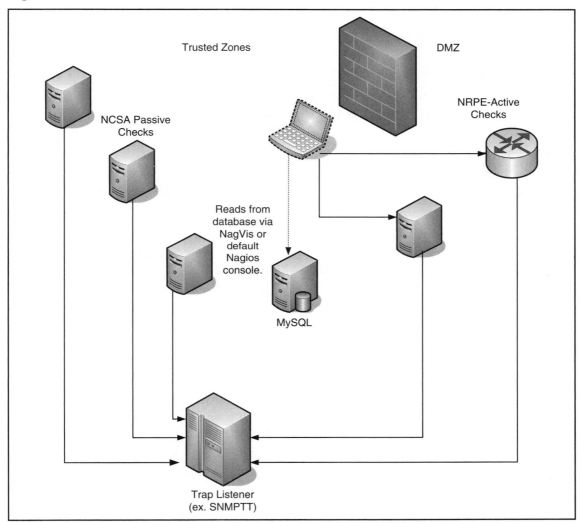

Select Advice for Integrating Nagios as the Enterprise Network Monitoring Solution

ACME Enterprises has established a network operations center (NOC) in each of their offices. However, the European office hosts the main Nagios monitoring server and serves as the main NOC. Like most enterprise NOCs, ACME defines three tiers of technical support. The first tier fields phone calls, opens tickets, and is the first line of technical support. Unlike the second- and third-tier NOC support teams, tier one offers limited help, but is accountable for observing and resolving problems reported by Nagios. All host and service faults as well as problems with Nagios itself should be captured in the service desk ticketing system. In contrast, the second and third tier NOC support teams have specialized skill they use to resolve escalated problems due to tier-one workload or technical capabilities. ACME dispatches problems to second- and third-tier teams based on application, hardware, or network issues. It is important to ensure that escalation policies are well defined and configured properly in Nagios. In other words, problems reported by Nagios should be exactly that—problems. Why? False positives causing "cry wolf" results teach your NOC support teams to ignore host and service alerts. The Nagios administrator or systems integration team within ACME needs to configure and thoroughly test all host and service checks to minimize the possibility of Nagios notifying when it should not. As with notification policies, this is an area of configuration that the ACME team should revisit regularly to minimize the number of false positives and ensure that SOC and NOC personnel can trust that when Nagios shows an alert an action needs to be taken.

The Nagios Software

Nagios software and monitoring plug-ins should be installed before the network monitoring system goes live. Host and service fault scenarios should be tested to validate that thresholds actually work. During the pre-deployment phase, all system and application dependencies should be captured so that status screens are not cluttered when dependent faults are the Nagios monitoring software should also be regularly audited for software upgrades. Software upgrades include the base Nagios software, custom plugins, and add-ons integrated with Nagios.

In larger organizations there will often be more than one person involved in writing and maintaining Nagios configuration files. The Nagios administrator (or multiple administrators, depending on the size and scope of the devices monitored by Nagios) needs to ensure Nagios is maintained post-deployment. Maintenance activities include updating Nagios configuration files and plugins and add-ons used by Nagios to monitor hosts and services. Why would Nagios configuration files ever need to be updated, you ask? In a networked environment the most common cases would include managed devices being decommissioned, replaced, or moved from one network segment to a different network segment that uses an IP address range, gateway, and network mask that differs from the original network segment. It is important to point out that managed devices that have been decommissioned or are no longer being monitored by Nagios represent another form of maintenance: "cleaning up" your configuration files! Who wants to see red covering the monitoring console resulting from decommissioned hosts in a DOWN state? Sure, Nagios is doing its job by reporting back that these unused hosts are unreachable, but the information is useless and does nothing more than clutter up Nagios status screens with meaningless alerts. If anything, reporting that a host is DOWN that we "know" has been decommissioned should immediately cause Nagios staff to delete the host from Nagios. We highly recommend that notifying the network monitoring staff is added as a mandatory part of the decommissioning process within any organization, as it is at ACME.

As with hosts that are decommissioned, hosts that are moved and service configurations that are changed require Nagios administrators to update the Nagios configuration as well. If this is not done in a timely manner, once again our Nagios console becomes cluttered with meaningless alerts, frustrating NOC staff and ruining any trust they have in the urgency of alerts sent out by Nagios. ACME makes sure that the network monitoring group is notified when service or host configurations are changed; the last thing they want is for Nagios to be known as 'the boy who cries wolf.'

Nagios Integration and Deployment

When a new monitoring system nearly ready to be deployed in production, a schedule to transition the system into the production operations center is necessary. A thorough testing effort can take place in an integration or development environment where users will be more understanding and forgiving of false alerts and misconfigurations. Once configurations are vetted in a development or integration environment, they can then be deployed to test and production environments to provide the information testers and NOC staff require to help them meet the needs of a customer. ACME sees the value of Nagios and makes use of it in all development, integration and production environments. We hope that your experience with Nagios is as fulfilling and useful as ACMEs' experience is. Good luck and happy monitoring!

Index